Natural Religion

Natural Religion

Frederick Turner

Transaction Publishers
New Brunswick (U.S.A.) and London (U.K.)

Library of Congress Catalog Number: 2006044537
ISBN: 0-7658-0332-1
Printed in the United States of America

Library of Congress Cataloging-in-Publication Data

Turner, Frederick, 1943-
    Natural religion / Frederick Turner.
        p.   cm.
    Includes bibliographical references and index.
    ISBN 0-7658-0332-1 (alk. paper)
    1. Natural theology. 2. Religion. I. Title.

BL183.T87   2006
200—dc22   2006044537

Prentice, disciple, master in our making,
Our work is that we build Thee, Thou high nave.
Sometimes a traveler, stern in his way-taking,
Glints through our hundred souls and, softly shaking,
Shows us a new way how to grip the stave.

We mount the swaying scaffolds of the tower,
The hammer hanging heavy in our hand,
Until our brow is kissed by one bright hour,
Whose beams announce the light of the all-knower,
Thou, like the wind that blows from sea to land.

Then there's an echo of those many hammers
That jar the mountain, blow by massive blow.
Only at nightfall will we let you go:
And then your still-becoming contour glimmers.
God, great art Thou.

From Rainer Maria Rilke's *Das Stundenbuch*
1. On the Monastic Life (1899)

translation by Zsuzsanna Ozsváth and Frederick Turner

Contents

Acknowledgements   xi

1.   Introduction   1

2.   The Problem   7
     A World of Different Religions   7
     They Fight   8
     They Seek a Common Element   9
     They Doubt   12
     They Become Pluralists   14
     They Syncretize   18

3.   Desiderata for a Religion of the Future   25
     Avoiding Holy Wars   25
     Taking Care with Abstract Metaphors   26
     Respecting Reason   28
     Avoiding the Trap of Signs and Wonders   30
     Using Ritual Rightly   33
     Obeying the Moral Law   36
     Acknowledging Higher Entities   43
     Rejoicing   45
     The Task before Us   46

4.   Religious and Scientific Truth   47
     Noah's Flood   47
     The Caduceus   51
     Bottom-up and Top-down   69

5.   Freedom, Values, and Strange Attractors   73
     Chance and Necessity   73
     Order Out of Chaos, Chaos Out of Order   76
     Meanings   83

	Problems in the Study of Society	87
	Values and History	92
6.	Time	97
	Not Enough Room in Space	97
	The Evolution of Time	101
	Gaia	107
	Time and Freedom	112
7.	The Information/Spirit Universe	125
	Mind and Matter	125
	Computability and Uncomputability	130
	The Three-Computer Universe	134
	Psychoanalyzing God	138
8.	A Brief History of God	143
	Summary	143
	The Early Stages: Nature Gods, Human Gods, and Collective Gods	145
	Markets, Cyberspace, and Angels	152
	A Digression upon Technology	164
	Divine Competition and Consolidation, and the Resurrection of the Dead	167
	The Last Times	172
9.	What Each Religion Brings to the Search	177
	Atheist Materialism	177
	Animism	182
	Ritual and Sacrificial Religion	184
	The Orphic Journey	193
	Reincarnation and the Afterlife	197
	The Historical Religions	204
	The Meditative Religions and Spirit Healing	212
	Transcendence and Time	214
	Prayer and Personal Religion	217
	My Christian Bias	223
10.	The Style of God	227
	The Real Presence	227
	The Poetic Idiom of the Divine	229

An Inordinate Fondness for Beetles: 238
   The Divine Language of Nature
The Queen of Heaven   240

Glossary   245

Further Reading   261

Index   275

Acknowledgements

The subject of this book not only demanded more knowledge, scholarship, and understanding than I am master of, as all my books have done; it also required greater enlightenment, wisdom, and depth of religious experience. Thus I must thank those whose minds I have borrowed from in two different ways: as usual for their intellectual help, but in a new way for their personal, moral, and spiritual qualities that I was compelled to model in my imagination if this book was to make any sense or carry conviction. But in a venture of this kind, error is not just a danger but an inevitable companion. And so I fear lest my many mistakes be attributed to my advisers and informants (whether they know that is what they are, or not) rather than to where they belong, which is to me.

I wish to thank Alex Argyros, an intellectual comrade who marvelously combines skepticism with the spirit of adventure, and Mihai Spariosu, whose insistence on the polymorphousness of possible worlds spurred me to criticize easy generalizations, and whose commitment to the irenic way challenged me to find peaceful solutions to the conflicts of apparently incommensurable worldviews. Bainard Cowan, Virgil Nemoianu, Zsuzsanna Ozsváth, Fred Curchack, Stephen Erickson, Larry Allums, Werner Dannhauser, John Cleese, Timothy Fuller, Michael Benedikt, John Alvis, Paul Hernadi, Steven Ealy, Emilio Pacheco, Frank Buckley, Paul Cantor, David Channell, Nicholas Gillespie, Harold Montgomery, Brian Rosborough, Edwin Watkins, Robin Fox, Yongzhao Deng, Karl Zinsmeister, James Cooper, Sandie Sanderson, Marleen van Cauwelaert, Jack Abecassis, Virginia Postrel, William R. Jordan III, Koen dePryck, Kanchan Limaye, Adam Bellow, Glenn and Virginia Arbery, Robert Royal, Lynda and Michael Sexson, Gail Thomas, and Ben and Daniel Turner deserve my undying gratitude for having put up with my strange speculations and given in exchange a deeper wisdom about life. Monsignor Don Fischer has been an indispensable guide. I would like to thank my artist and poet friends, especially Stefania de Kenessey, David Ligare, Frederick Feirstein, Burton Raffel, and Dana Gioia; Robert Sacks, the great interpreter of *Job*; and my students and colleagues at the University of Texas at Dallas, who keep me from totally losing touch with what is actually going on. Pat Howell has shown me new landscapes of the mind. Charlotte Turner's own spiritual pilgrimage has been an inspiration to me. I owe a debt to several great scientists, especially Istvan Ozsváth, Gregory Benford, Robert Turner, Ilya Prigogine, Roald Hoffman, and Edward Wilson, among others. J.T. Fraser has been a perennial source of wisdom. If my father, Victor Turner, were alive, he could have done this book ten times better than I, but his voice has been in my head nevertheless. My wife, Mei Lin, as always has been both what holds me up and what draws me further on. This book arose partly out of a conversation with my mother, Edith Turner, the anthropologist, over the question of religious metaphor. Her brilliant research on spirit healing raised the question of how "real"—and in what sense one meant the word—were the phenomena of religious experience.

I would like also to remember here my friend, the sculptor Frederick Hart, who is sorely missed.

Some paragraphs of this book, which I did not think I had the wit to substantially improve on, have appeared elsewhere: in essays I have published in the *American Arts Quarterly*, *Reason*, the *American Enterprise*, the *AWP Chronicle*, the *Journal of Social and Biological Systems*, *Papers in Comparative Studies*, *Lettre International*, *Kronoscope* (the journal of the International Society for the Study of Time), and in my books, *Beauty: the Value of Values*, *The Culture of Hope*, and *Shakespeare's Twenty-first Century Economics*. "The Lady of Cozumel" came out in *Edge City Review* and is included in my new collection *Paradise: Selected Poems 1990–2003*. The translations of Hungarian poetry are all by Zsuzsanna Ozsváth and Frederick Turner.

1

Introduction

Why write a book on religion? More to the point, why read one?

In the aftermath of the attack on the World Trade Center and the city of Washington the practical need for a reconsideration of religion, and especially of religious differences, is painfully clear. Religion did not go away when the Enlightenment showed us the path of human reason. It did not go away when twentieth-century science began to plumb the mysteries of the cosmos, when twentieth-century philosophy, psychology, and sociology explained the reasons for religious belief, when twentieth-century technology made possible a secular middle-class lifestyle for hundreds of millions of people, when twentieth-century secular regimes attempted to stamp religion out altogether. The twenty-first century has begun with a huge atrocity committed in the name of religion and the possible prospect of a religious war conducted with nuclear weapons and enveloping at least the countries between North Africa and Bangladesh.

Religion cannot be eradicated, even if it were desirable to do so. It deals with the most important things human beings know, and has its own profound claims to truth. Is there any way of showing that religious differences are not necessarily absolute, that hostility between religions is not justified by the logical demands of noncontradiction? This book explores this question, and brings in the new knowledge that modernity has given us as an ally, rather than an enemy, of religion.

The very sciences that once cast doubt on religion (or by describing the universe in terms of material determinism forced religion into a distorted and dualistic revision of its own theology) are, I shall argue, now providing us with a world picture that is strangely friendly to religious interpretations. Complexity theory seems to have given back to the world its autonomy, freedom, and mystery; cosmology

1

its origin; computational physics its ancient role as the vast thought of a vast thinker..

The core question this book asks and attempts to answer is: What would the universe have to be like, if all the religions were true? And its core claim is that the understanding of the universe that is beginning to emerge from the sciences is perhaps bizarre enough to match and to accommodate the bizarreness of a world in which all the religions really are true.

This book takes a rather different direction than that of most contemporary academic thought. It argues against relativism and pluralism (though in favor of a much closer embrace of different religious ideas than mere tolerance). It refuses to take the line that many contemporary advocates of worldwide spirituality have taken, which is the rejection of "western" modes of thought and an attack on global capitalism, technology, and progress. And it questions the longstanding agreement between secular rationalists and religious intellectuals, enshrined by Immanuel Kant, that the realms of fact and value, means and ends, are radically separate. The reward for these abandonments of conventional wisdom is, I will argue, well worth the sacrifice.

But we cannot write or read about religion in any meaningful way from the outside only, ignoring the inner experience of it.

"Thy life's a miracle." So says Edgar to his blinded father, Gloucester, in Shakespeare's *King Lear*. Gloucester has just attempted suicide, pathetically and unsuccessfully, by jumping off what he wrongly thinks are the cliffs of Dover. Edgar, disguised as a madman, has led his father to believe that the cliffs were real in order to heal him of his suicidal depression, and now, pretending to be a passerby, continues with the deception, commenting on the huge distance the old man has fallen and the crushing violence of the impact. Gloucester is persuaded to believe that he has been saved from suicide by divine intervention:

> Think that the clearest gods, who make them honors
> Of men's impossibilities, have preserved thee.

The ultimate purpose of any attempt at religious understanding is to bring home to oneself that simple fact: our life is a miracle. Suicide and martyrdom are important boundary-markers of the dark country of our deepest religious experience, whether we believe we serve the divine by our death, or the divine is the only beauty great enough to hold us back from the solace of self-destruction. Edgar's lie about the cliffs is the shell or envelope of a staggering truth, a truth so daily and customary that we fail to see it for what it is. How can this meat of which we are made, this hair-tufted, naked, nimble, rather feeble primate, with its noisy digestive system, have the amazing property of consciousness; how can it contain the gigantic dark continent of our dreams, our inner life, our metaphysical inner reflexivity? And as we see this we should also see what a miracle the world itself is, with its orchids, its slime molds, its elaborate Lego system of chemistry, its sperm whales and black holes and neutrinos, and its unimaginably vast distances, masses, sounds, energies, and voids; and marvelously, with the eyes and ears and other senses to perceive all the rest.

Though the miracle of ourselves and the world is almost always obscured from us except at moments of crisis, extreme grief, or ecstasy, that miracle contains, for anyone who has experienced it, a promise, that in some sense all shall be well and all manner of thing shall be well, as Juliana of Norwich put it. Religion—in its often blundering and sometimes murderously obsessive way—is, as I shall argue, our only real means of getting to grips with this huge promise and the huge problems that lie in the way of its fulfillment.

The great Hungarian poet Deszö Kosztolányi provides what is for me one of the most moving of all accounts of the way that religious experience can supervene upon the most rational and down-to-earth of lives. Kosztolányi was not in any sense a religious person, but a secular modernist literary man. I quote from it in the translation by Zsuzsanna Ozsváth and myself:

> But up there, my friend, up there is the lightening sky,
> a clarity, a glittering majesty,
> trembling, crystallizing into constancy.
> A heavenly dome
> the blue of my mother's eiderdown back home
> so long ago; the waterblot of monochrome
> that smudged my paper-pad with an azure foam,
> and the stars' souls
> breathe and glitter quietly in their shoals
> into a Fall night's
> lukewarm mildness—which precedes the colds and whites—;
> they watched the files of Hannibal, today
> look down at one who, having fallen from the rest,
> am standing at a window in Budapest.

And then I don't quite know what happened to me,
but a great wing seemed to swoop over me; the past,
all I had buried, bent down to me its breast:
childhood, infancy.

There so long stood I
to watch the vaulted miracles of the sky
that in the east it reddened, and the wind
set all the stars to quivering; sparks thinned
by the distance, they'd appear and disappear;
a vast thoroughfare
of light flared up; a heavenly castle door
opened in that fire;
something fluttered then,
and a crowd of guests took places to begin
deep in twilight shades of dawn
the measures of the last pavane.
Outside the foyer swam in streams of light, and there
the lord of the dance bade farewell on the stair,
a great nobleman, the titan of the sky,
the glory of the dancing-floor; by and by

there is a movement, startled, jingling,
a soft womanly whispering
miraculous; the ball is over; pages
ready at the entrance call for carriages.

Under a lace veil
streamed a mantle, fairy-tale,
from the frail
deeps of twilight, diamond-pale,
blued with such a blue
as the morning dew,
which a lovely lady dons for her surtout,
and a gem, whose hue
dusts with its light the pure peace of the air,
the otherworldly raiment she would wear;
or an angel pins, with virgin grace,
a brilliant diadem into her hair,
and a fine light chaise
rocks to a soft halt and she glides in,
quieter than a dream,
and, its wheels agleam,
on it rolls again,
a flirting smile glimpsed on the face of the queen,
and then the stallions of the Milky Way,
with glittering horseshoes gallop through the spray

of carnival confetti, each flake a star
of bright gold, where hundreds of glass coaches are.

Standing in a trance,
with joy I cried and cried out, there's a dance
in heaven, every night there is a dance;
for now a great old secret dawned on me,
that all the heavenly hosts of faerie
go home each morning on the glittery
and spacious boulevards of infinity...

...So, though today my body is distressed,
I feel that in the dust and mire, my friend,
stumbling among lost souls in a fruitless quest,
of some unknown and puissant Lord, yet kind,
I was the guest.

Tolstoy's Levin in *Anna Karenina* has got to this point when he runs across a major stumbling block: the variety of religions in the world. They cannot all be right, he thinks, or at least he does not believe himself to have the wit to see how they might be. So he chooses the Russian Orthodox Church, and in it he finds the ecstasy he seeks. But the theoretical problem remains, and with it the practical and historical problems of religious exclusivism, oppression, and even savage ideological carnage. Would it be just to seek one's own psychological and spiritual salvation at the cost of perpetuating a kind of polemical certainty that has historically been demonstrated to produce atrocity?

The problem is that the apparent contradictions among the various religions reward the hotheads, the bureaucrats, the fanatics, and the politicians among the religions, and punish the wise ones, the holy ones, the gentle philosophical systematizers, and the poets. This book is an attempt to solve that problem, to show in an entirely experimental, playful spirit—and in fear and trembling lest this very conception might be blasphemous—how maybe all the religions could be right, especially in the bizarre light of the new scientific understandings of cosmology, evolution, time, and chaotic self-organization.

There is a real tension in any good person's life between the imperative to perfect one's soul in mystical contemplative observance, and the call to work actively in the world for its betterment, feeding the hungry, educating the ignorant, healing the sick, and clothing the naked. Without the former where will we find the virtuous discipline to practice the latter?—yet without the latter what moral substance can be claimed by the former? Meanwhile the time and concentration needed for either seem to preclude any other goal. In the Jewish tradition of Talmudic studies that duality is sometimes termed the apocalyptic (perfecting the soul) and the prophetic (works of charity). Today that tension is especially acute, since—as I have argued elsewhere—it looks very much as if the best thing we could do in practical charity for our neighbor is intelligently seek our own material interests within a free market capitalist economy. Within particular religions this paradox is solved by a specific moment of personal revelation, such as Moses' in the burning bush episode of Exodus, Arjuna's in the Bhagavad Gita, Monkey's in *The Journey to the West,* the apostles' at Pentecost in the New Testament, and the ball-playing brothers' in the *Popol Vuh.* The acuteness of the problem—how to do our duty in the world, how to perfect our souls—is intensified into outright contradiction if we conclude that different religions are radically incommensurate and thus that either none of them is right, or only one is and we can't know for sure which one. Revelation is the place where the active and contemplative lives intersect, yet revelation is the specific part of religion that is undermined by the scandal of religious contradiction.

The enterprise this book sets itself is to remove that contradiction. But I am aware that it will be doomed if it sets itself outside the religious experience, aloof, ironical, detached, scholarly. One's own search for salvation and one's own partial and obscured experience of it cannot be the subject of a book addressed to an audience that includes many kinds of believers and unbelievers and trying to prove its point by public evidence. But it cannot be true to its subject if it dismisses private experience either.

2

The Problem

A World of Different Religions

The central subject of all religions is what has been called the divine. Even religions without gods at all identify a higher kind of being than what is given to ordinary experience. This book tries to imagine what that central subject must be like, and what the world must be like, if all the religions are true, in the sense that each of the world's religions is telling the truth about its own experience.

To do this is no easy task. We see this when we ask ourselves how people of different religions might deal with their disagreement; the various ways they could do so sum up neatly the core strategies of philosophers and theologians from many times and places. I count five broad ways by which people of different religions might negotiate their differences.

1. They might fight.
2. They might seek a common element in each of their experiences.
3. They might fall into radical doubt.
4. They might accept multiple accounts of reality.
5. They might syncretize their experiences, putting them all together into one.

The problem with fighting (1) is obvious. An abstract philosophical religion, which is what one would get if one adopted (2), would have none of the personal passion, rich storytelling, and ritual that make religion religion. Answer (3) is self-contradictory—doubt itself must be doubted—and answer (4) may paradoxically have led to the genocidal horrors of the twentieth century. The last way, the syncretic way, is what this book is about.

They Fight

The first way—to fight—has been the traditional route for many religious people, and has of course caused much human misery. Yet it has considerable justification. After all, each of them has actually experienced what he has experienced, and knows it to be true. What other reason might others have to question his reality but an intent to deceive or confuse? Surely the most belittling act of all is to devalue another's actual experience, to ignore the validity of his selfhood, to attempt to replace his point of view with one's own. The others must be enemies then, conspiring to rob one of one's vision, or worse, they themselves have been deceived by the Enemy of all truth and should be resisted by force if necessary.

And after all, one's actual experience of ultimate reality should be honored in its particularity, as Schleiermacher argued persuasively in his letter to religion's cultured despisers. If one's experience of the divine is in the burning of the paper offerings at one's father's Shinto funeral, or in the lighting of the Christmas candles, or the taste of Passover matzo, or the ecstasy of Vodun possession, or the circumambulation of the Ka'aba, or the sacrifice of a bull to Dionysus, or the screams of the prisoners upon the Chac-Mool of Tlaloc, or the wild ringing of the Orthodox Easter bells and the smell of roasting lamb, then one would be a fool to give that up for some generalization or other. One ought to defend that reality, to the death.

It is hardly necessary to list the holy wars and ideological slaughters that this approach has produced. Each tribe has its own fierce and dear and familiar deities, who preside over hearth and home, and protect their warriors as they go forth to righteous battle.

To say this is not to adopt a fashionable moral relativism. Certainly religious strife is required by some religions, and forbidden by others. The worst violence and atrocity in the last hundred years or so has been committed not by religion, in the strict sense of the word, but by atheist or at least radically secularizing regimes headed by people like Hitler, Stalin, Mao Zedong, and Pol Pot. Nevertheless, it cannot be denied that violence has been perpetrated in the name of religion. Examples are the Muslim jihads, the Christian crusades, the exterminations of Canaanites and Philistines by the chosen people in the Bible, the Inquisition, the German Thirty Years' War, the St. Bartholomew's Day massacre, the martyrdom of Ireland by the Protestant Cromwell, the bloody wars between Muslims and Hindus in Kashmir, the wars of the Buddhist Khmers, the ethnic cleansings of the Balkans, and of course the current wave of Islamic terrorism, stretching from Nigeria through North Africa, Western and Eastern Europe, Central Asia, the Middle East, Kashmir, and Southeast Asia, to New York and Washington. Whether the doctrinal differences between the participants are great or small is not the issue: Sunnis kill Shias with as much relish as they kill African animists, Christians, or western agnostics. What Freud calls the narcissism of small differences can even intensify the fury of the conflict in inverse proportion to the magnitude of the disagreement; the more we are able to identify with the other, the more perfidious the other's betrayal of the truth comes to feel. Jonathan Swift imagined a bitter war between the Big Endians and Small Endians of Lilliput over which end of a boiled egg should be cracked, and this conflict is not entirely implausible when we compare, for instance, the differences of Christian Serbs and Croats, or Northern Irish Catholics and Protestants.

Let those who wish to fight over religion, fight. If we wish to continue with such activities as writing and reading books, we must reject the fight option, except to defend ourselves against those who fight against us.

They Seek a Common Element

A second recourse of religious folk faced with religious differences would be to seek the abstract principle or ideal form that underlies the diverse doctrines, stories, rituals, and precepts of religion. But in doing so, much of the emotional and experiential detail of religion is in danger of being sacrificed to rationality and concord. Worshippers would become philosophers, seeking the essence or isness or Being or essence or quiddity that underlies all these diverse appearances, or perhaps, like William James, some common psychological factor embedded in human nature that urges us to worship. They would seek the highest common factor among all the different quantities given by the world religions.

Now such an approach, like the fight solution, has much to recommend it if we take the point of view of the participants. It is reasonable, peaceful, and shows a laudable tendency toward civilized compromise. It rises above the passions of the moment and of factional dispute. It moves from the notoriously unreliable and compromised world of the senses to the pure and abstract realms of the ideal forms.

Its major problem is that it misses the point of religion. The higher reality religion describes is not the same thing as the highest common factor of all the diverse doctrines about it. And this reflection should give us pause when we realize that many of the noblest attempts of human philosophy and metaphysics might fit perfectly into this description. The theological project of the Enlightenment, which claimed many of the greatest minds of Europe and America including Voltaire, Newton, and Jefferson, is a case in point. Their deistic deity is more like a principle of logic or mathematics than like the personal, time-embedded God of Job or of the disciple John—he is eternal, infinite, immaterial, omniscient, omnipotent, impersonal, characterless, a sort of shining colorless sphere that is not a physical sphere and does not physically shine. Earlier examples include the theological abstractions of Plato and of the Muslim, Hindu, Taoist, and Buddhist philosophers, who all sought a divine principle beyond time, change, expression, phenomena, multiplicity. The Sikhs found ways to reconcile the theology of Brahman with that of Allah by a resort to higher level of generality. The sub-Saharan African concept of the distant and uninvolved creator-god (whom I came across in my childhood under the name Nzambi) has the same abstract flavor, as does the North American Plains Indian notion of Wakan Tanka, the Great Spirit. In our own times we can cite the ecumenism of Baha'i, the Unification Church, modern Anglicanism, Unitarianism, and the New Age movement; Heidegger's notion of *Sein*—Being—is an especially fashionable example in intellectual circles.

Hard though it may appear, human beings have found it possible to worship this bloodless generalization of a deity. It certainly seems at first blush to be a more civilized religion. But worshippers of the abstract God can be at times as tyrannical as the idolators. The theistic concepts of "superstition" and "paganism" themselves are deeply intolerant ones, vital to colonialism. The abstracting monotheism of Akhenaton, of the armies of ancient Israel, of the Byzantine iconoclasts who gave their name to the whole category, of the Islamic holy warriors, of Savonarola and John Knox and Protestant missionaries all over the world, and the yet more abstract materialistic theology of modernism, have been responsible for their own share of atrocities.

Not that there might not indeed be something underlying and in common among the religions. The effort to find the underlying commonality of our experiences of the world has actually succeeded in producing brilliant answers, culminating in the inquiries of physical science. They include the idea of matter itself, and its language of molecules, atoms, elementary particles, quarks, strings, and topological manifolds. The problem is that none of them is God, or a god, or is even something especially sacred—and our sense of the sacred is crucial to religion. Given the fact that some numbers are primes, the highest common factor of all numbers turns out to be no bigger than one, which in itself does not give us the miracle of quantities and differences. The subtraction of what is not universal leaves nothing particular to religion; and in religion, the universal is only discovered in the particular.

But, it could be argued, genuine and splendid religious experience has taken place under the very theology of attributeless and indescribable divinity, the intangible Ground of Being. Some of us have, in fact, experienced God as eternal, impersonal, changeless, invisible. So the "common element" approach is not entirely wrong. The divine would be strange indeed if it can be experienced not only in the blood of a sacrificed chicken or the ecstasy of tantric sex or the striking of a temple bell, but also as the utterly nonsensory, the irreducibly inexpressible, the disincarnate. We have certainly come some way toward our goal—of a view of things that would include the particulars of all religions—when we recognize that the reality of the divine might be a strange Rube Goldberg contraption, and realize that the shining, featureless sphere of the philosophical religions is not necessarily an improvement. But this reality is one which some have indeed experienced as a shining sphere, which we must now add to our list of more full-blooded religious metaphors.

We must, therefore, respectfully and regretfully reject a simple universalism, in the sense of the highest common factor of all religions and ideologies. The highest factor contains so little content as to be useless. Let us not despair, however. This stage of our journey is necessarily the one where we encounter the difficulties of our project in all their apparent insuperability. Perhaps the difficulties themselves are part of the solution, as many of the wisest religious thinkers and mystics have suggested.

They Doubt

But why bother at all? Perhaps the best thing for us to do is to recognize that since our experiences differ so radically, the categories of our perception—the modes of time and space in which we sense things—cut us off forever from the thing in itself. Or perhaps we are not wrong at all, and our different experiences are all there is. Or there is no such thing as religious experience at all, and we are deceived by mystics and priests into thinking that there is such a thing. Or there is indeed religious experience, but it is no more than a state of unusual brain chemistry, and the true maturity of the human race will only arrive when we recognize this fact. Perhaps there is no reality underlying our perceptions. Perhaps there is no meaning, but only phenomena. Perhaps in our search for the divine, we are neglecting the immediate, warm reality of trees and love and bread and wine. Or perhaps our language and metaphorical systems determine what we are perceiving, for surely we cannot perceive what we cannot name; the limits of my language are the limits of my world, and whereof one cannot speak, thereof one must remain silent. The divine is like a unicorn, a nonexistent fabrication of language, a piece of nonsensical metaphysics. Or perhaps the world itself is only text. If contradiction is inherent in the very process of "giving an account of reality," perhaps the world is only the differences between those accounts, and the endless delay between the account and its confirmation, the deferring (*différance*) of certainty, the slippages between words and meanings.

Readers familiar with the history of philosophy in various cultural traditions will recognize these forms of doubt as corresponding to one or more of the multitudinous skepticisms of the world: Kantian, positivist, Pyrrhonian, Cartesian, phenomenological, existentialist, nominalist, solipsist, Wittgenstinian, deconstructionist, and so on. Again, one must admire the magnificence of the intellectual edifices that this approach has raised, even though they may appear absurd if we know that there is indeed an object of religious experience, because we have experienced it. The skeptical approach has fostered a critical attitude toward sense perception that has been indispensable in the development of science: if we had been incapable of doubting that the sun rises, as it appears to do, we would never have discovered the heliocentric theory of the solar system. If we had insisted on the apparent solidity of matter, we might not have found its atoms and voids. Morally the skeptical approach has been an excellent solvent or dissolver of tyrannical certainties and ethnocentric bias.

And we can indeed recognize in this approach a genuine element of much real religious experience. Zen Buddhists know the strange delight of recognizing that all is illusion, that we live in a floating world of change and appearance, that it is attachment to those illusory realities that is the source of pain, that the lotus of insight floats in the flow of mutability. Christian, Jewish, and Muslim mystics have reported a similar vertigo as they pass through the dark night of the soul, where all is in doubt and the self must be emptied of all it holds sure before it can encounter the divine. Existentialism, with its radical skepticism of all essences, will surely one day be recognized as a form of religion.

But even as we add this sensation of radical doubt to our list of the accounts given of religious experience, we must recognize the inadequacies of skepticism on its own, when unaccompanied by a faith that there is something to discover when the illusions are dispelled. Three such failings stand out.

One is that if the divine exists, there is a staggering arrogance in the assumption that because we experience it in different ways, it is not there. Gravitation is experienced in different ways—the motions of the planets, the flow of water, the falling of dropped objects, the feeling of the weight of our limbs, the heat of the sun (partly generated by its frustrated tendency to gravitational collapse). Evolution is experienced in even more ways, in every instinctive impulse of our bodies and minds, in every characteristic of every animal and plant, in family life, in mountains of limestones and in the renewal of a bacterial disease. The variousness of the evidence does not refute but confirms the existence of gravitation or evolution. Too radical a skepticism might discourage the kind of insight that Newton and Darwin were given.

The second inadequacy in the strategy of doubt is that it can lead to an irresponsibility about fact in general, an irresponsibility that has a major moral dimension. One of the great practitioners of doubt in recent times was Paul de Man. A leading deconstructionist, he had managed, strangely, to absolve himself of personal responsibility as a former Nazi propagandist; for what, after all, was de Man himself but a play of texts and representations? There was no reality in him to stand trial, there was no promiser or keeper of promises, no agent that could be held responsible. A century that permitted the Gulag, the Holocaust, the Great Cultural Revolution, and the killing fields of Cambodia has shown the inadequacy of equivocation as a refuge, and of skepticism about underlying realities as a moral stance. However distasteful certainty might be, it is our jury duty when called, as we all must be, to judgment.

The third failing is that religious experience is itself a real experience, and if as good skeptics we are to accept only our experiences as real, then by our own rules we are forced to accept the validity of the Loas of Vodun and the Kamis of Shinto and the angels of Catholicism along with trees and love and bread and wine—and where is our skepticism then? What is sauce for the goose is sauce for the gander. In Wallace Stevens' marvelous poem "Sunday Morning," the speaker urges his female companion to forget the ancient metaphysics of the holy sepulcher and ancient sacrifice, and join him in coffee and oranges instead of dashing off to church; his trump card is the immediacy and holiness of secular experience. But in T.S. Eliot's "The Waste Land," it is that very same secular experience that is the "unreal city," the place of shadows, and it is the almost impossible commitment to religious sacrifice that is full of existential vitality and immediacy. Both poems are convincing; neither feels like propaganda or special pleading. Our skepticism about inferring transcendent realities from the various flows of experiences must, to be consistent, apply most strongly of all to the philosophical program of skepticism itself.

They Become Pluralists

A recent variant of the "doubt" strategy for dealing with different worldviews is pluralism. We simply give up the struggle for consistency and accept the validity of radically incommensurable worldviews. We should therefore accept each of these worldviews as equally valid ways of knowing. Each ethnic group, gender, or sexual preference community has its own unique closed hermeneutic system, incomprehensible to the others, making up together a rich multicultural diversity. We should cultivate an ethos of tolerance, and not attempt to expropriate the visions of others. Each worldview, in the words of Michel Foucault, the best-known exponent of this view, is an "episteme," that is, a system of knowing, and the world is completely passive to how it is known. After all, any word in a given language only "means" its paraphrase in other words of the same language, whose meanings in turn are glossed at some finite number of removes by means of the very word we began with; a dictionary nowhere refers anywhere outside the world of texts. Even pictures are visual conventions, no more truly representational than other words or symbols (hence postmodern artworks made of verbal slogans and postmodern architecture made of coded art-historical references). Ostensive definitions (pointing at something and naming it) will not get us out of our semantic box, as Wittgenstein argued, because pointing is itself already a semantic convention. And the crucial issue, then, is who decides what means what—who has the power to enforce his own meaning.

In this view the world as a transcendent reality outside our views of it does not exist. The assumption that it does is, in the opinion of multiculturalist and postcolonial critics, a subterfuge, a regime of power and knowledge, designed by the rich, powerful, heterosexual, male, and ethnically privileged to oppress the underprivileged, the weak, the female, the sexually "deviant," and the ethnically other. Reality is socially constructed. Some scientists, like Paul Feyerabend, have given their support to this idea. There is even support for the position in physics itself, if we interpret the observer principle of quantum mechanics as implying that reality is constructed by how we see it—and then add the sociological observation that we see things the way our culture tells us to. The world is text, filled with contested sites. (The reader will pardon my use of the characteristic vocabulary of this discourse: nothing gives the flavor of it so well, for it is a style of thought as well as a position, as unmistakable as the vocabulary of the evangelical polemicist, the communist, or the business school marketing consultant.) We are familiar with this position in, for instance, some versions of medical anthropology, which hold that bacteria and viruses are no more valid explanations of disease than spirit possession or a bad combination of humors.

Again, as with skepticism itself, we should take this very inviting position with a grain of doubt. Suppose the real world might actually exist? Gravitation still works in Tibet and the Amazon jungle, local beliefs to the contrary notwithstanding. Wouldn't it then be intellectual suicide, rather than tolerant pluralism, to silence one's own quest for the reality beyond the appearances?

And is the position really consistent? For surely pluralism is itself a worldview, one which tacitly proposes itself as—if not an underlying generalization or core principle for all the others—a bag in which all the others can be put, even if unexamined. But this bag role privileges pluralism; and therefore pluralists must decide whether other regimes of power and knowledge, other epistemes than the pluralist one, are inside or outside the bag. Some of those regimes might be jihads, witch hunts, inquisitions, Communist or Nazi hegemonies. If they are inside the bag, they must be controlled and protected from one another by some kind of single superordinate authority or world policeman or New World Order, the very antithesis of political pluralism. If they are outside the bag, in other words if their moral authority cannot be challenged by a pluralism that recognizes itself as just another worldview among many that are equally valid, then one would be unable to protest their oppressiveness. One would have to accept clitoridectomy, or suttee, or Scientological denials of medical treatment to children, or local racism and homophobia—or the Holocaust, the Gulag, the killing fields, and suicide bombers—as all part of life's rich multicultural pageant. Or should the regime of religious tolerance itself be an absolute and exclusive view of reality that should be defended to the death?

Thinkers like Richard Rorty and Jürgen Habermas have sought to find pacific ways for us to live with our differences, at the cost of not taking anything in the world seriously enough to be worth the defense of one's convictions. But at root the pluralist response to the problem logically entails a sophisticated version of the first answer—to fight. If non-pluralists should not be persuaded, and if their values are radically and untranslatably different from mine, as pluralism contends, they cannot be trusted for one moment. I am in what Hobbes called a "state of nature" with respect to them, with no sovereign authority over us to protect us from one another, no factual or intersubjective court of appeal. If I declare that I am a pluralist, I am ipso facto declaring that I accept no moral authority and may be dangerous. My advice to the reader who accepts the validity of the pluralist answer is: if you have power and wealth, prepare powerful weaponry in secret, conceal your disagreement with others, and then suddenly and covertly launch an overwhelming attack on your enemies, silencing them forever by death. In the academy, fail them or deny them tenure. Machiavelli would be an excellent guide in this endeavor.

If, however, you are politically, ethnically, or in gender terms disenfranchised, disadvantaged, and therefore weak, it would be suicidal to subscribe publicly to the pluralist view of things—given that you truly believed in it. Your best recourse would be to pretend to adopt one of the other strategies, build support, and silently bide your time until you get into power. Thus those who sincerely espouse pluralism, if our logic is correct, must be one of the following: silent about their views, fools, or in absolute power. Pluralism is an excellent view to espouse publicly if you do *not* really believe in it, for it implies that one is holding oneself back by sheer goodness of heart from crushing the supporters of other views, which, since they are not in error according to pluralist doctrine, constitute a real threat to one's own claim to be right.

But the pluralist position is flawed in even deeper ways. Contemporary pluralism is partly based on Wittgenstein's apparent refutation of any relationship between facts and propositions—his brilliant demonstration that pointing is itself part of the realm of arbitrary human signs and thus cannot connect us with, and found our propositions upon, nature. This idea has been expanded by Willard van Orman Quine into a critique of reference in general, and by some followers of Thomas Kuhn, Jürgen Habermas, and Paul Feyerabend into a universal questioning of the unique validity of science. If language is essentially untestable by physical reality, any account of the world in language is as valid as any other, provided it meets whatever practical or political goals human beings are using it for.

But this analysis rests upon a prior assumption, that language, in the sense of arbitrary, mutually understood signaling systems, is unique to human beings and thus has reference only to human meanings and conventions and not an objective reality. But what if pointing, or some version of it, is not unique to human beings, but a common feature of higher and lower animals at least? Even bees dance to indicate to their hive-mates where the nectar is. If pointing is a natural signal, and reference a common means of organizing information among animals and other organisms, the great Cartesian barrier between mind and matter, meanings and facts, the realm of language and the realm of nature, breaks down. New games-theory and replication-dynamics research in the biological selection of social behavior (reported in such useful works as Brian Skyrms' *Evolution of the Social Contract* and Elliott Sober and David Wilson's *Unto Others: The Evolution and Psychology of Unselfish Behavior*) shows that adaptive constraints actually require the emergence of arbitrary signaling systems among animals.

At a lower level, the decoding of the DNA molecule reveals an uncanny resemblance between the way DNA "means" and the way language does—with DNA versions of words, sentences, lexicons, surface grammar, deep syntax, morphology, phonology, and even semantic change over time. If reference and meaning are perfectly natural, and if the constraints of evolutionary survival insure a reasonable correspondence between an organism's signaling system and its natural environment, then there are naturally better and worse systems of discourse, and multiple epistemes can be referred to a more general standard as a test of their accuracy. Thus epistemological pluralism—the belief that there are incommensurable, mutually contradictory, yet valid ways of knowing the world—cannot get any support from epistemological skepticism—the belief that nature cannot be known at all because only humans possess the signal systems that embody knowledge, and those signals are arbitrary and thus have no natural connection with a putative physical reality.

Pluralism can indeed be defended as a temporary posture of laudable humility, maintained until a larger picture emerges. But it can have no defense as a description of nature, which has had thirteen billion years to adjust and fine-tune its signaling systems with respect to one another, so that now they are largely translatable into each other. Our own signaling systems come of the same lineage, are robust parts of nature themselves, and have been subjected to the same veridical tests as any other organ, structure, or behavior common to the world of evolutionary adaptation. Thus pluralism is useless in trying to understand whatever divine emergent properties nature makes manifest.

They Syncretize

Jihad, abstract universalism, total skepticism, and pluralism are all inadequate, as we have seen, to the problem of religious diversity. What then? Perhaps we need to go back to the question and examine it more carefully. Perhaps we should accept the validity of all true religious experience in its particularity, including the inner meaning and expressive appropriateness of all religious ritual and myth. Perhaps the object of religious worship need not be the bland featureless sphere, the all-purpose generalization, the most likely and acceptable explanation—nor a plurality of incommensurable narratives, each quite plausible when taken in its own context. Could it instead be as detailed, complicated, odd and unique, and ad hoc as

history itself, with its staggering variety of ceremonial hats, its tobacco mosaic viruses, its assassination at Sarajevo, its palmetto trees
and stag beetles and astrolabes, its meteor impact at Chicxulub, its
shoes and ships and sealing wax, its cabbages and kings? But we
have been put off, perhaps, by the sheer Rube Goldberg unlikeliness
of the thing that results.

Suppose that what we experience in religion is actually as weird
in its own way as the composite of all the religions would be. This
book is an attempt to visualize it—to fill in, as it were, plausible
connective tissue between the various religious worldviews, to show
how they might in fact be consistent with each other. The word for
such an attempt is syncretism.

This position is not the same as what theologians call "indifferentism" (or sometimes "relativism")—the failure to recognize the
uniqueness and validity of true religion. Indifferentism would correspond to the attitude of one who was so weak-minded that he was
prepared to believe that Christ was Buddha was Krishna was
Mohammed—a trimmer's expedient avoidance of mental work. A
syncretist would argue instead that different religions have indeed
touched parts of the reality, and they are not the same part. There is
only one Christ the redeemer, only one Buddha, only one Krishna,
only one Mohammed. When the great mystics of each religion have
reported their experience, however, there is always a residue, a sense
of something huger and stranger still, in their encounter with the
divine, that their own categories and language could not compass.
Perhaps other religions have touched and described that overplus,
but again in their own terms, so that what is familiar to the Hindu
mystic is part of the dark cloud of unknowing to the Christian mystic; what is clear to the Christian is part of the mystery of Allah; what
is the everyday wisdom of the Sufi is an insoluble koan to the Zen
sage, and what is plain to the Zen sage is a dizzy strangeness to the
master of the Upanishads. But what if we could, now, put those different experiences together into a single pattern?

This project is not new. In fact some of the greatest civilizations in
the world have been based upon just such a synthesis. The ecumenism
of the Roman Empire before Constantine is a good example. Despite repeated and brutal attempts by the Imperial authorities to suppress cults deemed subversive, the very nature of Roman polytheism was such that it could easily absorb foreign materials and make
them its own. Every time the Romans came across a new religion

and deity, they promptly baptized it into their pantheon. The Persian god Mithras was worshipped by Roman centurions manning Hadrian's wall in northern Britain, along with Apollo, Minerva, and Venus. The African god Ammon was interpreted as another avatar of Jupiter. Pompeiian frescoes sport images of the Egyptian Isis. Indeed, the Greeks before them had done the same thing. The marvelous conversation reported in Plato's *Republic* takes place on the occasion of the instauration in Piraeus of the Thracian goddess Bendis.

Hinduism has likewise exploited this special talent of polytheism, so as to give generous welcome to alien deities. Images of Mary and Jesus can sometimes be found among the multitude of sculpted gods and goddesses in ancient Hindu temples. But monotheism can also be syncretistic. Jesus and Mary are great saints for the Muslims. When Dark Age Christian missionaries came to Northern Europe they happily adopted large elements of the existing animist, totemist, and polytheist religions, bequeathing us such ritual remnants as harvest festivals, Halloween, Yule logs, holly, mistletoe, the names of the days of the week, Easter eggs, the word "Easter" which comes from the fertility god Eostre, and the sobriquet for God himself, "Lord," from the Anglo-Saxon chieftain's title *hlaford*. The same blending is going on in Christian Africa, in the Catholic festivals of the contemporary Maya, Quechua, and Huichol, in the cargo cult, and in the rituals of Umbanda and Vodun. One of the three names for the Jewish deity is *Elohim*, whose root is cognate with the Mesopotamian god Enlil, and whose plural form is explained by scholars as a fossil of ancient polytheism.

For me the most delightful syncretism is that of China, wherein three deeply different religions, Confucianism, Taoism, and Buddhism, have been genially merged while preserving their individual differences. Wu Cheng-En's great prose epic *The Journey to the West*—which tells how the holy but rather nerdy priest Tripitaka, helped by the irrepressibly comic god Monkey, carries the sacred scriptures of Buddhism over the Himalayas from India into China—celebrates and cements that union. Its hallmark is a very peculiar and at first off-putting blend of holy seriousness, slapstick comedy, rousing adventure story, tall tale, and postmodern self-reference, full of odd, charming Chinese metaphors, practical jokes, puns, riddles, and anecdotes. The mood or tone of the book is itself part of its meaning: holy seriousness must include a certain hilarity, sacred foolery, and nonsense, lest it seek to trap the mysterious and multitudinous wind of the spirit and thus belie what it would reveal. I would hope readers of these words might come to this book in the same spirit—as Philip Sidney put it, the true poet "nothing lieth, for he nothing affirmeth."

The old syncretisms, however, could not assimilate the exclusivist certainties of iconoclastic monotheism. Egyptian polytheism, which had successfully negotiated the integration of the religious cults of the Valley and the Delta, could not digest the fanatical monotheisms of Akhenaten and of Moses, and was forced to excrete them. The Roman Empire could not ever bring the stubborn Jews to heel, and was itself eventually swallowed by Christianity with its claim of a unique God and a unique path to salvation. Polytheistic Athens found it necessary to give the hemlock to its greatest philosopher, the monotheist Socrates. Monotheistic Islam replaced polytheistic Hinduism in many Asian regions. Christianity replaced the old gods of pre-Columbian America. Across Africa Islam and Christianity gain millions of converts among the local syncretist populations. Even the great Chinese syncretism has been challenged to its roots by the new monotheism of Marxist dialectical materialism.

The urge to oneness in conceiving of the fundamental ground of being has triumphed, and for good reasons. Science itself could never have developed in a polytheistic universe; the inquirer into physical truth must be absolutely confident that the whole world makes one kind of sense, at least at some level. If nature has as many languages as the gods of a polytheistic pantheon, one would never know what language a given fact was couched in, and the test of consistency with other facts, which is the core of scientific investigation, would be doomed from the start. And our actual experience of the success of science and of technology based on it has confirmed the "one physical truth" hypothesis over and over again. The authorship page of almost every article in the scientific journals is mute testimony to the cultural universality of science—the names are from everywhere on the globe. Every smart young person in the world who wants to find out about physical reality ends up accepting the basic premise of science, the assumption that the world is consistent and thus is one.

The problems of polytheistic syncretism are not just problems of knowing, but also of feeling and willing. The very activity of retrofitting one's religion with a succession of new deities and narratives, when unaccompanied by some deeper insight, leads to a loss of seriousness, of sincerity; and even to a loss of compassion, since every mode of feeling is being equally affirmed and thus none is taken especially seriously. There is something a bit cold-blooded about pre-Christian Roman religion as it developed away from its virtuous republican roots toward empire, a coolness shared by those sects of Christianity that emulate the tolerance and easy assimilativeness of classical Rome. The playfulness and comedy and tolerance we have praised in the polytheist must somehow be accompanied with as much love, moral depth, and passion of feeling as could be boasted by a religious fanatic, or our project will have failed.

If we must reject simple jihad, universalism, skepticism, pluralism—and even the relativism that homogenizes the real difference between religions—some kind of syncretism is all that is left. We must somehow integrate radical unity with the demonstrable plurality of religions in the world and of our experiences of its deepest meaning. It will not be enough for us to simply baptize every different creed as we encounter it. Sooner or later there will be a Masada that we cannot conquer in that fashion. What is needed is some court of appeal to which all the pleaders can turn: that court is nature as discerned by science.

Science is the great validator of the unity view of reality, as poststructuralist pluralists recognized when they assailed "western rationality" in defense of their ideas of cultural relativism and the pluralist social construction of reality. But as this book will argue, science may also offer rich views of the nature of the physical universe, and of time in particular, that go a long way to solving our problem of radical diversity in people's experience. A tree—the great metaphor of biological evolution, and the hidden metaphor in the "supersymmetry" model of the elementary particles—has one trunk but many branches. And if time can branch, then there might be room for many narratives without inconsistency. We will not need relativism or pluralism as correctives to our tendency to ignore the multiplicity of things and perspectives, if our view of the single reality of the whole is capacious and branchy enough.

What is the difference between syncretism of this kind, and the pluralism and relativism characteristic of the contemporary academy? Basically, the syncretistic approach continues to hew to the line that there is a difference between right and wrong. Given apparently contradictory but internally consistent accounts of reality, it does not accept the contradictions but turns to scientific knowledge of the world to resolve them. And it recognizes that there are other means of resolving them than by the substitution of one for another, including simple addition. The discovery of black swans in Australia need not lead us to deny that swans are colored, or divide the world into white swan and black swan epistemes, or discard the category "swan" and the reality it lives in altogether; we might, as nineteenth-century naturalists did, simply add black swans to our list of kinds of swan.

The "naturalistic syncretism" that this book argues for is, in the end, not much different from the naïve acceptance of a single reality that is the default option of our sensory and cognitive systems. It took four billion years to evolve that realism, presumably against every alternative calibration of the nervous systems of living organisms. It is an argument, then, that has already won.

3

Desiderata for a Religion of the Future

Avoiding Holy Wars

Let us try to construct a list of requirements that one might make for an imaginary syncretistic religion of the future. These "requirements" or desiderata are not intended to limit the scope of our inquiry so much as the opposite: to indicate the formidable variety of elements that should be included. One limiting condition is, however, implicit: views that lead directly to holy war and religious persecution are avoided, as part of the very mission of this book. The terrorists, political power addicts, profiteers, and murderous psychopaths that parasitize religion as they parasitize government, business, the academy, and every other human enterprise will have no justifications for their activities. But even so, most religious conflicts are not between good people and evil ones, but between the good and the good, and are the more terrible for that fact; and the purpose here is to show that such good folk are not necessarily at real odds with each other, and can in good conscience desist from their strife. Everybody knows that the wise and holy people who most paradigmatically represent their religions are grieved and tormented by the scandal of religious violence. Those people will receive encouragement. There will, moreover, be none of that superior enlightened baiting of religious enthusiasts that turns them into hotheads, rendered stubborn by the imputation of stupidity, ripened for martyrdom and murder by cultured contempt.

This desideratum has a special relevance since the events of 9/11, when murderous and evil religious violence, once thought to be an extinct relic of the past, seems to have thawed out from the chill of secular humanism. The hegemony of secular humanism, revealed as a kind of religion in itself, is now over, and at least one other religion, once held in its spell, has rediscovered its old capacity for hatred. It is thus urgent that some other way of defusing the bloody violence of religious strife be found. Secular humanism, as events in Holland and Britain have shown, is no protection against Wahhabist murderers. Like atheist communist terrorists before them, Islamist terrorists will cheerfully use the freedoms and opportunities offered by civilized democratic societies to try to destroy them. Something stronger than secular humanism must be brought to the defense of decent civil society. Only a new religious spirit, one which is inclusive not out of intellectual uncertainty and confusion, but out of confidence that all genuine human views of things are views of the same thing, will rally us to the great effort of defeating terror.

Taking Care with Abstract Metaphors

The "requirements" for a syncretistic religion of the future will be much less tender and considerate with the relatively recent theologies that have attempted to rationalize and philosophize religion, than with religion's traditional stories, devotions, symbols, and rituals. There will be no particular loyalty here to the essentially mathematical analogies that have been used in the more intellectual reaches of the major world religions to define the divine—metaphors such as infiniteness, timelessness, immateriality, changelessness, and extensionlessness, and even such notions as eternity, omniscience, omnipotence, and perfection. Those concepts are hostages to the philosophical and scientific systems that created them, and have either changed their meanings with scientific progress and new mathematical discoveries, or been rendered obsolete altogether.

For instance, what do we mean by "infinite?" Even nineteenth-century mathematics gave us a theoretically "infinite" series of Cantor transfinite numbers of higher and higher cardinality. In this century we now have, among other candidates for the term, Einstein's important distinction between infiniteness and boundlessness, new proposals for the topology of black holes and other singularities that are infinite in various different senses but spatially very small, and the infinite depth of detail revealed as the fractal attractor of a nonlinear dynamical process is plotted within a finite mathematical space. Which infinite is God? Again, timelessness could plausibly be posited as a term of praise for God when time was defined as a privation of being, the realm of fate, the regime of determinative cause, or the arena of thermodynamic decay and the increase of entropic disorder. But when, as now, time appears to be the crucial ingredient of any conceivable being (since all being is, as we now think, made of vibrations), when time is now the dynamic medium of evolutionary creativity, the only realm where spontaneous self-organizing emergence can take place—would we really want to deprive God, by definition, of any participation in time's life-giving waters? Do the great classics of religion—Exodus, the Book of Job, the Bhagavad Gita, the Gospels, the Koran, *The Divine Comedy*, *Paradise Lost*—make any sense at all if God is incapable of dialogue with human beings, of changing his mind, of being in a story, of a significant sequence of actions? Can a timeless God be free in any meaningful sense?

In like fashion, it is hard to see how three characteristics posited of God by abstract theology—omniscience, omnipotence, and perfection—can coexist, given the moral horrors of the world. This is the ancient problem of theodicy—how can God allow these things to happen? The usual answer, that God wants his universe to be free, seems lacking on two counts. The first is the suffering of innocents, especially children, on account of which Dostoyevsky's Ivan Karamazov respectfully hands back his ticket to heaven. The second is more complicated, but can be usefully framed in terms of the story of the Garden of Eden. Of all the universes God could have created, there were clearly some in which Adam and Eve freely chose disobedience, and thus all the evils and sufferings of the world. But if Adam and Eve were really free—which is the whole point of this explanation—there must equally have been potential universes in which they were freely obedient, and thus they and their descendants lived forever in perfect happiness. If God is both omniscient and omnipotent, he would know which universes would give rise to free and obedient Adams and Eves, and which would not, and he could have chosen to actualize one in which the Fall did not happen, through the free choice of our parents. Thus God deliberately chose the world of suffering and evil, and is therefore responsible for them, and so cannot be perfect. No less a thinker than Kant declared the impossibility of theodicy, given the existing definitions of God. It is said that during the Holocaust a jury of rabbis put God on trial for it and convicted him. But the conclusion of the story—they went on worshipping him nevertheless—suggests that there may be something wrong with the metaphors of omniscience, omnipotence, and perfection, at least in combination, especially with respect to the assumptions about the nature of time that they embody.

Let us thus be less than punctilious in our treatment of abstract theology, secure in the conviction that the intellectual systematizers that created them were more concerned for the elegance of their correspondence with truth as they knew it than with its continuity with the revelations and traditions of religion as such. They and their followers should not be offended on religious grounds if we set aside some of their metaphors, since they themselves were quite cavalier in their own reinterpretations of scripture, tradition, and liturgy. And since their loyalty was to the truth rather than to the then current authority, they would, if they were around to do so, be more likely to applaud further progress in thought, when carried out with their own saving humility, than to condemn the breach in their own authority. The magnanimous Aquinas, the wise Maimonides, the paradoxical Ibn Arabi, the gentle Gautama would surely rejoice at the continuation of their most quixotic of professions.

Respecting Reason

But though the desiderata of our hypothetical religion of the future will not include an insistence on those mathematical metaphors derived from science and philosophy, it will also put out of court any requirement that its adherents abandon reason and the critical reliance on evidence. A good rule of thumb would be the common sense embodied in old legal precedent in a jury trial: one should not have to accept any proposition that would not be recognized as a reasonable assumption when assigning legal liability. It is not a defense to argue that one expected one's daughter to levitate when one dropped her off the roof, because the I Ching had suggested that she would, or to cite religious grounds for denying her a needed blood transfusion.

On the other hand, though our religion should not forbid the reliance on reason and evidence, it should not require it either: there must be room for Abraham's terrifying consent to God's demand for sacrifice. Abraham's offer of his son must be supererogatory; if Abraham had refused, it would have been fair of God not to choose Abraham for a special revelation and destiny, but it would not have been fair for God to condemn him. At the same time, if God had been silent upon Mount Moriah, and Abraham had gone ahead and sacrificed Isaac, our perspective would argue that the killer should then submit himself to the human law, and humbly accept whatever punishment or censure such law would impose for his action, without attempting to defend himself on the grounds that God had told him to perform it. Part of his sacrifice to God would be precisely such submission. But the onus of moral justification would then pass to God: and to say this is not against the spirit of those same scriptures. In the most extreme of all Divine Justice mystery stories, Jehovah appears before the bar when Job demands a court hearing, and justifies him before his false counselors, who had insisted that God could not be called to account. There is the same submission of the Divine itself to the best efforts of human justice in the *Oresteia*, where Athena delegates the trial of Orestes for his mother's murder to a jury of Athenians.

God's own submission to human justice is itself voluntary, supererogatory, since he would in strict justice be free to do anything he wanted with his creation, being the owner of it in an absolute sense. Kant makes the point that it is his holiness, what we might interpret as his artistic integrity in his role as creator (and not his sense of justice, or even his goodness, that is, his bias in favor of his creations) that prompts him to yield to Job's subpoena. God's finest creation is Job's sense of justice; Job's courage in facing God is Leviathan, Behemoth, the great mystery of a creation that takes on its own being and entelechy. Paradoxically, Job's first reaction to his catastrophic losses—"The Lord giveth and the Lord taketh away: blessed be the name of the Lord"—though it concedes God's just right to do what he has done, does not make a sufficient demand upon God's generosity, God's voluntary propensity to abandon executive privilege and enter the narrow confines of the human courtroom. The rest of the great drama of Job tells the story of how God does just that. Thus even in the most terrifying old religious stories about human reason and the human sense of justice, the divine concedes these human claims. A religion of the future should do no less.

Justice is based upon an assumption that reason is valid. But we now know from the work of the logician Kurt Gödel that a system of reasoning cannot prove its own axioms; that the axioms, so to speak, are hanging arbitrarily out there, with no logical necessity at all, generating a universe of reasoning to be sure, but with no explanation in themselves. Reason cannot prove its own validity. Before we reason, we must first make a leap of faith to believe in reason. We can certainly argue about what set of axioms produces a universe that best fits our experience, or produces a moral system that creates the best kind of culture and society. But the very logic in which the argument is conducted is itself founded on the same set of completely inexplicable rules. The decisions we make here are like the decisions we make when we choose the rules of a game, not like when we adjudicate a contested move in a game; they hinge on how we like the game that a given set of rules creates, not on whether a rule has or has not been violated. This book itself, by its very nature as a book, assumes a relatively peaceful society with an economic system that can get books to people who want to read them, and the political freedom to do so, and the wealth to afford such leisure, and the atmosphere of tolerance that can accept disagreement. Any book, qua book, that does not make these assumptions is an act of bad faith. But it is an act of faith either way, to write—and to read—a book. We are already committed.

The difference between religious and nonreligious people is not the difference between faith and reason. It is the difference between those who recognize that an act of faith implicitly precedes anything we do, and those who do not. Both religious and nonreligious people can be believers in reason, and it is perhaps more important to believe in it than to admit that one's belief is a matter of faith. Socrates in the *Phaedo* branded as a great sin the practice of what he called "misologic"—the disbelief in reason. He was right to do so. But it is a sin, not a mistake.

Avoiding the Trap of Signs and Wonders

A subtler negative requirement for our hypothetical religion concerns miracles and magic. Any religion that relied for its acceptance fundamentally upon miraculous or magical events as proofs of its validity would be hostage to technological obsolescence. If those miracles can be duplicated by human technological advances, they are no longer miracles: they are no longer contradictions to nature that compel belief. Today we can levitate (in helicopters), communicate at great distances (radio, telephone, Internet), create visions without substance (film, TV, holography), restore vision to the blind (cataract and nerve surgery), view the past as it happened (old newsreels), heal paralytics, destroy cities in an instant, bring the medically dead back to life, create earthquakes, make machines that think, circle the earth in minutes, bear other people's babies or posthumously sire our own, part oceans, reattach limbs, feed six billion, induce visions in the brain, build temples in three days, and travel to the moon. Thus if we base the authority of the founders or saints of our religions on such feats, our religion begins to look like a contest of technological prowess—how did the saints or gods miniaturize their equipment so cunningly, what was their power source, were they using lasers or superconductivity? And our religious worship is reduced to a request to be entertained by futuristic conjuring tricks before their time. Arthur C. Clarke's famous dictum to the effect that any sufficiently advanced technology is indistinguishable from magic can be turned around to mean that any merely miraculous religion is just an anticipation of future technology.

The great religious founders were right to warn us against our appetite for signs and wonders. My interchangeable use of the terms "magic" and "miracle" is intended to drive home this point. Healers of the next millennium may well for convenience carry their nanotechnological healing machines around in their own bodily tissues, and as a matter of course heal blindness by thinking a moment, mixing their spittle with a little dust to feed the nanomachines, smearing it on the blind person's eyes, and asking them to wash it off later. One day we may by sophisticated neurotransmitter control be able to induce mystical trance states and suspended animation—and in doing so we may only be repeating the traditional psychic technology of the yogi or Tai Chi master. Imaging techniques already give us primitive forms of telepathy, in that we can see a patient thinking; military and prosthetic control interfaces connect nerve impulses to electromechanical devices; one day we may be able to link directly the electromagnetic signatures of synaptic circuit firings in two people, so that they can literally share their thoughts. Eventually we may be able to halt the fraying of the telomeres at the ends of our chromosomes, control the processes of apoptosis, replace our brain cells, and become biologically immortal. If the criteria that define deity are such achievements as these, we would have become God; and if so, what would we do when we needed something larger, better, more valuable, and more beautiful than ourselves?

This caution against miracles is not intended as debunking, either of the miracles themselves or of the technology that we have been devising to replicate them. The meaning of the miracles is, as the dull old theology always preached, spiritual and moral, not the heap powerful juju magic that the despisers of superstition imagine it to be. The real question is what the miracle means, the deep poetry of its intricate metaphor, so insubstantial to the literalist, so blindingly real to the person of spiritual maturity. Miracles are, rightly, reminders of the much greater miracles of our everyday existence, obscured to us by custom and complacency. As the alchemists came to understand, magic was only truly valid if it induced a transformation in the soul as well as in matter—and if one had the transformation of the soul, who would need gold or even everlasting life?

If Mozart is sitting composing a concerto and his dead father Leopold appears to him, which is the greater miracle, the father's apparition or the son's artistic power of music? Any good twenty-second-century virtual reality geek will be able to project a ghost; but the concerto is irreplaceable. If Moses was merely a bio-warfare superhero, I submit that the talents of Pharaoh's tomb artists were more miraculous than his powers. The meaning of the Passover is more marvelous than the plagues and floods and scourges that passed over the chosen ones. Your own mind, that meat computer reading these lines, that little flash of annoyance, is more marvelous than any magic; and the transubstantiation you will perform at your next meal, metamorphosing bread into synaptic circuitry and thence into thoughts, is as astonishing a sacrament as any in the Church's catechism. Not that sacraments and magic are insignificant: but their right use is to astonish us by their trickery, like Edgar's on the cliffs of Dover, into a sudden Zenlike recognition that our lives are indeed a gift, a miracle.

The answer to the technology/miracle problem is that we should take technology itself more seriously from a spiritual point of view. Jesus, Lao Tse, Mohammed, Buddha used technology both in their lives and in the metaphorical medium of their revelations. Jesus himself, a carpenter, was a technologist by profession, and his parables are full of the machinery of his agrarian and pastoral society. The three leading technologies of the Roman Empire in Jesus' time were perhaps masonry, carpentry, and metallurgy; the equivalents today might be telecommunications, computers, and biotechnology. An analogous contemporary Jesus might be a pharmaceutical engineer or computer chip designer before taking up his ministry. Our problem is that modern technology grew up in a relentlessly secular cultural medium, and thus we have been blinded to its spiritual and moral significance. Technology does in fact do something miraculous—it literally extends the dominion of mind over matter, it innervates matter with mind, and in so doing it incarnates the spirit in the physical world. It is the only practical means of fulfilling the great moral injunctions of religion—to feed the hungry, heal the sick, clothe

the naked, enlighten the ignorant; it is the very instrument of the divine in this world. Thus we can revise our caution about miracles and magic: we should indeed take seriously the magic of the religious founders, to the extent that we are prepared to accord appropriate spiritual significance to technological progress. And this means insisting that our technological progress should indeed constitute spiritual improvement, and criticizing it when it doesn't.

Using Ritual Rightly

Continuing with our list of desiderata: our religion must avoid any claims to exclusive salvation based on other than moral grounds. That is, justification cannot be based upon an exclusive language, doctrinal credo, a specific ancestry, special foods, or food taboos, one's presence in a particular location, a ritual practice such as baptism, or a bodily modification such as tattooing, footbinding, circumcision, or clitoridectomy. Why this stipulation?

We are well aware by now of the furious passions that can be aroused by doctrinal differences—one of the reasons the nation-state emerged in the Renaissance was to protect the murderous zealots of different Christian sects against each other. More recently we have had our noses rubbed in the atrocities of scientific racism, the belief in justification based on ancestry. More recently still, large numbers of young Muslim men have shown themselves willing to murder unknown men, women, and children while committing suicide, on the basis of religious belief. These evils are not simply the result of the corruptions of modern society, since such crimes are as old as history itself; they plainly contain a powerful instinctive element.

One of our most persistent irrational reactions is extreme disgust at the ritual practices of others. People in one group tend to find the intimate practices of another sickening and uncanny. Cremations and purifications in the Ganges, so ordinary and dear to Hindus, feel bizarre to non-Hindus. Anti-Semitism flourished upon lurid depictions of *The Protocols of the Elders of Zion* and dark evocations of the strange garments, the caftan or gabardine of "the Jew." Catholic relic cults appear grotesque to outsiders. Pictures of Shaker dances and Unification Church weddings and the Muslim Hajj at the Kaaba in Mecca have a horrible fascination for the nonparticipant in those faiths. The idea of the Eucharist disgusts many Muslims. "Savage" tribes are thought of as cannibals; "inferior" subcultures, like Appalachian mountain folk, are thought of as incestuous; the rituals of

Saddhus, Black Baptists, Vodun worshippers, and Freemasons are experienced by outsiders as strangely obscene. The soul food of the other is often nauseating: grits, haggis, kishke, borscht, bread pudding, wichiti grubs, kimchee, escargots, and so on can have for outsiders the queasy associations of somebody else's breast milk. Orthodox Jews and Muslims find pork-eaters unclean. Hindus are revolted by western eaters of beef. Perhaps that disgust is a derivative of the fear that any member of a highly ritualized social species must instinctively feel about being left out of his own group's language, accepted lineage, holy place, and ritual practice. Such exclusion would mean sterility and death to a hunter-gatherer.

Ancient and atavistic loathings and terrors divide us enough already, and do not need to be reinforced by theological doctrines of exclusion from communion based on nonmoral criteria. But we are a ritual species; and our own dear tongue, family lineage, ritual clothing, food, holy places, bodily scarrings, and so on are vital to the construction and maintenance of a sane self. They also constitute the essential inner discipline we need to counter those parts of our nature that we inherited from very ancient ancestors, whose genetic interests were vested in their own individual survival and reproduction rather than in those of the group. Our tens of millions of years as members of a cooperative social species, genus, family, order, and class were preceded by hundreds of millions of years as members of a phylum and kingdom largely devoted to individual genetic selfishness. Thus our lusts, aggressions, greeds, and mendacities need to be tamed not only by the inheritance of more recently evolved tendencies toward altruism, gregariousness, truthfulness, self-control, honor, and love, but also by the codes embodied in group ritual and tradition. The evolution of our brains not only made it easier to be social and cooperative, but also to lie, defect, cheat, and plot. The huge and terrifying psychological sanction of exclusion from the ingroup, itself based on ancient instinct, is the most powerful of our weapons against the evils of our nature.

Local religious customs and taboos can not only give us the freedom of self-discipline, an identity, and a psychological core, but somehow also conduct us toward the great central mysteries of our lives. The world would be a sadly poorer place without Three King's Day in Mexico, the nose-rings of the California teenager, the ritual honey beer of the Ndembu, the dreadlocks of the Hasid or the Rastafarian, the family shrine of the traditional Chinese home, the

Passover matzo, the gentle presence of the sacred cow. Without the language of what is dear and profound and ancient and holy, how could we represent to ourselves that deepest good and beauty and truth that alone makes life worth living?

Thus the challenge is to retain local identifiers, customs, and observances, with their beauty and comfort, and their value as codes of communication, instruments of social cohesion, and liberators from the demons of our nature, but to do all this without allowing them to be a source of hatred between communities. We may be encouraged by the fact that when human beings are not economically under the gun, and when they are secure in the habits and practices of their society, they are often driven by boredom to seek foreign shores— "to seken straunge strondes," as Chaucer puts it—in pilgrimage, tourism, or education abroad. By the time that we are all middle class, as seems likely by the end of the twenty-first century, the problem of local ritual practices may go away—not because such practices have disappeared or lost their sacramental meaning, but because they have become powerful tourist attractions. In Santiago de Compostela, the great Galician pilgrimage destination, it is not unusual to see rituals from Mexico, Germany, Ireland, Africa, and Spain all going on at once, in which the participants are simultaneously performers, tourists, worshippers, students, and consumers.

To suggest a more complex and mixed attitude toward ritual is not to diminish religion, but to echo the great sages of all religions, who insist that we not fetishize ritual and set the service before the god. Indeed, we miss the meaning of the ritual if we treat it as a fact, a practical necessity; we become like dogs eating sacramental bread out of ordinary canine hunger. We also miss the meaning if the ritual becomes a merely automatic custom. Ritual should always be challenging, a "new and shocking reevaluation of all we have been," as T.S. Eliot puts it. Rituals ought to be bizarre and strange, in the same sense that art should always, in the words of Ezra Pound, "make it new"—and Pound understood, as his followers sometimes did not, that to make it new is often to revive the old. The ancient liturgy of the Passover contains a series of awkward questions, to be asked by the youngest child, that raise once again the meaning of the ritual as opposed to its mere practice. Devout Buddhists call Buddha "shit on a stick" for the same reason; one koan goes: "See the Buddha, kill the Buddha." Even the Buddha himself should not be fetishized. Christ, the second person of God, is depicted as a baby suckling at his mother's breast, a scandal designed to shock us out of legalistic observance; as anyone knows who has had one, babies demolish any routine and force the household into a constant state of improvisation. The devout tourist may be a better pilgrim than the dweller who worships by rote.

Though our imaginary syncretistic religion should be fully embodied in practice, ritual, human physical life, local custom, local history, local folkways, and local tradition, its very variety should act as a defamiliarizing shock, to push us through that last small door in the ritual that leads us to the presence of the divine. Thus claims to exclusive salvation based on place, language, race, specific ritual practices, and so on are paradoxically in contradiction to the value of the local and specific.

Obeying the Moral Law

One of the few characteristics truly common to all religions is a code of conduct or moral law. Even existentialism, with its profound suspicion of any essential authority, insists on what would be called virtues in another religion—honesty, attention, courage, love, compassion, and so on. Thus a requirement for a moral system should not in itself be controversial. But which one?

There are many today who believe that human values are constructed by society. Among those of us, myself included, whose livelihood depends upon that concept—anthropologists, teachers, parole officers, psychoanalysts, politicians, artists, sociologists—the notion of social construction is hard to resist. For such professionals, there is a great temptation to exaggerate the differences among societies in various parts of the world as regards morality, and in the nineteenth century the sudden influx of undigested anthropological information that followed the establishment of colonial empires did seem to indicate that morality changes from one place to another. Professional considerations aside, we are better able to quiet our consciences if we can tell ourselves that the slightly smelly thing we are doing would be perfectly acceptable in Samoa or the Amazon jungle. But more mature consideration and further research have shown that underlying the surface variations in human codes of conduct there are robust universals that prohibit murder, theft, lying, incest, adultery, and so on, and that enjoin such virtues as cooperativeness, truthfulness, generosity, and self-control. Like language, which has been shown by Noam Chomsky, Derek Bickerton, Steven Pinker, and others to have a universal deep structure and developmental process, morality is a human instinct. The work of games-theory replicationists like Skyrms, Sober, and Wilson, which I have already mentioned, proves that group selection not only can work, but can by good Darwinian selective processes bring about positive inclinations in individuals of many species toward altruism and cooperation. The psychological outcome of selection for such virtues would be a conscience; we are, by this logic, most likely to be happy if we are good.

The notion of a moral instinct is opposed not only by the social constructionists—who, rejecting any biological givens in human psychology, want all morality to be a matter of local social ideology—but also by many hard-line biological determinists, who want to see the physical universe as devoid of value, meaning, direction, and freedom. Indeed, the two groups collude in supporting our existing educational system. But the rule that moral values cannot exist in the physical universe is nothing more than a rule, an unfounded article of metaphysics. Why should a value not also be a fact? After all, human values and faiths can literally move mountains—consider any large military or engineering or architectural project. Yet humans are part of the physical universe; and why should we deny factuality to those values yet ascribe it to neutrinos, for instance, which are so insubstantial and ineffective as to pass through the earth without affecting it at all?

Evolutionary materialists, like Richard Dawkins, like to argue that the gene is completely selfish, and that since all life depends on genes, all life is essentially selfish, bent only on survival. For Dawkins the fundamental unit is the selfish gene; for single-cell biologists, it is the selfish cell; for more traditional Darwinists, it is the selfish individual. (One could argue that even Dawkins is not fundamentalist enough, and that the primary unit should be the selfish codon, the selfish nucleotide, or the selfish atom.) Despite their theoretical differences on what the fundamental unit is, selfishness believers are agreed that from the fundamental unit on up, no new properties of the moral kind can emerge. Does this mean that because the letters of this sentence on the computer screen are made of featureless dots, they themselves are featureless dots? Or that because water is made of two dry gases, it is not wet? The assertion that life is essentially selfish is metaphysics, as I shall show.

The key idea in evolution is survival; yet living organisms by definition are dying all the time; they live by dying, which is metabolism. Biological "survival" is a grand, breathtaking, and accurate metaphor, but only a metaphor. Nothing of a gene is surviving in material reality when it reproduces; what "survives" is a piece of abstract information, the sequence of nucleotides on the DNA chain. My liver dies and resurrects itself every forty-eight hours or so. It is no more "surviving" than a flame. A chunk of granite that has survived in good hard fact for a billion years would, if it could, both laugh and shudder at the lunatic claims of a living organism to be surviving by hatching its eggs, or even by eating and excreting. Yet life is very effective—there is as much limestone around as granite, and limestone is the corpses of living organisms. A mere phantom—a pattern of information—can move mountains; for the crustal plates of the Earth and the eruptions of volcanoes are now driven by the boiling and fizzing of life-created rocks as they are subducted into the mantle. And if so abstract, so spiritual a thing as that pattern can masterfully determine the structure of large chunks of matter and the whole surface of our planet, why should not the even more abstract and metaphysical entities of goodness, freedom, soul, and beauty?

Our genes determine our bodies and brains, and they determine how we think and feel and behave. True. But our feelings and thoughts determine our behavior, which determines how our brains and bodies grow, and whom we choose as a mate, which determines how future genes will be distributed in the species. Suppose that beauty, value, meaning, freedom, planning for the future, teleology, soul, and so on were complete nonsense, but, were a species to operate *as if* they were real—by nurturing its young, self-sacrifice, ritual celebration and the like—such a species would be at a competitive advantage with others. In all the games that nature provides for us to play, cooperator groups, if they are clever enough, will outbreed equally smart noncooperators. In order to keep up, the other species would in turn be forced to develop teleological behavior, and thus the core value assumptions of teleological behavior as a guide to preserve consistency. Eventually every part of the world would be filled with organisms and structures that acted *as if* the universe were meaningful, valuable, and full of intentional design. Concede still that all of those value-abstractions are still complete nonsense. But that concession is now a purely metaphysical one, with no practical or scientific relevance. Those abstractions will have become laws of nature. Good hard empirical science would tell us that of course the universe is a work of God in progress. A belief in the meaninglessness and valuelessness and directionlessless of the universe would then be an act of purely religious faith, maintained in the face of the cold hard facts of meaning, design, love, progress, and beauty. The austere and faithful biological materialist, in his sackcloth and ashes, could then say with the mystic, "Credo quia absurdum est'"—I believe because it is absurd.

We might devise a sort of test, similar to Alan Turing's well-known Turing Test for artificial intelligence, for purposive teleological value-oriented behavior. It could go thus:

If any entity—for instance the gene pool of a species, a band of social animals, an individual animal or plant—cannot be distinguished in its actual behavior from one which is acting purposively according to values and intentions and planning for the future, then:

That entity must be deemed to be acting purposively according to values and intentions and planning for the future.

But if morality is an aspect of our biological nature, the relationship between morals and religion begins to appear in a new light. Part of the evolution of religion itself may have been to cement a system of social controls that backs up our emerging moral instincts, and sanction selfish defectors from the common good. Again, this is not to diminish either religion or morality, but to root them more deeply in this real evolving universe. The only authority for the idea that the divine might not be so rooted in the universe is the taboo against mixing fact and value. And this taboo was one of the articles of the unwritten treaty that resulted from the Enlightenment standoff between religion and science.

If biology in itself can give a solid foundation for morality, do we even need religion any more to provide supernatural sanctions for moral behavior? Let us see how far a purely naturalistic morality can get us; our religion of the future should indeed endorse the rules that result. We must have a moral law, formal or informal, and a practice of virtue to give it effect, since we are creatures of habit and are much better at doing things we have already rehearsed. Our religion must base its moral law on the values inherent in the common cultural and genetic inheritance of the human race—that is, to be a good member of the religion should also mean that one is a good human being, a good primate, a good mammal, a good animal, a good piece of matter, a good arrangement of energy. Evidently part of the religion's mission would be to find out what "good" means in each case. For example: to be a good human being is to fulfill one's obligations; to be a good primate is to play one's proper part in the troop; to be a good mammal is to nurture one's young; to be a good animal is to maintain one's health and to maximize the representation of one's informational structure—at this level of organization, one's genes—in the next generation; to be a good piece of matter is to survive; to be a good piece of energy is to have a certain magnitude and a coherent vibratory structure. The highest level of this moral hierarchy, fulfilling one's obligations, indeed already covers most of the Ten Commandments, including the injunctions against murder, lying, theft, adultery, and so on.

It might perhaps be argued that religion is better off without a moral law and sanctions for behavior, since modern secular democratic society, with its institutions of research, education, publication, and law enforcement, can now recognize our biological need for morality and include it in the human rights agenda of life, liberty, and the pursuit of happiness. We can only be happy, it appears, if we are good; and the right to the pursuit of happiness would thus include the right of access to moral instruction and the right to live in a cultural environment that encourages good morality. We have already come some way in this direction in the United States and Europe, with legislative and judicial decisions on civil rights, public education, abortion, child pornography, truth in advertising, antitrust, public health, the environment, drugs, tobacco, divorce, child support, family leave, and so on that reflect implicitly moral intentions. Indeed, so pervasive is the moral thrust of modern government that it has already come into direct conflict with the second of the great rights, that of liberty. Can religion now shrug off the age-old burden of maintaining moral standards and leave it to the government?

The answer must be yes and no. Government can institutionalize moral principles and enforce them at some cost to life and liberty in wars and policing and taxes. But government cannot by itself make real progress in morality. If Aristotle and Cicero are to be believed, some moral improvement comes from the civic experience of public service in a republic. But the republic of Athens murdered Socrates and the male population of the island of Melos, the republic of Germany elected Adolf Hitler, and the republic of Serbia elected Slobodan Milosevic. It could well be argued that what moral advances one does see in a republic actually derive from the participation of its members in a free marketplace, which enforces in its own decentralized ways the virtues of civil society, and the carryover of the values inherent in contract making, business reciprocity, and negotiation into the practice of politics. At best, perhaps, government can act as a somewhat inefficient moral ratchet, preserving moral gains made elsewhere. This is no mean task, with its own kind of honor and its own quiet nobility; we need Mr. Smith to go to Washington and Mr. Atticus Finch to defend the innocent. But Messrs. Smith and Finch cannot and should not in their capacities of legislator and lawyer explore the borderlands of spiritual discovery.

It would certainly be a relief to religion to be able to shuck off onto courts and parliaments some of the role of nanny, of fusspot, of maintainer of the respectable status quo, and thus have its hands free for the much more challenging adventures to which its mission calls. Immanuel Kant has shown us that there is something base about a merely prudential morality—the cupboard love that does the right thing in calculating pursuit of a reward. Religion has rather uncomfortably threatened its flocks with the torments of hell and bribed them with the delights of heaven, and it would be a blessed respite not to have to do that any more. Indeed, that role is corrupting in many ways—even the denial of the carrot-and-stick morality can be a perversion of its own, implying that an action is only good if one doesn't enjoy it or profit by it. The true forte of religion, as one can clearly see in its masterworks, the teachings of Buddha and the prophets and Christ and St. Francis and the like, is to actually set the bar of goodness higher, or even change the nature of the game itself, and thus—since happiness comes from being good—to invent or discover higher joys.

The religion of the future may thus be freed up to go on from mere obligation—without denying obligation's foundational role in morality—to richer fields of profit. In Plato's *Republic* Socrates quickly reaches the limits of morality as envisaged by the solid citizen Cephalus, who defines justice as giving each man his due. Though Socrates himself could scarcely have foreseen it, the further adventure into the mystical realms of the sun that he sets off on then was to result in almost unimaginable moral discoveries in the future. For after all, giving each man his due was in his time quite consistent with slavery, wars of conquest, the subjection of women, infanticide, imprisonment without trial, the withholding of the franchise from large classes of people, marital rape, and genocide. Without the openings into further realms of value that were provided by the religious imagination, good government could happily have gone on permitting or encouraging these practices. The Christian concept of the individual soul, the Islamic concept of the moral and responsible society, the Protestant conscience, the Enlightenment notion of intellectual freedom, the achievements of modern liberalism, all had their initiating spark in the religious imagination, especially in that fiery place where art, philosophy, theology, and mysticism cannot be clearly distinguished.

Certainly religion should endorse the rendering unto Caesar what is Caesar's, and even surrender to courts and legislations what were once its own moral discoveries. But its major moral duty is to continue the evolutionary development that we have already seen in the emergence of animal, mammal, primate, and human codes of valuable behavior, into higher realms of challenge and delight. Thus the separation of church and state has a function beyond its initial necessity, which was to keep the citizens of a multiconfessional society from each other's throats. It opens up a realm of play, of theological experiment, that is the crucible of new value. Modern democratic society takes much moral enforcement upon itself, and thus renders religion in some senses unserious and toothless; but it is precisely this lightening of the stakes that makes religion once more free to sail the universe of the divine imagination. The danger is that the state, together with the political realm that supports it, will begin to imagine that it too is capable of moral discovery, and can legitimately innovate in the ethical world. The results are horribly clear in this century: they range from the moralistic totalitarianism of Hitler, Stalin, Mao, and Pol Pot to the less serious but deadening orthodoxies of fifties Americanism and nineties political correctness. The best the state can do for morality is to reflect the moral principles of its electorate, trust that art and religion will go on refining those principles, lower taxes, and open free markets so as to maximize the flow of ideas and values, and hope for the best.

The reader may have noticed that freedom, which is one of the highest values for many religions, and which many would argue is a precondition of morality, is not explicitly on this list of desiderata. The reason is that many religions—Calvinist Protestantism, Greek polytheism, Stoicism, and Epicureanism, most brands of scientific materialism, some forms of Hinduism, and some traditions of Islam, for example—seem to find the idea of freedom oversimplified, and insist on apparently contradictory ideas of predestination, *tyche*, necessity, material determinism, karma, kismet, or fate in general.

Interestingly, these religions by no means advocate irresponsible conduct, and since freedom and responsibility are definitionally bound up together, there must be some rich complexity that these traditions have glimpsed that may deepen our understanding of freedom. Let us therefore assign freedom to the *agenda* of religion, rather than to its *principles*.

Acknowledging Higher Entities

All religions acknowledge something more important than the immediate interests of the self in the present moment. That higher entity, or ultimate concern (in Paul Tillich's phrase), or *mysterium tremendum et fascinans* (in Rudolf Otto's) can be identified in various ways. Nature religions find it in the coherences of the physical world; vitalistic religions find it in the life force or the planetary ecosystem; personal religions like Judaism, Islam, Krishna Consciousness, and Christianity find it in the personality of their God or gods; social religions like Confucianism or Marxism find it in the spirit of society or the dialectic of history; materialistic religions find it in the irreducible properties of matter; mystical religions, like Buddhism, find it in the core of Being itself. Even Existentialism, seeking to avoid any reference beyond the here and now, cannot help hypostasizing experience or community or the benign indifference of the universe.

For a view of the world to be religious, it must recognize something greater than the self. If religion is defined this way, it would be hard to find any coherent standpoint that was not religious; and this itself shows a promising ecumenism that warrants us in adding such a proviso to our list of desiderata for a religion of the future. That "something greater" must be comprehensible enough for us to know when we are pointed in its direction and to provide a guide for conduct. But it must also be mysterious and unfathomable enough to be plausible: for if it were plainly understandable, our limited self's mind would be able to contain it in its entirety, and thus it would not be higher or greater than the self. This consideration should act as a caution in our project to imagine what the complete picture of the divine might look like: new mysteries should emerge in the new, more synoptic view, even as the old puzzles are removed. In resolving difficulties that divide religions from one another, we should not pave over the central mystery of religion, but rather extract the fences and territorial claims that religious controversy has already put up within it.

If this proviso is valid, it suggests that the unity of the physical world, the vital energy of life, the mysterious inwardness of the person, the larger cultural entities of society and history, the fundamental laws of the material universe, the nature of Being, and the immediacy of experience might all be different parts of the same very strange and complicated whole. Thus we have a further guide for our theology, in that we cannot leave any of them out or set up one at the expense of another. For instance, we must find a way of reconciling religious views like those of the Quakers or the Existentialists, in which the connection with ultimate concern is very much through the individual, and in which the dangers of communal agreement and ceremony are strongly emphasized, with views like those of peasant Catholicism, or Umbanda, or Black Baptist Protestantism, or Confucianism, in which the major unit of connection with the divine is the group, ritual and collective feeling are given a very positive valence, and too great a tendency toward private devotion is thought of as selfish or perverse. Likewise, we must find ways to accommodate both the divine immanence of nature religions and the divine transcendence of supernatural religions, both the expressiveness of the ikon and the purity of iconoclasm, both the passionate feeling of communicating with one's personal savior and the wise and dispassionate peacefulness of meditating upon the impersonal ground of being.

But if there is something higher than the self, and if the self desires to communicate with it, another interesting proviso appears: the need for some equivalent of sacrifice, prayer, contemplation, and worship. To communicate is to trade; and sacrifice is the word we use for trading with the divine. We are social animals that exist in an ecosystem; our fundamental nature is based on reciprocity. We could not exist as human beings without trading with each other and the world; sacrifice is whatever gift we give to what is higher than we are to express ourselves to it and indicate our awareness of its gifts to us, even if those gifts are merely those that come from being included in a larger whole. Prayer is talking to that higher entity; contemplation is trying to look at it; worship is appreciating it for what it is. In this light, sacrifice, prayer, contemplation, and worship are simply the ways we find of avoiding a churlish insensitivity to the gift of existence. How we do it varies hugely, from the painstaking care with which a scientist measures the radiation of a star, to the holy bloodshed of the Aztec pyramid, from the sudden awed hesitation of the bridegroom in contemplation of his beloved's beauty, to the lighting of a candle or the striking of the Shinto temple bell.

Rejoicing

The words we have for joy, ecstasy, and the like would scarcely be meaningful without a religious context to give them substance. Consider the sequence: satisfaction, contentment, pleasure, happiness, delight, joy, rapture, ecstasy. As the words indicate greater and greater levels of desirable feeling, they simultaneously transform from implying the mere absence of pain or desire to implying the presence of some positive good; from implying beneficial states of metabolism to implying experiences that transcend bodily sensation; from connotations of physical appetite satisfaction to connotations of spiritual union with the divine; from the adequately *here* to the demandingly *beyond*.

The joyful experience of the divine or ultimately real is at the core of all religions; it is the mystical engine of religious motivation. Our religion of the future must incorporate, express, and enable in its narratives, rituals, imagery, and practice the feelings of mystical communion, vision, insight: what the English mystic Richard Rolle described as *calor*, *cantor*, and *dulcor*—warmth, song, and sweetness. We should pay attention to the characteristic descriptions of that joy, which might be listed as follows:

Its odd relationship with sensory and emotional delight, as a sort of litotes: spiritual joy is not physical pleasure, but it is not *not* physical pleasure either; it is not passion, and not *not* passion.

Its physical manifestations in trance, trembling, dance, glossolalia, and so on.

Its superficial similarity to drug-induced states of rapture.

Its close kinship with and frequent accompaniment of suffering, grief, pain, and shame.

Its complex link with both moral goodness and sin.

Its loose but frequent connection with the beauty of nature and art.

Its not-always-reliable association with the traditional practices of asceticism, physical discipline, ritual, meditation, and contemplation.

Its inwardness.

Its transience and fragility, its vulnerability to being easily interrupted and distracted.

The dark night of the soul that is often the portal through which it is reached.

Its connection with prophecy, new knowledge, inspired or shamanic speech, and artistic inspiration.

The Task before Us

The criteria I have listed in this chapter so far are relatively easy to arrive at, digest, and justify. They involve either prudential considerations, such as the ability of religious communities to coexist with each other and with secular society, or widely accepted universals of religion.

The greater difficulties of this project appear when we consider matters of specific doctrine. For instance, many would cavil if we laid it down that our religion of the future need not insist on any of the following: monotheism, polytheism, theism, the immortality of the soul, the Devil, reward and punishment in the afterlife, a personal savior or supreme prophet, the forbidding of images, etc.— since there are major religions which do not include them. Others would object if we stipulated that our religion must, at the same time as not insisting on them, also acknowledge their validity, since they are doctrines (according to the stipulation that is the premise of this book) under which true religious experience has taken place, and many of them, such as the immortality of the soul, the existence of good and evil spirits, and a supreme deity, are very widespread. We can, for instance, affirm the powerful claim by some of the world's greatest religions, that the divine has indeed revealed itself in a personal savior, while pointing out that this savior is divine revelation in the medium of history, and that there are other divine revelations in the media of story, morality, ritual practice, bodily meditation, personal vision, and so on.

There is a delightfully cynical old saying, variously attributed to La Rochefoucauld, Oscar Wilde, and Gore Vidal, that to be happy it is not enough for us to succeed: our friends must fail. A variant of this applies, unhappily, to some religious authorities: it is not enough for my religion to be true: all the others must be false. For those who cannot be cajoled out of the purity of this position, this book will be a waste of time. But even for the others, somehow asserting the truth of all religions must appear to be impossible. What kind of strange beast could correspond to all of those descriptions? Let us turn to science for the beginnings of an answer.

4

Religious and Scientific Truth

Noah's Flood

The question "How could all the religions be true?" implies two prior questions. The first concerns the relationship of religious truth to scientific truth: In what sense is a religion true? The second question—in a way, a restatement of the first—concerns the problem of how to pack all those religious truths into the same universe: What would the universe have to be shaped like to contain them all?

In answering the second question we are in luck. The universe as contemporary science sees it in such diverse disciplines as mathematical logic, cosmology, particle physics, quantum physics, nonlinear dynamics, information theory, thermodynamics, evolutionary theory, chaos and complexity theory, and the study of time, is beginning to look very promisingly like a Rube Goldberg contraption itself—just the sort of place where one might expect to find such a beast as the one the religions have got a feel of.

But first we need to clarify how we should expect a religious assertion or story to be true. In doing this we must walk a fine line between reducing religion to a set of beautiful metaphors on one hand and requiring an exact and literal facticity for religion, a facticity that *science* invented, that traditional religion never claimed, that would put the letter above the spirit, and that would make nonsense of the parables of Jesus and the stories of Krishna alike. If Jesus is literally, as he says, the door to the sheepfold, where are his latch and hinges? Who decides which of the scripture's words are metaphors, which literal truths? Only authority can, and who certifies the authority?

Let us look more carefully at the relationship between scientific truth and religious truth. Are they two alternative and contradictory explanations of the same universe, one true, one false? Do they describe, without contradiction, two completely different universes? Or do they describe the same universe, in different ways? If the last, how are we to describe that difference, so as to avoid bringing the two views into unnecessary conflict?

In the exhausted standoff that followed the bloody religious wars of the Renaissance and Reformation, science and religion agreed to confine themselves to separate territories—science to the realm of fact, religion to the realm of value. That truce allowed for the great intellectual achievements of the Enlightenment, including the foundations of physics and chemistry, and the U.S. Constitution. But it also, perhaps, led to an uncertainty about what is good and true and important in the human sphere, an uncertainty whose consequences we see about us in education, the family, and public morality; and perhaps to a denaturing of scientific knowledge, a stripping from it of human significance and thus historical meaning.

Today there are signs that the *cordon sanitaire*, the quarantine between religion and science, can no longer be preserved. The logic of religion itself has led its moral theology back from the otherworldly contemplation of the divine to a renewed concern with the world of physical reality and human history; there have been too many scandals of religion standing lost in prayer at the sidelines while Holocausts, Gulags, famines, ethnic cleansings, and other human disasters cried out for practical action and attention to real facts. Meanwhile science has given birth to technologies that can no longer be viewed as value-free—reproductive interventions, recombinant DNA manipulation of the genes of animals, plants, and humans, mood-altering drugs, and suchlike; and has begun to speculate in a scientifically legitimate and testable way about issues that are of intense concern to religion, such as the origins of the universe and the possibility of artificial intelligence. Scientific historical scholarship has turned its attention to the actual life of Jesus. Most basic of all is the issue of evolution. Must we go through again the horrors of contested claims to fundamental truth?

William Ryan and Walter Pitman in their book, *Noah's Flood: The New Scientific Discoveries About the Event That Changed History* (New York: Simon and Schuster, 1998), have given us, without entirely meaning to, a very optimistic answer to this question, at least in the special case of the Great Flood. The book tells two stories—one, over tens of thousands of years, the epic saga of how human civilization in Asia and Europe survived and flourished in the huge climatic and geological changes that succeeded the last Ice Age; the other, over a couple of centuries, how religious and historical scholars, archeologists, oceanographers, earth scientists, and climatologists pieced together the first story. It turns out that religious accounts and scientific accounts complement each other very nicely. The key event is the catastrophic flooding of the Black Sea basin, by salt waters from the Mediterranean that broke through the Bosphorus about seven thousand years ago, driving the human civilizations that flourished on the rich coasts of the shrunken lake into a great diaspora, an event that shows up in the myths and legends of dozens of nations. Ship-borne survivors of the flood could indeed have fetched up on the foothills of the mountain range that includes Mount Ararat.

The story of how the deluge was discovered is deeply instructive as to the proper relation of religion and science. In the nineteenth century there were two camps on the issue of the flood: a fundamentalist camp, which hoped to use the new geological evidence that large areas of dry land had once been under water as support for the Biblical deluge; and a secular camp, which saw the new geology as sweeping away centuries of superstition and revealing the flood story as a mere fable. As the evidence mounted, the secular camp seemed to be vindicated; there could have been no world flood, and the geological history of the planet appeared to be one of gradual accumulation and incremental evolution rather than one of dramatic divine interventions. But meanwhile brilliant and courageous young scholars and archeologists, braving the dangers of the turbulent Middle East, had begun to unearth the literature and history of the ancient Fertile Crescent, revealing strong historical evidence for some kind of deluge. And as the twentieth century brought in more and more sophisticated techniques of dating, geological analysis, and data management, a different picture of world geological history began to emerge, one full of natural catastrophes, sudden changes of climate, and, yes, enormous flood events.

The upshot, the discovery of the Black Sea flood, has bad news and good news for both camps. The secularists have to face the disquieting fact that the things that you're liable to read in the Bible ain't necessarily false; the Biblical literalists are faced with a flood that was not a worldwide event. Science is vindicated in the book by the demonstration of its careful process and self-critical concern for accuracy: time and again the researchers that Ryan and Pitman interviewed were forced by the evidence to accept explanations totally opposite to their own opinion and the consensus of their colleagues. The libel current in postmodernist humanities departments, that scientists only find out what they want to find, is once again triumphantly refuted. Scientists are genuinely surprised by facts, which proves that facts really exist and are not a figment of people's imaginations or an artifact of their methods and worldview.

But the religious account of the world is also vindicated. For though the flood was not a worldwide event in a literal sense, the evidence seems to be that the great diaspora of human cultures—spreading new methods of agriculture, pottery making, techniques of architecture, and the Indo-European group of languages across huge areas of Asia, Europe, and Africa—could be said to be one of the originating events in world civilization, and indeed of global importance in terms of human history. The religious account gives us two things. One is the hint without which the scientific investigation might never have happened, the big picture into which might be fitted such otherwise unconnected observations as the currents of the Bosphorus, the coral growth in the Caribbean, the mysterious "stone things" that the boatman of the land of the dead uses for navigation in the Gilgamesh Epic, the depression of the Earth's crust caused by the weight of glacial ice, and the heroic statuary of the Sumerians. The other thing we get from the religious account is the meaning, importance, and thrust of how people took the flood, what it did to them and how it affected their later actions. The very thought that the species life of humanity itself might be ended by some natural catastrophe was perhaps as important as the first realization by some intelligent and introspective cave dweller of his own personal death, and perhaps our own realization after Hiroshima that we could be the agents of our own extinction. If the flood was not worldwide, its implication was. The covenant with God or the gods that occurs in all the religious accounts, and thus the beginning of human history as itself a meaningful process, is both epochal in importance and inaccessible to natural science alone.

The significance of Noah's flood is that now we can see side by side what kind of physical event might lie behind a religious story, and what kind of real significance a scientific fact might have when seen in the light of religious meaning. Religious faith does not mean shutting the eye of reason; and scientific knowledge, though not the beginning nor the end of understanding, is the connective tissue, the vital middle, that connects the two. The great achievements of the Renaissance were based on the unremitting desire to reconcile faith and reason; perhaps we are ready to take up that grand mission again, in a more peaceful and ecumenical way. There is no substitute for that pursuit. The truth can never harm what is of deepest value to the soul.

The Caduceus

There is an even more remarkable example of the relationship between religious and scientific truth in the symbol of the caduceus: the snake-staff of Hermes, Mercury, Moses, and Aesculapius.

The symbol was already ancient when it appears in the mythology of the Hebrews, Greeks, and Romans. Snakes twine about the terracotta arms of tiny Minoan goddesses. The Sumerian court physicians of circa 2,000 BCE carried a staff entwined with two serpents as a sign of their office. The mediator-god Ningizzida, whose symbol is the snake-entwined staff, is depicted in bas-reliefs from the Mesopotamian city of Lagash conducting the king, Gudea, into the presence of the supreme god Enki. (John Armstrong: *The Paradise Myth* [Oxford University Press, 1969]—a most useful book for this study.) The iconography of the Edenic serpent, coiled around the Tree of Knowledge, may be older still, and the story of the serpent in *Gilgamesh*, which, clearly in the same tradition, steals the herb of immortality that the hero has obtained, may be as much as 7,000 years old. The twined-snakes visual motif can also be found in ancient Hindu diagrams of the *chakras*, or energy centers, in the human body. Where the snakes intersect—at the caste point between the eyes, the heart, the navel, the genitals, and so on—the chakras are found. It may even be implied by the yin-yang symbol of East Asia. In Norse mythology, the roots of the world-tree Yggdrasil are gnawed by the world-serpent Nidhoggr.

The snaky rod is called the *karykeion*, or messenger's staff, by the Greeks, and the *caduceus* by the Romans. In its earliest Greek form it appears as a forked stick, the branches knotted to form a loop, but later the staff is twined about by two serpents in a helical embrace, the heads facing each other. This is the form it takes in Roman iconography. The visual motif of the snake-encircled tree is a pervasive motif in Roman funerary statuary, where a hero, almost always accompanied by a horse and a dog, pours a libation with his consort to the psychopomp, Mercury. It is also familiar in the story of Hercules, who must contend with a serpent coiled around the tree when he goes to fetch the golden apples of the Hesperides. The myth scholar Jane Harrison believes that the combination represents Life, and she is clearly right as far as she goes. But the equally strong death associations—the snake/tree seems to grow at hellmouths, between life and death—should make us question further.

There are various Greco-Roman myths of the origin of the caduceus. One is that Hermes came across two snakes fighting each other, and found a way to turn their war into love. He took a staff, given him by Aesculapius, and threw it between the snakes, whereupon they twined around it in the familiar double helix. At once they ceased their conflict; war turned to love, hostility to copulation.

It will be immediately evident that this myth is closely related to the story of Tiresias, who, seeing two snakes mating, killed the female, whereupon he turned into a woman. Seven years later he again saw two copulating snakes, and this time killed the male, upon which he reverted to being a man. Zeus and Hera, who had been arguing about whether men or women derived more pleasure from sex— Zeus maintaining that women did, Hera that men did—took the opportunity to ask Tiresias, who had experienced sex as both a man and a woman. He replied that women derived ten times more pleasure from sex than men. Hera, angered by this response, blinded Tiresias. A different version of the tale of Tiresias' blinding also casts light on its meaning—that Tiresias was punished by Athena, the goddess of wisdom, as Actaeon was by Artemis/Diana, for watching her bathe naked. In any case, as compensation for Tiresias' blindness, Zeus conferred on him the gifts of prophecy and longevity.

What are we to make of this rich mess of tales? The copulating snakes stories clearly establish the meaning of the caduceus as, generally, life itself; more specifically, life as reproduction, and more specifically still, life as sexual reproduction. By an amazing coincidence, the fundamental life-symbol of the ancient world happens to be a pretty exact diagram of the DNA molecule, in which two strands of bases or nucleotides, strung along a chain of phosphate groups, coil in a double helix around a central sequence of weak hydrogen bonds. I argue that this correspondence is more than a coincidence.

Some versions of the copulating snakes myth seem to indicate that the sexual harmony of opposites is achieved against a background of sexual strife—a strife which is itself acknowledged in myth terms to be necessary and beneficial. There is an echo in the story of

Tiresias' punishment of the more dreadful fate—foretold by Tiresias in Euripides' play—of King Pentheus, who likewise gazed upon forbidden female sexual mysteries. The "moral" of that tale, as of the related story of the dismemberment of Orpheus by the Bacchantes, is that there must be a complementary balance between the warring powers of Apollo and Dionysus. Tiresias' attempts, before he has acquired this wisdom, to restore peace by removing one side or the other in the battle results in a compensatory and catastrophic metamorphosis of his own sexuality; and the strife of Zeus and Hera is the cause of Tiresias' distinguishing gifts of prophecy and long life. In some sense, then, the gift of knowledge is related to the tension between sexual hostility and sexual amity, and to the sense of shame experienced by all three characters (and by Athena in the observed bathing myth). The parallel with the Biblical story of Eden is obvious.

The central element of the myth is a snake wrapped around a tree—the supreme symbol of the disruption of order and protean transformation, embracing the supreme symbol of stability, order, and continuity. The snake, whose venom can both poison and, in the hands of a physician, heal—which dies but is reborn when it sheds its skin—is linguistic slippage personified. But it is reconciled symbolically in the caduceus with the staff or tree, whose ancient significance is suggested by the fact that the word "tree" itself is derived from the Indo-European root *deru-*, which also gave us the words true, trust, and troth—the keeping of promises and the continuity of meaning.

The speculations of contemporary evolutionary biology on the origins of sexual reproduction show interesting resemblances to the meditations of these ancient Mediterranean mythmakers. Geneticists suggest that sex arose out of conflicts on the micromolecular level between viral invaders and the host DNA, and between the need for genetic stability and the need for genetic variation. Ethologists and sociobiologists attribute the elaborate ritual behaviors and ardent pair-bonding of sexually reproducing species to conflicts between territorial/aggressive drives and simple copulatory drives, some—for instance, Konrad Lorenz—even suggesting that the pressure cooker of sociosexual selection and competition drove the emergence of higher cognitive faculties and self-awareness and the concomitant extension of lifespan required by species that must learn the complexities of social sexuality. Tiresias the shaman, the ritual adept, acquires his expertise in the future and his longevity, just as the human species apparently did, through an elaboration of a sexual dialectic; a dialectic found, in an even more economical form, in the Hebrew identification of sexual with mental "knowing."

The other major branch of Greek and Roman myths that deal with the caduceus involves its exchange for the lyre, the contract between Apollo and Hermes. What does the trade mean? To answer this question we must come to a deep understanding of the meaning of the lyre and the meaning of the god Apollo. In yet another story, the caduceus came into the possession of Hermes/Mercury by means of an exchange. Mercury had already invented the lyre, using forked sticks and the shell of a turtle. He traded the lyre to Apollo, who gave him in exchange the caduceus, which was originally in his possession. Apollo then gave the lyre to his son Orpheus, who later used it as the essential talisman to pass as a living man through the gates of the underworld in his quest for Eurydice and return unharmed. The lyre was, of course, the instrument by which Greek poets marked the metrical divisions of their oral poetry—the ancestor of the instrument by which modern Serbian and Bosnian *guslers*, or oral poets, punctuate their epic verses on the battle of Kosovo. In myths and folktales trading usually indicates symbolic equivalence, or at least a further, leaked-over, meaning for each of the objects traded.

The tradition in which Apollo, not Hermes, was the original possessor of the caduceus, is also supported by the fact that Aesculapius, the god of medicine, is another possessor of the caduceus (now the symbol of the *pharmakon*) having got it, presumably, from his father Apollo. Apollo was originally not a very "Apolline" god at all, being associated with plagues and arrow wounds, and nicknamed "Smintheus," the mouse-god. In ceding the caduceus to Hermes and taking on the lyre instead, he is being cleansed of his more earthy and organic Dionysian connections and prepared for his role as the sun god of reason and order. Likewise, he slays the serpent Python and takes over the Delphic cult from the old chthonian goddesses who governed it before; but the ancient associations cannot be dispelled. The oracle is a woman, not a man, and she uses the laurel leaf, from the tree of the nymph Daphne who rejected Apollo's advances, as her psychotropic agent to achieve the oracular trance.

The best and most succinct gloss I know on the subject of Apollo's lyre is Rilke's third sonnet to Orpheus (first series), which I quote in A.J. Poulin's translation:

A god can do it. But tell me, will you, how
a man can trail him through the narrow lyre?
His mind is forked. Where two heart's arteries
intersect, there stands no temple for Apollo.

Singing, as you teach us, isn't desiring,
nor luring something conquered in the end.
Singing is Being. For a god, it's almost nothing.
But when do we exist? And when does he spend

the earth and stars on our being? Young man,
your loving isn't it, even if your mouth
is pried open by your voice—learn

to forget your impulsive song. Soon it will end.
True singing is a different kind of breath.
A breath about nothing. A gust in the god. A wind.

Rilke remembers that the lyre, like the caduceus, began as a branched stick. The journey of the poet is the shamanic one: to pass down the branches of the mind's—not the body's—arterial tree into the underworld. Shamans need certain specific skills, that are symbolized in the old underworld stories by the golden bough, the lyre, the clue, the magic flute, the shamanic drum or bagpipe, the spirit-doctor's rattle, or the mask of the angakoq. These talismans refer to the ancient techniques of the arts—melodic structure, poetic meter, dramatic mimesis, the picturing power and pattern design of the visual artist, storytelling, and so on. New research is showing that these artistic forms have a double nature, a twofold loop structure like the figure eight or the infinity sign, with one feedback loop inside, within the neuroanatomy of the human brain, and one feedback loop outside in the cultural tradition.

Poetic meter, for instance, is culturally universal on all continents and in all societies from the most technologically simple and isolated to the most advanced and cosmopolitan, with one interesting exception—the Western free verse of the last eighty years. The human poetic line, with this one exception, is always about three seconds long, rhythmically shaped by regular patterns of long and short, heavy and light, or tone-changing and tone-unchanging syllables, and by such devices as rhyme and alliteration. The three-second line is tuned to the three-second information processing cycle in the brain, which preserves three seconds of short-term memory before storing its essentials as long-term memory and forgetting the rest. If this internal cycle is driven by the external rhythmic stimulus of poetic meter, significant changes in brain activity and brain chemistry occur, as studies of the effects of ritual chanting have shown. The right brain becomes just as active as the left, the limbic system is awoken, and a cocktail of neurotransmitters is released, whose known properties combine alertness, relaxation, pleasure, and challenge. Listening to poetry literally makes us smarter—just as listening to Mozart has been shown to do by recent research.

The Orphic poet uses his lyre as Theseus used his ball of twine, to enter the labyrinth of the human racial past and to return. As Rilke says in sonnet 17:

> Deep down, the oldest
> tangled root of all that's grown,
> the secret source
> they've never seen.
>
> Helmet and horn of hunters,
> old men's truths,
> wrath of brothers,
> women like lutes . . .
>
> Branch pushing branch,
> not one of them free . . .
> One! oh, climb higher . . . higher . . .
>
> Yet they still break.
> But this one finally
> bends into a lyre.

In a few brief lines Rilke here recapitulates the entire Darwinian evolutionary tree of humankind, with glimpses of the growth of primitive hunting technology, the rituals and social structures of kinship, the Venus of Willendorf, the first arts. Through tragic waste and amputated branches the process refines itself into freedom and spirit. The lyre actually grows out of Darwin's tree of evolutionary descent, as its flower (and perhaps as the seed of a future tree).

Thus the lyre itself, in the sense of poetic meter and the other traditional artistic techniques, was both a product of the evolutionary process and, as it articulated itself, the guide of evolution. The human species is, technically, a domesticated species: the domesticators being ourselves and the method being artistic ritual leading to differential reproductive success. Like the human race itself, which eventually renounced its ancient eugenics and called upon its ritual adepts and priests to be celibate, Rilke too rejects the merely sexual compulsions that were human evolution's first fuel— "learn to forget your impulsive song." No temple to Apollo stands at the blood's meetings of three ways; the temple is raised at another crossroads, where the mind's Oedipal questionings lead us to forbidden knowledge of our own origins. But the mental branching grows out of the biological; the tree of knowledge is a branch of the tree of life.

Thus one meaning of the trade of caduceus for lyre is that the caduceus, the mechanism of life, can develop into the lyre, the art of poetry, or that poetry is at bottom the further workings of the mysterious language of living organism. The myth is thus a myth of the origin of language. In modern terms we might say that the trade recognizes the deep parallelism between the discrete combinatorial generative system of DNA and those of human grammar and human poetic meter, and celebrates the latter as an outgrowth of the former. Poetry is fast evolution. Biological evolution is slow poetry.

Another meaning implicit in the trade is the idea of trade itself. The very transaction by which the meanings of the caduceus and the lyre are brought into relationship with each other is itself part of their significance. Mercury was among other things the god of commerce. The Latin *merx* meant merchandise, in the sense that merchandise was something under the purview of the god. His name is cognate with mercenary, merchant, mercantile, commerce, and market itself. It is also the root of mercy; but how can the market be merciful? Isn't it counterintuitive that mercy—and *merci*, the French word for thanks—should come from the same linguistic root as mercenary? What does the legendary ruthlessness of the marketplace have to do with the free gifts of compassion? If, using the excellent *American Heritage Dictionary*, we follow the etymology of this root back to its Etruscan origins, we find the same ambiguity all the way down. The Old French *merci* meant forbearance to someone in one's power; the Late Latin *merces* meant reward, but also God's gratuitous compassion.

Those who in the Marxist tradition persist in seeing the market as impersonal and merciless, are comparing it by implication with the intimate world of uncounted cost and unquestioned trust that they believe exists in the family, in a friendship, in a traditional tribal village, or in a nonprofit organization dedicated to some higher voluntary purpose or liberal art. Perhaps the market is less forgiving than such communities, though anthropologists, sociologists, and novelists have charted the often ruthless politics and unyielding cruelty of families, villages, and universities. But communities of this kind are not the alternative to the market, nor has the market shown any sign of putting an end to them—they flourish still as they always did, and their sphere in society is proportionally no smaller in relation to the market than it ever was. There are two real alternatives to the market. One is the way that communities actually treat strangers and outsiders, and the way communities traditionally treat each other, when they are not trading with each other or governed by a higher authority: that is, by enslavement, murder, and war. The other is the utopian rule of an abstract justice in which there could be no room for mercy, since any communication or gift or exchange other than the application of the law would amount to corruption and favoritism. The market is the place where one can begin to communicate with strangers, where one can negotiate, where there is time to haggle and latitude for error, where a loan can be prolonged (with a "grace" period) because the lender wants his money back, where defeat does not mean extinction but the opportunity to pull off a better deal another day. It encourages a basic level of civility, and requires of those who would profit by it a preparedness to take risks in trusting others, even if the risk taking is the margin for error in the quantification of risk when one is estimating the interest one should charge on a loan.

Mercury is an extremely interesting god in this context: as well as being associated with markets, he was the divine messenger, the god of travel and of thieves, and the psychopomp, that is, the god who conducted the souls of the dead to their final destination, whether Hades or the Elysian Fields. Perhaps we can make sense of him thus: being the spirit of communication and exchange, he is that which allows whole systems of connected feedback to come into being. He is thus the patron of change, since systems can change only to the extent to which they can communicate within themselves and with other systems. Merchants, the "middlemen" of human exchange and often the carriers of news, information, new science, and socially disruptive ideas and diseases, take Mercury to be their leader. The marketplace is the place where both goods and ideas are exchanged, and thus it bears the god's name. Naturally all the illegitimate and cheating forms of communication and exchange—lying and stealing—are also under his aegis. Mercy is kin to thievery; both are unjust. Naturally, too, Mercury conducts human consciousness—itself the product of the internal communication of self-awareness and the external communication of exchange with other human beings in the marketplace of life—across the greatest threshold of change, from life to death.

When we look at some of Mercury's other attributes and associations, he becomes more interesting still. He gives his name to the metal that is liquid, quicksilver, that cannot be held in one place but runs away. Mercy—the things of Mercury—is essentially liquid. It "droppeth," as Portia says in *The Merchant of Venice*, "as the gentle rain from heaven," and is not "strained," however fine the mesh by which we try to strain it out. In alchemy, mercury was one of the two primary opposites, sulphur—a solid—being the other, whose true union through the evolutionary process of alchemical metamorphosis produced perfect gold. Mercury's planet was the harbinger of the two great diurnal changes, day into night and night into day, and thus the link between the day world and the night world: again, Mercury is the reconciler of opposites.

One final detail of the visual iconography of the Greco-Roman caduceus now comes into focus. The two snakes are usually shown facing each other. Thus the image is one of self-reference, of feedback, like the familiar "hall of mirrors" effect created when two reflecting surfaces face each other. Sometimes the two snakes are bearded, denoting wisdom, maturity, and the self-knowledge expressed in the phrase "*nosce teipsum.*" Thus the caduceus contains within itself an intriguing suite of significances, from the purely biological, through the economic and the artistic, to the realms of self-consciousness and the soul.

The significances I have adduced here for the caduceus might arguably seem tenuous or at least idiosyncratic to the Greco-Roman tradition. But a similar constellation of meanings emerges when we turn our attention to the mythology and commentary of the Jewish tradition. Here my scholarship is even more incomplete, but the material is so rich that even a superficial treatment reveals highly suggestive parallels.

The Hebrews' version of the caduceus is a staff—Moses' rod—which can metamorphose by magic into a snake, and can by the power of Jahweh turn back into a staff. The distinction between the two transformations is emphasized by the story of Moses' contest with the Egyptian magicians in Exodus, in which the Egyptians, like Moses, are able to turn their staffs into snakes and bring plagues upon the lands, but Moses' staff-snake eats up the snakes of the magicians. The *Zohar*, a remarkable Kabbalistic work from mediaeval Spain, expatiates: the Egyptians cannot turn their snakes back into staffs or dispel the plagues, whereas Moses can reverse the process. The Egyptians are good deconstructionists, but only Moses can manage the necessary reconstruction.

I believe the *Zohar* is right in discerning a symbolic correspondence among the many rods, wands, or staffs by which the power of Jahweh is exercised in the Hebrew Bible. Moses' rod is usually associated with the mediator-angel Metatron in Jewish folktale and mysticism; the legend is that the rod or staff was originally a branch of the Edenic Tree of Life, and was plucked from the tree by the angel. (Angelo S. Rappoport's *Ancient Israel: Myths and Legends* [Bonanza Books, New York 1987] is a useful source.) Metatron is evidently related to the Mesopotamian god Ningizzida, who is like Metatron a messenger, a mediator between the divine and the human, and a psychopomp. Ningizzida is sometimes depicted with the two snakes emerging from his shoulders.

Moses first obtains the rod during his exile in Midian, when he is commissioned by the Lord of the Burning Bush to lead the chosen people into freedom, and his lips are circumcised by the fiery coal of Jahweh. When Moses raises the rod, the Israelites are victorious in battle. He uses it to part the waters of the Red Sea, and to strike the rock and create a spring of life-giving water during the sojourn in the desert of Sinai. More mysterious still is the role played by the staff when the chosen people begin to doubt the promises of God, and they are bitten by snakes and fall sick. Moses, taking the role of Aesculapius, then constructs a caduceus—a bronze snake upon a staff—and raises it up before the people. Whoever merely looks upon the serpent is cured. Recalling this ancient episode near the beginning of the Gospel of John, Jesus likens himself, as healer, to this serpent fastened to the tree; and thus we may see the icon of the crucifix as itself a version of the caduceus, with the cross as staff and the savior as snake.

In much Western iconography, the snake is symbolically equivalent to the newborn child, especially the foundling child or the child born outside the normal limits of society. Moses' name is the Egyptian term for "son of," a constant reminder of his strange foundling status, his origin among the bullrushes of the great snake of the Nile, and his adoption by the Uraeus-wearing daughter of the Pharaoh. Milton, in the Nativity Ode, likens Christ to the infant Hercules, who strangled snakes in his cradle. I have seen Celtic crosses in Galicia, the Celtic region of Spain, which on one side carry the crucified Christ, but which on the other carry, also crucified as it were, the Virgin mother, in exile, with her baby child.

In the Jewish Bible the rod reappears again and again. Of particular interest is its role in the story of Jacob and Laban. In the story Jacob serves as the ranch manager for his uncle and father-in-law, Laban, who is a hard man who reaps where he does not sow. Jacob is so expert and creative in his work that he makes Laban rich, and despite the fact that Laban keeps changing the rules of his employment, Jacob ends up with both of Laban's daughters and huge flocks and herds of his own. He serves seven years for Laban's elder daughter Leah, seven years for the younger daughter Rachel, and six years for his share of Laban's flocks and herds. Jacob's peculiar expertise seems to be in animal breeding: he mates the most vigorous stock in his uncle's herds and improves the breeds. His knowledge of stockbreeding is symbolized by the rather mysterious procedure of setting up a peeled branch before the herds when they come to drink; this peeled branch is interpreted in the Kabbala as being related to the Metatron-rod of Moses. Like Moses' healing bronze snake/staff, the peeled branch is efficacious simply by virtue of being held up and seen. As we have already noted, the caduceus is an exact diagram of the double-helix DNA molecule. Jacob is evidently a ancient expert in recombinant DNA. Simply to know how snake and staff can be reconciled is sufficient to produce healing and fertility. Jacob's genetic expertise, the story insists, is taught to him by God, who also promises to bless Jacob himself with a multitude of descendants.

Again, there is an interesting relationship here between scientific fact and religious truth. In modern Egypt snake-charmers have a special trick; by winding a cobra around a stick they can induce in the animal a kind of rigid paralysis or trance state. The snaky rod can then be handled with safety as a single object. But the moment the stick is flung to the ground, the trance is broken and the snake begins to move again. Evidently this ancient practice is at the core of the Moses staff story. Moses' difference from the priestly snake-charmers is that he can reverse the process. What the story is getting at, then, is the art of taming or domesticating animals. Moses not only can do it, as the priests can, but he can understand it and thus do it backwards. Likewise, in the Jacob story, there are otherwise inexplicable details that science can illuminate and that at the same time give insight into the meaning of the science. Jacob has agreed with Laban that he can keep for his own all the piebald or particolored animals that are produced by the flock. Under the guidance of God he sets up his peeled staff in front of the ewes when they give birth, whereupon they produce piebald offspring. What is going on? New studies of Russian fur-foxes and of animal domestication in general give us an answer. If animals are bred specifically for tameness—that is, tractability and fearlessness with respect to human beings—the tamest offspring of wild parents being bred with each other, the tamest of those matings bred in turn, and so on, many wild species can swiftly be domesticated. But with the trait of tameness comes a group of other characteristics: a tendency to curly and shortened tails, floppy ears, curly hair, neotenic or infantile behavior, a neotenic tendency in the shape and relative size of head and body, and above all, piebaldness or multicoloredness in the coat or skin. Thus the story of Jacob is a story about selective breeding for domestication; and perhaps even more remarkably, it is a story about how humans selectively domesticated ourselves, and then became conscious of that process itself and were able to assist it. For after all, the whole point of the story is who is going to be the ancestor of the tribe.

The rod of Jacob and Moses is connected in the *Zohar* with the institution of circumcision, the process by which a Hebrew male was enabled to give birth to himself a second time and be reborn in the spirit. In the *Zohar*, as the anthropologist Harriet Lyons interprets it in a brilliant unpublished Oxford B.Litt thesis, the peeled branch of Jacob is a willow-sapling whose bark has been removed to reveal a part white and part red inner body. This wand, which combines the red of transgression with the white of purity, is associated with various mediating figures: Metatron, the mediating angel; Jacob himself, who mediates between the gentleness of Abraham and the severity of Isaac; the Sabbath, the time that mediates between ordinary human time and the time of God; the Shekinah, the mystical female spirit of the chosen people, who as the bride of Jahweh mediates between individual Jews and God; and the male and female principles in general. Circumcision in this view symboli-

cally provides a man with an orifice like a woman's through which
he can give birth to himself a second time. Moses, significantly
enough, as a foster-Egyptian, was not circumcised. During his return from the land of Midian to Egypt the angel of God, angry at his
impurity, takes the form of a great serpent one night and swallows
him down to his feet—almost returning him to the animal womb.
Moses' wife Zipporah rescues him by circumcising their baby son
and smearing the blood upon Moses' feet. In so doing she
transgressively takes the role of the male *moyl* or *mohelet* who per-
forms the *briss* (*Berit Mila*) or circumcision ceremony. Furthermore,
this is a symbolic circumcision of Moses himself, as she explains
when she says to him: "truly now thou art a bridegroom of blood
unto me." Jacob's rod, then, is part of a symbol-complex which includes both biological life and the cultural or spiritual transcendence
of life.

Thus among other things the Jacob story is about what one might
call traditional evolutionary theory. Success is defined as reproductive success; Jacob is the fittest in these terms. He himself sires twelve
sons by various women. He prospers by acting as a selective force
on his herds, accelerating their evolution by what in modern terms
we would call genetic engineering. What the story says about God is
that God is the spirit of evolution and the true guide for what will
survive into the future. But God, like Laban, reaps where He does
not sow: a rentier, so to speak, an owner of the means of production
who gives employment to his workers. God, like Laban, is a kind of
friendly adversary whose demands for repayment create the economic discipline and stimulate the technical ingenuity that ensure
prosperity, and whose arbitrary tests warrant the survivor as the right-
ful heir to the future. The Bible story hammers this point home by
having Jacob wrestle all night with a man (usually interpreted as an
angel) who actually turns out to have been God Himself. Jacob suffers a torn sinew in his thigh from this battle, but gets in recompense
a divine blessing, and a new name: Israel, that is, the position of
ancestor to the whole nation. Jacob, the great saver, is saved.

Jesus' parable of the talents is clearly a gloss upon this story. The
kingdom of Heaven, he says, is like a wealthy man who goes traveling and lends his three servants money (reckoned in weights of
specie called talents) until his return. The servant that gets five talents uses the money to trade, and doubles the money to ten, which
he gives to his master on his return. The servant that gets two talents

also doubles the money, to four, and renders it to his master. The wealthy man praises these two servants and promotes them, effectively making them partners in his firm. The third servant buries his talent in the ground and repays it unrisked and unenhanced, explaining that he was afraid that the master, who has a hard reputation of reaping where he has not sown, would blame him if he lost the money in a risky venture. The master condemns him, and orders the one talent to be taken away and given to the servant with ten talents, explaining angrily that the one-talent servant should at least have "put the money to the exchangers"—played the financial market—so that he could have given it back with usury (interest). "For unto every one that hath shall be given," Jesus concludes, "...but from him that hath not shall be taken away even that which he hath."

In the parable, the Master expects a return on his money equivalent to what a competent money manager could get by playing the financial markets over the period of time the Master is away. The interest rate represents the cost of time. In present-day scientific terms the cost of time is the increase of entropy, or thermodynamic disorder. In human life the increase of entropy shows up in the process of aging—including the onset of menopause, which is a key element in the Jacob and Laban story and in the whole related cycle of stories in Genesis. We, and the physical world around us, wear out over time. The order that we inherit is a loan, which not only must be repaid, but also carries with it a finance charge; the repayment is death, and the finance charge is aging. But two of the servants in the story manage to beat the entropic market rate. Jesus says that they do it through trade, which means that if he has the Jacob and Laban story in mind, which he surely must, Jesus equates trade with the process of evolutionary husbandry practiced by Jacob. In other parables of production, such as that of the sower, Jesus explicitly outlines the process of natural selection that enables one seed to bring forth a hundredfold while another brings forth only fortyfold and another none at all. Thus trade, or productive business, is the continuation of the natural process of creative evolution, and it is one way in which we can use the investment loan of our lives and the available resources of nature to beat the interest rate of entropy.

These economics coincide closely with certain leading ideas in contemporary cosmological physics. The universe is subject to the increase of thermodynamic disorder over time; the demands of Laban and of the Master in the parable cannot be denied. But other processes are at work. The enormous pressure within the dense primal fireball causes it to expand. As the universe expands, it cools. The cooling process itself triggers spontaneous symmetry breaking, as when crystals suddenly form in a supersaturated cooling solution, or frost-flowers blossom on a winter windowpane. Crystals and frost may seem very symmetrical, but they are much less so, forming along specific planes and axes as they do, than the omnidirectional symmetry of the liquid or vapor that gave them birth. That symmetry-breaking can give rise to higher levels of order, embodied in more and more complex molecular forms whose asymmetries paradoxically provide a whole new field of opportunities for new kinds of symmetry to emerge. These forms must in turn compete with one another for survival, and thus further elaborate themselves, until in at least one place in the universe they generated the amazing variety of living organisms, including Jacob's rams and ewes, and Jacob himself. Thus the evolutionary view of the universe corresponds nicely with the Biblical conception that life is a debt to be repaid with interest, but also an investment, which if properly used can yield a return superior to the interest rate.

What is it, in the Hebrew tradition, that the "caduceizing" of a human being by circumcision enables him to do? It is not only to have the wit for selective breeding and breeding money by trade; nor is it only to be certified as cultural, as "cooked," so to speak, and thus separated off from raw nature. It is, paramountly, to be qualified for Yeshiva and the interpretation of the Talmud. As with the ritual of married sexual congress, the right time for that gentle disputation over the Law is at midnight on the Sabbath. It is the place where Jahweh celebrates his nuptials with the Shekinah. The interpretation of the Book is the Hebrew equivalent of the Greek ritual of poetry and drama; the peeled rod is ritually exchangeable for the celebration of the meaning of the word, the singing of the divine verses, just as the caduceus is exchangeable for the lyre.

We can, therefore, summarize the meaning of this ancient symbol in terms of a cascade of transcendences. The snake-encircled tree is certainly a symbol of life; but it is also a symbol of the transcendence of mere life by means of a dialectic which includes death itself. The snake venom can kill or cure. The tree merely grows— though it branches, and thus opens up a future richer than the past. But the snake renews itself, changing its skin in a symbolic death and rebirth, unpeeling itself from itself. The snake breaks the rules.

In biological terms we see imaged here the moment of evolutionary transition from asexual reproduction to sexual reproduction—an innovation which, in evolutionary history, carried with it a complementary invention, genetically programmed death by aging. Sex and death are one process; programmed death clears out each older generation to make room for the next generation, created as true unique individuals by the genetic reshuffling of sex. After billions of years of glacially slow asexual evolution by mutation and selection unassisted by sexual recombination, sex made possible the acceleration of evolutionary change in the last few hundred million years that came with sexual selection and social behavior. Success in territorial and mating ritual, a criterion meaningful only at the level of social interaction, could begin to act as a powerful selective pressure of its own on the genome not only of other species but its own, reversing the traditional causal flow from genotype to phenotype. Species could domesticate themselves to their own social requirements. In one case at least, the human, the sociocultural tail came to wag the genetic dog; the innovation represented by the snake became coupled to the biological conservatism of the tree of descent. Thus in a further sense the caduceus symbolizes also the coevolution of biology and culture.

The next step in the cascade of transcendences is the emergence of market exchange as a pseudosexual system of ideational recombination. The market is in the realm of mind the equivalent of the interbreeding gene pool in the realm of biology. Like the tree, it branches out into new products, technology, bioengineering, systems of bondmaking, marketing, and exchange; and like the snake, it renews itself reflexively and transgressively, engendering its own critique at crucial points of class or ethnic or gender struggle. Indeed, this step in the cascade of significances is the hardest for the academic humanities to accept, since the humanities themselves were created by the market partly as an institution to critique the market.

The final step in this cascade of meanings is suggested on the Greek side of the Mediterranean by the morphing of tree into lyre, the exchange of caduceus for lyre. On the Hebrew side it is symbolized by the rite of circumcision—the caduceizing of the male Jew that qualifies him for the poetic hermeneutics of Torah study. The pun on hermeneutics is intentional; Moses has long been associated with Hermes Trismegistus, the mythical Egyptian sage from whom we derive the terms "hermetic" and "hermeneutic." The creation and interpretation of poetry is the final significance of the caduceus. Genetic evolution is slow poetry; poetry is fast genetics.

Two objections might be raised to this set of interpretations. One is that by multiplying meanings I have deprived the symbol of any particular significance—what is in common among all these different referents? The other, more commonsense still, is how on earth people living millennia before even the invention of the microscope and the Darwinian discovery of evolution—let alone the identification by Watson and Crick of the double-helix structure of deoxyribonucleic acid—could have made the biological connections I have suggested.

The answer to both objections is the same. The double helix is one of the best natural symbols—perhaps *the* best—of the processes of creative replication and feedback that underlie organic life, the evolution of sex, the coevolution of genes and culture, the workings of the market and the self-reflection of poetry and hermeneutics. Those processes are in their broad macroscopic outlines obvious to any thinking observer. But the caduceus is more than a symbol, it is an explicit diagram. A circle is clearly the simplest picture of a negative feedback loop, which cycles back to its beginning state and then repeats the procedure. If we add to the circular motion a linear movement—the simplest possible diagram of an irreversible change—we get a helix, which is the natural symbol of positive feedback, where repetition makes a difference and thus iteration can transform as well as reestablish. If the helix in turn generates its dialectical antithesis, we get a double helix and at the same time a more stable form, since each snake plays the role of figure to the other's ground. We also get a sort of printing system, whereby one snake serves as the "symbolon" of the other, the incomplete half of the coin or *bulla* from which the other half can be reconstructed or identified. The staff or tree between the two snakes is now the natural symbol of dialectical synthesis—and the loose ends, the heads and tails of the snakes, are the natural diagram of the partial open-endedness of the system.

Nature, then, could scarcely help "choosing" the double helix as the shape of its life-molecule; it is the geometrical essence of feedback, self-reference, and replication with cumulative and adaptive variation. And the sages of our human past were compelled both by their own evolutionary heritage and the economy of the diagram's descriptive power to choose the same form.

The tree—in particular, its branchings—is in turn the natural symbol of any process of differentiative growth, of hierarchical function, of the reconciliation of the many with the one, of ordered relationship between local and global, and of family descent. Its three-way joint is a diagram of father, mother, child; of major premise, minor premise, and conclusion; of any logic gate such as a transistor or a grammatical copulative, with input, output, and control; of the branch point of the human body, where legs and torso meet at the organs of generation; of a decision on a decision-tree or a deadline on a schedule-tree; of free choice itself in irreversible time; of biological speciation; of the crystallization process by which the early cosmos of supergravity collapsed out into the four forces of physics and the complexities of the periodic table as the universe expanded and cooled. Hesiod's account of the birth of the gods, the Genesis story of creation, and all other creation accounts I know of, contain this implication of a branching out from the one into the many. Sophocles' *Oedipus Rex*, with its elegant pattern of three-way joints, contains most of my list, especially in the form of distortions or mutilations of the productive three-way junction: the baby Oedipus' stapled feet; the meeting of the three roads from Corinth, Thebes, and Delphi where Oedipus encounters and kills his father; the place to which Oedipus returns when he consummates his marriage; the catastrophic feedback loop in his family tree; the four, two, and three feet of the Sibyl's riddle, whose answer is its answerer and thus whose input gate is its output gate; the collapse of the syllogistic method Oedipus uses for his detective work when the conclusion turns out to be the major premise, the detective the criminal; and the terrible stapling together of one branch of the future with the past that is created by an infallible oracle of what is to come.

Recent developments in the study of the fractal geometry of nature, initiated by the French mathematician Benoit Mandelbrot, lend confirmation to the intuitive connection of tree and snake. What Mandelbrot showed was that nonlinear equations—equations in which the answer on one side of the equation was fed back as one of the terms on the other—tended to generate shapes when plotted in space that were utterly unlike the closed and continuous finite forms of classical geometry. They were, in essence, branchy—they developed themselves on an infinite cascade of scales into finer and finer articulations. Thus tree-shapes are the sign that a snakelike feedback process has produced them, and the "dragons" of fractal geometry (as Mandelbrot christened them) are what are painted when any self-referential branching process is given its head and allowed to play itself out.

Indeed, when we examine the sheer geometry of the caduceus, the combination of snake and tree seems almost overdetermined, and its cascade of significances inevitable. We thus have a symbol with wide cultural distribution, one which may even be culturally universal in Irenaeus Eibl-Eibesfeldt's sense of the term. I suspect that Kukulkan/Quetzal and the other coiled serpents of Mesoamerica, may have the same basic iconography, and that study will reveal equivalents throughout the world. One of the interesting aspects of this particular human symbol is that in certain ways it overwhelms the comfortable distance we like to keep between the investigator or scholar and the material that is studied. Our own hermeneutics, our own investigation of the ideational womb from which we came, is predicted by the symbol itself.

Bottom-up and Top-down

We can, then, expect two characteristics of religious truth. One is that by alerting us to the big picture, the grand scheme of things, religious assertions and stories can lead us to put together the isolated details of scientific fact in a way that makes sense and that can provide the basis for further scientific research. Without the old religious myth of the Trojan War Schliemann might never have found Troy nor, having found it, recognized its significance for the whole Eastern Mediterranean world. In order to think at all a human mind must have a place to stand, a set of certainties against which it can get purchase as it tests the reality of what it investigates. That place of stand and purchase may be implicitly or explicitly provisional—indeed, scientific honesty compels us to concede that our standpoint may be temporary. But whatever that place is, we must have faith in it for the time being. Mathematical logic, as demonstrated in Gödel's Incompleteness Theorem, shows that any axiomatized system must contain propositions that are true but not provable—that axioms cannot prove themselves but must be risked if we wish to engage in reasoning. Other things being equal, one unprovable axiom is no worse than another—whether it be the primary reality of matter, the proposition that I think, therefore I am, the social, cultural, or semiotic construction of reality, the originating dismemberment of Tiamat, the mathematical irrationality of Planck's constant, the will to power, or as Jonathan Edwards believed, the proposition that space itself was God. An axiom is only a hypothesis upon which we are willing to set our weight, ground upon which we are prepared to plant. Thus reason can only operate on the basis of faith; and religion is the discipline that deals with what kinds of faith have borne valuable fruit. If religion is belief without proof, and if Gödel is right that no system of proof can prove its own axioms, and if we all have at least provisional beliefs, then we are all religious whether we like it or not.

The other characteristic of religious truth is that it can provide the human, historical meaning for events, a meaning that is as efficacious—in terms of city-building and population migration and technological transformations of the surface of the planet—as any physical force. The power of belief and commitment is cold, hard fact. Such efficacy is a proper concern of science, whose mission is to give an account of any observable phenomenon. Let that account be as reductive as the observations will justify. Science will and should always prefer reductive, bottom-up explanations, since this is part of the method that distinguishes it as science. We cannot be sure something has a higher-level cause until we have eliminated lower-level ones, and it is easier and more reliable to establish or disprove lower-level ones than higher-level ones. But the method should not dictate the findings of the method. The very fact that science divides itself into disciplines such as physics, chemistry, and biology, whose focus is on different levels of complexity, is eloquent testimony that higher-level systems cannot be adequately described in terms of lower-level ones, and thus that systems, as well as the components of systems, can be causes. If physics, which deals with more fundamental entities than chemistry or biology, could do the work of chemistry and biology, there would be no need for chemistry and biology. Science's glory is to establish top-down causality by assuming all causality is bottom-up, and signaling honestly when the assumption turns out to be invalid.

Religion, as a kind of knowing, starts from the opposite side: its study is of top-down causes, and its core method is the detection of top-down effects upon us. Historically it was not until recent years that science has been able to exhaust enough of the bottom-up causes in the world so that it could begin to look at systemic and top-down ones. Up to that point the artificial separation between science and religion could be preserved. But now scientific disciplines such as global climatology, plate tectonics, ecology, cognitive science, chaos and complexity theory, fetal development genetics, neurochemistry, and the like are routinely investigating large global and systemic causes, and so in many cases intersecting with religious concerns. Thus religious and scientific truth can no longer be separated; religious and cosmological questions are relevant to each other.

5

Freedom, Values, and Strange Attractors

Chance and Necessity

The dualism of science and religion, fact and value, mind and matter has produced profound mental obstacles that have hindered our intellectual and moral progress until recently. One of our most subtly paralyzing dualisms is the apparently harmless one between order and disorder. The idea of liberation—artistic, moral, intellectual, political—under which we have labored for so many years, is especially prone to the corruptions of this dualism. For instance, if order means predictability, and predictability means predetermination, and predetermination means compulsion, and compulsion means unfreedom, the only way we can be free is if we are disordered. The failed political, aesthetic, and moral hopes of the last two centuries have been founded upon a deep discomfort with the idea of order, and what are taken to be its close relatives: hierarchy, foundationalism, norms, and essences—even with value itself, if value is conceived of as being anything other than momentary individual preference.

We have found ourselves forced by the logic of the duality to choose the random, the disordered, the arbitrary, the *acte gratuit,* the unconditioned, the weightless, the unfurrowed—over the ordered, the intelligible, the shapely, the traditional. Our art featured aleatory music, chance splotchings of paint, the random word choices of "language poetry"—John Cage, Jackson Pollock, John Ashbery. What, after all, were the alternatives? We could submit ourselves to the Transcendental Signified, the old man with the white beard, Nobodaddy Himself, the ancestral authority figure who bars the doors against our franchise, our potential for achievement, our free play of art, our sexuality, our political identity, and self-expression. Or we could accept that the world was a dead machine and we were merely parts of that machine, linear and deterministic. We would thus be fated to some kind of mechanistic social order determined by our genes, by the physics of our energy economy, by economic necessity or psychological drives. Indeed, it began to look as if the second alternative was just a new avatar of the first, that the scientists and psychologists and sociologists and businessmen and commissars who preached materialist determinism were really just the old, white-bearded patriarchs and racial oppressors in disguise.

Nobody wants either a random universe or a deterministic one, for freedom and value and meaning appear impossible within them—though great philosophers in the tradition of Nietzsche have struggled to assert them nevertheless. But given the potential for abuse inherent in the deterministic position, it seemed safest to opt for a definition of freedom as a random relationship between the past and the future. The problem is that if this were the case, memory and experience would be completely useless, because to the extent that I act on the basis of past experience, I would not be free. Any connection with tradition would be oppressive.

The postmodernist solution was to make meaning and value completely arbitrary, imposed at the whim of the individual. At least we could individually *perceive* events as meaningful and valuable. One person's perception would be as good as another's, so there could be no political repression. And then—it began to look promising—we could hold the universe to be unknowable because inherently random, and dismiss all science and all objective knowledge as irrelevant, or simply the means to rationalize the political interests of the powerful. Did not quantum theory, if we squeezed it a little and did not look too closely at its beautiful mathematics, be made to say something of the same kind? Were not the white lab-coated ones condemned out of their own mouths? And this is more or less the present state of deconstruction and discourse analysis in the arts.

But then, the knots and toils we tied ourselves into when we tried to profess views such as these! We had discovered a new sin: involuntary hypocrisy—hypocrisy when we were most desperately trying to avoid it. When we opted for simple disorder and randomness, we were faced with the problems of how to *mean* the destruction of meaning? How to publish the discrediting of publication and public? How to achieve institutional recognition when institutions are the legacy of the past and thus based on sadistic repression? How to attack hierarchy in a language with a syntactical tree and grammatical subordination? How to critique a work of art as good or bad? How to get paid for paintings or sculpture where payment must be in the coin of "alienated labor," and private ownership of art is the quintessence of commodification? How, even, to act with a body possessed of an immune system of quite military rigor, and a nervous system strikingly unified under central control?

And can freedom, seriously, be the same as random or disordered behavior? According to thermodynamics the universe becomes more disordered over time, that is, less intelligible and less able to do work. Is freedom just our little contribution to the universal process of increasing entropy? Is it our job as free beings to assist in the destruction of this beautiful ordered universe about us? Intention takes a highly organized brain; can the only free intention be that which would tend to disorganize that brain and disable intention itself? What becomes of responsibility if freedom is randomness? Can we take credit for what we do that is good, if there is no responsibility? Can there be such a thing as justice, for instance, if we cannot be held responsible for our actions?

Until recently the best that we could do with the available intellectual tools in cobbling up a reasonable account of the universe, and of our own freedom, was to devise some kind of combination between order and randomness, linear determinism and disordered noise. The title of Jacques Monod's book on biological evolution, *Chance and Necessity*, puts it well. Perhaps we could describe both the emergence of new species and the originality and freedom of the human brain as a combination of random mutations and relatively deterministic selection.

But even here there were deep and subtle theoretical objections. Evolution seemed to proceed in sudden jumps, not gradually; a new species did not seem to emerge slowly but rather leap into being as if drawn by a premonition of its eventual stable form. Another objection: without the right suite of species, the ecological niche wouldn't exist; but without the ecological niche, the species wouldn't. How do new niches emerge? Again, from a purely intuitive point of view even four billion years didn't seem nearly enough to produce the staggering variety and originality of form to be found among living species—birds of paradise, and slime molds, and hermaphroditic parasitical orchids, and sperm whales, and all. Most disturbing of all, it became clear that the process of development, by which a fertilized egg or seed multiplied and diversified itself into all the cells in all the correct positions necessary for an adult body, was not a mere following of genetic instructions embedded in the DNA blueprint, but was an original and creative process in itself, which produced a unique individual out of a dynamic and open-ended interplay of cells. How a cell develops depends not on a specific instruction from its genes, which after all contain instructions for it to become any part of the body—a piece of an eye, of a liver, of bone, of skin, of brain—but on how the *surrounding* cells are developing, and what chemical messages they give out as they do so. The miracle was that the interplay could produce something in the end remotely resembling its twin siblings, let alone its parents. It was as if the individual organism were *drawn* toward a beckoning form, and that the genes were not so much blueprints *specifying* that form, as gates *permitting* the developmental process to rush to its conclusion.

And the same kinds of problems arose if we tried to apply the chance-and-necessity model to the working of the human brain. Maybe "nature and nurture" don't exhaust the inputs. Can it make sense to speak of *internal* inputs, or forms that *draw* an appropriately prepared human brain into a specific competence, like language? There seemed to be a huge mass of internal, newly emergent laws and principles in such systems that we have hardly begun to understand—and where did they come from, all of a sudden?

The dualism of order and disorder was coming under increasing strain. But within the arts and humanities the traditional avant-garde hatred of any kind of essentializing, hierarchizing, (biologically) determinist, transcendentally significant, and totalizing Order was so ingrained that the more shaky that dualism became, the more passionately it was asserted. The problem the avant garde was honestly trying to solve was that the only alternative to repressive order that seemed to be offered was random disorder, or on the psychological level, whim.

Order Out of Chaos, Chaos Out of Order

Suppose we were to try to specify what an escape from this predicament might look like philosophically. We would have to distinguish between two kinds of order: a repressive, deterministic kind, and some other kind that would not have these disadvantages. We would also have to distinguish between two kinds of chaos, one which was simply random, null, and unintelligible, and another that could bear the seeds of creativity and freedom. If we were really lucky, the second kind of order might turn out not to be the antithesis of the second kind of chaos; they might even be able to coexist in the same universe; best of all, they might even be the same thing!

The extraordinary thing that has happened—an astonishing stroke of good luck, an earnest of hope for the future—is that there really does seem to be the second kind of order, the second kind of chaos. And they do seem to be the same thing.

This new kind of order, or chaos, seemed to be at the heart of an extraordinary range of interesting problems that had appeared as philosophers, mathematicians, scientists, and cybernetic technologists tried to squeeze the last drops of the imponderable out of their disciplines. They included the biology and brain problems already alluded to; the problem of how to describe catastrophic changes and singularities by means of a continuous mathematics; the problem of how to predict the future states of positive feedback processes; Gödel's paradox, which detaches the true from the provable; the description of phase-changes in crystallography and electrochemistry; the phenomenon of turbulence; the dynamics of open systems and nonlinear processes; the observer problem in a variety of disciplines; the failure of sociological and economic predictive models because of the rational expectations and second-guessing of real human subjects; the theoretical limitations of Turing machines (in certain circumstances they cannot turn themselves off); the question of how to fit the fractal geometry of Benoit Mandelbrot into orthodox mathematics; the classification of quasicrystals and Penrose tilings; the whole issue of self-reflection, bootstrapping, and positive feedback in general; and most troubling of all, the question of the nature of time.

In choosing the term "chaos" to describe this new imaginative and intellectual arena, the discoverers of it pulled off something of a public-relations coup without perhaps fully intending to. They could have called it "antichaos," which would have been just as accurate a term, in fact a better one, as its implied double negative—"not not-order"—suggests something of its iterative depth. But "antichaos" would have sounded too much like law 'n order to avant-garde artists and humanists, who would have dismissed it as yet another patriarchal Western mystification. Indeed, some humanists have taken "chaos" to their bosom, as they once did quantum uncertainty, as a confirmation of their pro-random, pro-disorder bias.

A brief—and necessarily oversimplified—explanation of chaos theory, and the related field of complexity theory, may be helpful to readers unfamiliar with these developments (the glossary may be useful for readers who wish to refresh their memory of this account). Chaos theory is a body of understanding devoted to the tracing of hidden order within apparent disorder, and the discerning of disorder within apparent order. It includes such concepts as fractals, catastrophes, bifurcation, iteration, attractors, dynamical systems, nonlinearity, feedback, and the butterfly effect. Related to chaos theory is complexity theory, which is devoted to complex systems, with many elements and/or nonlinear relations. Such concepts as emergence, dynamical processes, self-organization, etc., link it closely with chaos theory.

In a nonlinear dynamical process—often called a feedback system—the various elements all affect each other and there is no clearly determinable origin or priority of cause and effect; or a system affects itself and thus governs its own behavior. Nonlinear processes can include positive feedback, in which a very small initial fluctuation can snowball up into a catastrophic change; this phenomenon has been called the butterfly effect, denoting the possibility that, because of the sensitive dependence of complex nonlinear systems on their initial conditions, the beating of a butterfly's wing in Brazil could trigger larger turbulences which would in turn escalate into a hurricane. The point where an ordered system begins to become disordered is usually called "bifurcation."

The "attractor" of any dynamical system is the form that its various behaviors trace out in its "phase space"—an imaginary space whose axes are the various variables required to describe an object. Those variables could include the three dimensions of its location, and its speed, momentum, direction, temperature, pressure, density, etc. Obviously this tracing out often requires more dimensions than the familiar three of space, making the whole hard to visualize; and thus phase spaces are usually carefully edited to show only the variables of interest to the observer, or those which make a significant difference to the object's behavior. For instance, a swinging pendulum, gradually slowing through friction, traces out a simple spiral when its speed and direction are singled out as the axes of its phase space. Complex dynamical feedback systems in which all the elements are interacting demonstrate irregular behaviors that are often called chaotic. The phase space tracings of such chaotic behaviors can be elegant fractal forms, called "strange" attractors. These include the Lorenz and Hénon attractors. Likewise, when in a nonlinear mathematical equation the solution to the equation is fed back again into the equation as one of its original variables the result is sometimes a set of values which—when plotted in a phase space denoting how quickly the solutions increase to infinity or converge to a single value—a "fractal" form of great beauty is generated.

A fractal is an irregular geometrical shape that continues to reveal significant detail at any scale of magnification and cannot be represented by classical geometry. Fractals are said to be "self-similar"—that is, like coastlines, branching trees, river tributaries, or clouds, they show similar shapes at different scales, whether "close up" or "far away." This property is also called "scaling symmetry" or "internal symmetry," since this is a symmetry denoting invariance under changes of scale, rather than invariance under changes of angle or rotation. Since such forms can have the odd property of filling up the space available to them with more and more detail, a line densely kinking to fill up a plane, or a surface densely folding to fill up a volume, they seem to defy the conventionally absolute distinctions between one-dimensionality and two-dimensionality, two-dimensionality and three-dimensionality, and so on: mathematicians have thus been able to classify fractals in terms of how densely they fill the next dimension up, thus generating the concept of a fractal dimension. As well as one-dimensional lines, two-dimensional sheets, and three-dimensional volumes, for instance, there might be forms like electrical discharges, corals, or lung bronchi that would have a fractal dimension of 1.85 or 2.37.

The most familiar of all fractals is the Mandelbrot Set. The mathematician Benoit Mandelbrot discovered this set, usually represented by a colored diagram of surprising beauty (the "radiant snowman"). It is obtained by taking a field of complex numbers (i.e., ones with both real and imaginary components), squaring each one, adding the result to itself, and then feeding the end product back into the equation as the initiating variable. The initiating numbers are color coded to indicate how quickly they either increase to infinity or approach some limit, and displayed on a graphic plane. A subset of the Mandelbrot Set, or a blowup of some part of the visual representation of the set, is called a Julia Set. Like its parent set, it reveals infinite varieties of new detail at different scales. The Mandelbrot equation is a classic nonlinear equation in the sense in which I am using the word. The iteration, or repeating of an operation or process, is essential in many branches of chaos and complexity theory.

Iteration need not produce a dull uniformity of product, but can generate unexpected new forms of order.

This capacity to create new forms of order has been dubbed by the Nobel Prize–winning chemist Ilya Prigogine "self-organization": a process in which through the interaction of all its elements with each other and with themselves, a relatively stable system emerges. The rolling boil of a pot of heated water is a good example of the result; another is the Great Red Spot of Jupiter, a storm that has raged in the same form and at the same latitude for hundreds of years at least; a third is a living organism, whose gestating cells have through their mutual interaction specialized themselves to produce a functioning plant or animal. There is evidence that the brain establishes coherent and retrievable memories in the same general way.

These areas of new research have led to a general theory of "emergence." The core concept of emergentism is that new forms of being, such as life and mind, can come into being by natural processes which, crossing certain thresholds of size, complexity, etc., must organize themselves into different kinds of entities displaying new "emergent" properties. As a simple example, the dry gas oxygen, when combined in sufficient quantities with the dry gas hydrogen, produces water, which displays the emergent property of wetness, with its specific characteristics of forming drops and a meniscus, clinging to surfaces, etc. One molecule of water is not wet; yet when enough are added together, wetness emerges. This book generally accepts the emergentist position, but does not draw from it the conclusion that a creator is unnecessary. Rather, however, the creativity is immanent in the process of emergence itself; from a theological point of view, the exquisitely adapted forms of the world are not so much the products of an external designer, as the lineaments of a divine biography.

In order to understand the deeply liberating point of chaos (or antichaos) theory, we will need to go into the differences between deterministic linear order and chaotic emergent order, and between mere randomness and creative chaos. Let us begin by considering an odd little thought experiment.

Suppose we were trying to arrange a sonnet of Shakespeare in the most thermodynamically ordered way, with the least entropy (thermodynamic disorder). We cannot, for the sake of argument, break up the words into letters or the letters into line segments. The first thing we would do—which is the only sort of thing a strict thermodynamicist could do—is write the words out in alphabetical order: "a compare day I Shall summer's thee to?" As far as thermodynamics is concerned, such an arrangement would be more ordered than the arrangement in Sonnet 18: "Shall I compare thee to a summer's day?..." as composed by Shakespeare. Here, in a capsule, is the difference between deterministic linear order and chaotic emergent order.

We could even test the thermodynamic order of the first arrangement by a further experiment. Suppose we coded the words in terms of gas molecules, arranged in a row, the hottest ones corresponding to the beginning of the alphabet, the coldest ones to the end, and so on in alphabetical order. If left to themselves in a closed vessel the molecules would, because of the increase of entropy over time, rearrange themselves into random alphabetical order (the hot and cold would get evenly mixed). Just as in a steam engine, where the energy gradient between hot steam and cold air can be used to do work, one would be able to employ the movement of molecules, as the alphabetized "sonnet" rearranged itself, to perform some (very tiny) mechanical task. And it would take somewhat more energy than we got out to put the molecules back into alphabetical order, because of the second law of thermodynamics.

As arranged in Sonnet 18 those words are already in more or less "random" alphabetical order. Yet most human beings would rightly assert that the sonnet order is infinitely more ordered than the thermodynamic, linear, alphabetical one. And in other respects the poem does seem to exhibit the characteristics of order. It could, if damaged by being rearranged, be almost perfectly reconstituted by a person who knew Shakespeare's work well. The sonnet can "do work:" it has deeply influenced human culture, and has helped to transform the lives of many students and lovers. It is an active force in the world precisely because it does not have the low-entropy simplicity of the alphabetical order that might enable it to do mechanical work. Here lies the basic distinction between "power" in the mechanical, political sense, and the mysterious creative influence of art.

But though we have distinguished between the two kinds of order, it is equally necessary to distinguish between the two kinds of chaos. Otherwise we would be in the predicament of someone like Stanley Fish, the "reader-response" theorist, who has been forced by the "order-disorder" dualism into asserting that any random sequence of words, chosen perhaps by flipping the pages of a dictionary, would possess a richness of interpretive potential equal to that of the sonnet; and thus that the very idea of text is either meaningless or extensible to everything in the universe.

If reader-response theorists understood information theory, it would be enough to show that their mistake is to confuse "white noise" with "flicker noise." White noise is made up of random amounts of energy at all frequencies. One could certainly imagine that one was listening to the sea when one heard acoustic white noise; there are even devices that make white noise to soothe people to sleep. But there is nothing there to understand or interpret. On the other hand, flicker noise, which does not at first sound very different, is the "sound" that a system makes that is ordered in itself and at the same time highly unstable and going through continuous internal adjustments by means of feedback: a good example is a pile of sand onto whose apex new grains of sand are being dropped one by one. There are many one-grain avalanches, fewer multi-grain avalanches, fewer still mass avalanches, and only the occasional collapse of a whole slope. The sequence of these avalanches obeys laws and forms an elegant fractal pattern when plotted on a graph. What one hears when one hears flicker noise is the combination of these events; and if one analyzed it carefully, one might be able to work out the size of the grains, the interval of their deposition, and so on. There is real meaning to be extracted. Our reader-response theorist refuses to extract it.

But this example is perhaps rather abstract. Flicker noise is not just the "sound" made by piles of sand. It is also what we get when we "listen" in a crude way to highly complex organic systems. For instance, suppose we take the temperature of an animal: that reading is flicker noise. The temperature is made up of a combination of fantastically organized and intricate metabolic processes; yet it is indistinguishable from the "same" temperature taken of a simple chemical reaction, or of a random mixture of unrelated processes, which would be white noise. The problem is that a thermometer is a very crude instrument; but it is not enough to do what reader-response theorists would do, that is, to accept its crudity as accuracy, and to make up for it by imagining all kinds of exotic meanings for the animal's temperature that had no necessary connection with its organic metabolism. What makes it a crude instrument is precisely that it makes no allowance for the nature of what it is measuring.

Another example of flicker noise is what you would "hear" from a set of electrodes applied to someone's skull if the electrical signal were translated into sound. Just because one could imagine that the squeaks and booms and whistles one would hear resembled perhaps the song of humpback whales, that would not mean that the sound "meant" humpback whales. But this mistake is exactly analogous to much contemporary art criticism and interpretative theories of literature, the arts, or history, which discount the inner personal intentions and meanings of the author, whether the author authorizes a poem, a piece of music, a painting, or an historical act. By discounting those personal meanings, and perhaps substituting the crude statistical measures (the "temperature") of gender or race or class interest, we may avoid the bugbear of authorship—authority—but we lose any understanding of what it is we are dealing with: we cannot distinguish a living organism from a stone, and are in grave danger of treating them the same.

Meanings

In the realm of artistic value, the idea of nonlinear systems generating emergent forms of order can prove very illuminating. When, in the move away from traditional societies to the modern state, we abandoned the old religious notions of the soul, of beauty, virtue, higher values, honor, truth, salvation, the divine, and so on, we suffered a genuine loss. But perhaps now we can re-found some of those beautiful notions upon a new-old basis. The strange attractor of a chaotic system can look very like a Platonic ideal form: though any instance of the outcome of such a system at work is only partial and apparently random, when we see all instances of it, we begin to make out a beautiful, if incomplete and fuzzy shape. Might not virtues, ethics, values, and even in a way spiritual beings, be like those deep and beautiful attractors?—and might there not be larger systems still, including many brains and the interactions of all of nature, that would have attractors not unlike the Divine as described by religion?

Meaning itself can be redefined in terms of the relationship of strange attractors to the physical processes they describe. Any nonlinear dynamical system, when triggered by a stimulus, will generate a sequence of unpredictable events, but those events will nevertheless be limited to their attractor, and further iteration will fill out the attractor in more and more detail. The brain itself holds memories in the form of such attractors, the dynamical feedback system in this case being Hebbian circuits of neural connections. Thus we can picture the relationship of a word to its meaning as the relationship of a given trigger to the attractor that is traced out by the feedback process it initiates. When the word "refers" to a perceived object—say, a smell or a sight—that object is one that can trigger a subset of the full attractor, as a Julia Set is a subset of the Mandelbrot Set. Thus a single word can trigger a "meaning-attractor," sections of whose fine detail can also be triggered by various sensory stimuli. This description rather nicely matches with our Proustian experience of connotation and poetic evocation, and with the logical form of generalization. It accords with the results of linguistic experiments concerning the relative strength by which a given example—say, a duck, an ostrich, or a sparrow—is recognized by a speaker as belonging to the meaning of a word ("bird"). It also explains the difference between ideas and impressions that exercised the philosophical imaginations of Locke and Hume: the richly detailed subset evoked by the sight of an object would certainly make the general sketch of the whole set evoked by the word look somewhat pale by comparison.

Since the trigger—whether the word or the sensory stimulus—is itself part of the feedback system, it is encompassed by its description, which is the attractor proper to it when it is allowed to iterate its effects upon a complex neural network. Thus the represented, the representation, and the experiencer of the representation are all part of the same physical system. The usual critique of physical descriptions of representation—for instance, John Searle's Chinese Room analogy for artificial intelligence—is that however a given object is represented inside the physical system, it requires a smaller system inside the system to see it and know it, or, as John Eccles believes, a detachable nonphysical soul. The chaotic-attractor theory of meaning holds out the promise of an intelligible physical description of meaning that does not require an inner homunculus or the intervention of a metaphysical deus ex machina, with further attendant problems of infinite regress—how does the god in the machine perceive and know the representation?—to make it work. One way of putting this is that the issue of reflexiveness, of self-reference or self-inclusion, has been transferred from the metaphysical level where it can only be interpreted as a barren infinite regress or reductio ad absurdum, to the physical realm where it can be studied as we study turbulences of other kinds, with their own emergent properties and self-generated orderliness. The reflexiveness, we feel intuitively, should be there in any account of meaning; the trick is to keep it from messing up our own thinking about it, and place it where it belongs, in the operation of the brain itself!

It remains to suggest how this "attractor theory" of signification might work itself out in the etymological history of a language, and express itself in terms of phonology, morphology, and metaphor. The social and cultural dimension of language, like the neurosensory dimension, has the form of a nonlinear dynamical system with strange attractors pulling it toward certain "archetypal" forms. Those forms could be seen in the odd "targetedness" of the great soundshifts that periodically convulse a language; they can also be observed in the way that metaphorization will take parallel paths in different languages, so that when a colorful idiom from another language is presented to us, we can almost always find an equivalent in our own. Thus the words "spirit" in English and "Atman" in Sanskrit have identical metaphoric histories, as do the words "kind," "nature," and "genus," all of which came together again in English, having led separate lives in Germanic, Latin, Greek, and other tongues for thousands of years since their original common root in Indo-European. Metaphorization and sound-changes are every new human generation's way of committing a sacrificial impiety against the tongue of its ancestors, an impiety that commutatively atones for the crime of the ancestors themselves in similarly appropriating the language for themselves from their own mothers and fathers. And since meaning dies the moment it ceases to cut slightly against all previous usage—a valuable if overemphasized and not entirely original contribution of Deconstruction—it is *constituted* by this continual low-level feedback between the language and the world it contains.

Such might be the rudiments of a new, evolutionary poetics and a new nonlinear theory of meaning and representation. Obviously I have only scratched the surface here; the point is that we do not need to sit helplessly in the morass of late poststructuralist despair and misologic, and that there are still worlds for the literary humanities to conquer.

And there are practical implications of this model of meaning. (By now such phrases as "model of meaning," with their invitations to further reflexive iteration, should hold no terrors for us, since we hold a clue to the labyrinth, a clue whose own windings are equal to the windings of that dark place we would discover.) One implication is that many of the characteristics of the relationship of word and meaning are already present in the relationship between a percept and the experience of it. If a sense perception can generate a sort of "Julia Set," then in a way a sense perception is like a word. That is, we share with other higher animals the elements of a sensory language that preexisted the more encompassing kind of language that uses words. Or we could put it the other way around, and say that language is just a larger kind of sensing, using internal triggers to evoke larger attractor-sets than any percept could. Obviously we have here a further reason for exploring our relationship with our animal friends: it is a way of understanding the fundamentals of our own language, of discovering that ur-language we share with other parts of nature than ourselves. One huge advantage of that ur-language is that it is not riven by the linguistic boundaries that divide the more fully human languages like English and French from each other; and if we learn to speak it better, we may find more common ground with cultural Others as well as with biological Others.

In one sense, of course, we already possess such ur-languages, in the shared imagery of the visual arts and in the "universal language" of music. But the theory of meaning proposed here suggests that there is something analogous to music and visual imagery that underlies language itself, obscured by its more recent evolutionary achievements, to be neglected only at the cost of a vitiation and graying of our expression and understanding. I came to this conclusion by an entirely different route a few years ago, while translating the poetry of Miklós Radnóti with my remarkable colleague Zsuzsanna Ozsváth. In the following section I shall discuss the discoveries we made together, and in this way give body to the critical and linguistic theory proposed here, especially to the concept of the ur-language. Suffice it to say here that poetic meter turns out to be a sure road to the ur-language, or to change the metaphor, meter is the lyre or golden bough or magic flute that enables us to enter the underworld of that language and to return with intelligible gifts for the community. Meter, like music and visual imagery, is an ancient psychic technology by which human nature and human culture are bridged; appropriately, and as we might imagine from our discussion of the fractal harmonics of Hebbian synaptic circuitry, meter is a rhythmic and harmonic system in itself, a way of inducing the wave functions of the brain. The lyre through which Rilke traces

Orpheus in the *Sonnets to Orpheus* is the poetic form of the sonnet itself.

If the words of a poet can induce in another's brain the same strange attractor that they proceeded from in the poet's brain, an extraordinary possibility presents itself. This possibility is that when those harmonics are in our heads we are actually sharing the thoughts, and indeed the subjectivity, of the poet, even if he or she is dead. The poet lives again when his or her attractors arise in another brain. Poetry, then, is a kind of artificial intelligence program, that springs into being when booted correctly into any good human meat-computer.

Problems in the Study of Society

The notion of the strange attractor can be useful not only in understanding artistic and poetic values, but also in the much more down-to-earth realms of history and sociology. Any analysis of historical events we make, or any theory of social behavior we formulate, is itself one of the determining factors in the situation it describes. Thus there is no "meta" position, no detached Olympian viewpoint from which objective assessments can be made, and therefore no escape from the apparent chaos of mutual feedback. Even economists are just another group of competitors over what constitutes value.

Not that this struggle for ontological control is a blind one. We would be totally ineffective at it if we were not able to assess the motives and assume the worldview of others. And even this would not be enough. Our imaginative model of the other must contain its own image of oneself—the gift, said Robert Burns, is to see ourselves as others see us; and that image itself must contain its own assessment of the other. And our outer negotiations take place not just between our own persons but also among the entire dramatis personae of the inner drama by which we estimate the future. The confusion is not one of blindness, but of too much sight; not of randomness, but an excess of determinants; not of chaos, but of an order too complex to be explained before the next complicating event comes along—of which the next, complicating, event is the best explanation.

Indeed, this capacity to impose our interpretations on things is not only our predicament but also what enabled us to second guess, predict, and control the simpler systems of nature, such as the biological, chemical, and physical ones. We bought our power over the rest of nature with the essential uncontrollability of human events. We can control nature to the extent that we stay one step of reflexivity ahead of it. Nor is even nature innocent, but is itself the resultant and living history of a cosmic evolution which pitted many forms of reflection against each other; the marvelous cooperation of nature is a prudent and subtle form of mutual feedback. Even so, when we find we can reduce another organism to a successfully testable set of laws and predictions, it is a sign that we are dealing with a lower order of reflection than our own.

Thus to attempt to do so with human beings—to educe and apply the laws governing them and to predict their actions—is, in human terms, a viciously aggressive act, an attempt to get control at the expense of others' freedom. It implicitly reduces human beings to the level of lower animals, even to that of inanimate things. But this indeed is what much social and economic history, much sociology and progressive political theory, have attempted to do. The promise such studies held out was not lost on those with the sweet thirst for power. Transformed into political programs those systems appeared in our century as the great totalizing regimes—Marxism, Fascism, National Socialism, International Socialism. We should not be surprised at the vigorous counterreaction of human cultures against such systems.

In the light of this analysis it now becomes clear why, with the best will in the world, all principled revolutions have ended up diminishing human variety and freedom in their societies. For a revolution to be truly freeing it must be unprincipled, in the sense that its intentions do not rest on a predictive theory of human social behavior. Principles in this sense must be sharply distinguished from values, which are much more complex products and guides of human history, including within them the nonlinear flexibility and creativity of their past. The American Revolution was an unprincipled revolution, which is why it succeeded when so many failed. But unlike most later revolutions it did not question the great values of human life, and indeed recommitted itself to them. Such principles as the American Revolution possessed, enshrined in the Constitution, really amount to a declaration of regulated intellectual anarchy or unprincipledness. The separation of powers, which is, more than equality and more even than democracy, the central message of the Constitution and the thematic undertone of every article, is an intuitive recognition of the reflexive, self-organizing, unpredictable, feedback nature of history, which by reinterpreting its initial conditions is able to forget them.

Separation of powers makes politics into a drama, not a treatise. Perhaps the true hidden presence behind the Constitution is William Shakespeare. All the world's a stage. We are all actors, in both senses of the word. Our inherent value derives from that condition, not from Kant's notion that we are ends in ourselves. We can still keep our dignity even if we are, for immediate purposes, means, as long as we are actors in the drama. Even if their function is to serve, the crusty boatman or witty nurse or pushy saleslady are interpreting the world from their own center, are characters, dramatis personae, to be ignored by others at their peril; and are thus free.

But of course even this formulation which I have made is itself a part of the situation it describes; it is a speech in the play, to be evaluated by your own reflexive processes of assessment. Let us see whether the line of thought it prompts is a more or less freeing one than its competitors.

We immediately run up against a large problem. Does this critique of historical and human studies mean that they must revert to the status of chronicle and appreciative observation? Like amateur naturalists, must their practitioners only be collectors, without testable hypotheses or laws? Should we just admire the exquisite coiled turbulence of human events, wonder, and move on? The French historian Fernand Braudel is almost such a historical naturalist; there are moments as one contemplates his great colorful, slowly roiling paisley of Mediterranean history, seemingly without direction or progress, that one could wish for little more out of history. Should not the historian be a sort of Giacomo Casanova, a *picaro* among the courts and sewers of eternal Europe or China, remarking and "thickly describing" the choice beauties to be seen on one's travels?

On the face of it, a very attractive approach; but it abdicates that very activity—holistic understanding and the enrichment of the world by interpretation—that characterizes the human *Umwelt*, the human species-world, itself. The admonition not to totalize is the most totalitarian command of all, because it essentially dehumanizes history. The feedback process of human culture is a feedback of what deconstructionists would call totalizations. The open-endedness of history is created by the competition and accommodation of various candidates for the last word, the dernier cri, the formula of closure (including this one); it is an ecology of absolutisms. Nor is this ecology a random play of flows, without direction or growth; technology, records, and enduring works of art constitute ratchets which prevent any return to earlier, less complex states of the system, just as genetic inheritance did in earlier ages. Thus history is an evolutionary system, with the three factors required for evolution to take place: variation (provided by the unpredictable paisley of reflexive events), selection (provided by the competition and accommodation of "totalizations"), and inheritance, a conservative ratchet to prevent what is of advantage from being lost.

We are already embarked on the venture of making sense of things. The only way open is to seek forms of understanding and descriptive categories that are proper to our own level of reflexive complexity. To do this is essentially an artistic, a constructive, a performative, a religious activity, and it cannot fully depend on the capacity for calculation by which we claim to understand the rest of the natural world. History is an art, even a technology, even a liturgy, as much as it is a science; and it is so not only in the activity of historiography, but also in that of research.

I am suggesting, in other words, that what is going on is a change in our fundamental paradigm of historical and human study. And here another set of major scientific advances comes into play. Most workers in the historical and sociological fields still accept the cultural determinism that was one of the first naive responses of the West to the cultural diversity of the newly discovered nonwestern world. Thus for them the units of historical study, human beings, are tabulae rasae, blank sheets to be inscribed by cultural conditioning or economic pressures.

More recently, however, in fields as diverse as cultural anthropology, linguistics, twin-studies, paleoanthropology, human evolution, psychophysics, performance studies, neuroanatomy, neurochemistry, folklore and mythology, and ethology, it is becoming clear that we human beings bring to history and society an enormously rich set of innate capacities, tendencies, and exclusive potentials. We uncannily choose, again and again, the same kinds of poetic meters, kinship classifications, calendars, myths, funerals, stories, decorative patterns, musical scales, performance traditions, rituals, food-preparation concepts, grammars, and symbolisms. We are not natureless. Indeed, our natures include, genetically, much of the cultural experience of our species in that period of one to five million years of nature-culture overlap during which our biological evolution had not ceased, while our cultural evolution had already begun: the period in which unwittingly we domesticated and bred ourselves into our humanity. The shape and chemistry of our brains is in part a cultural artifact. We are deeply written and inscribed already, we have our own characters, so to speak, when we come from the womb.

Having taken away one kind of rationality from historical and human studies, we may be able to replace it with another. But in so doing are we not committing the very sin, of reducing a self-organizing and unpredictable order to a set of deterministic laws, of which we accuse the determinist historians? Are we not replacing cultural or economic determinism with biological determinism? Not at all. First, to understand the principles governing the individual elements of a complex system is, as we have seen, not sufficient to be able to educe laws to predict the behavior of the whole ensemble. The beautiful paisleys of atmospheric turbulence are not explained by the most precise understanding of the individual properties—atomic weight, chemical structure, specific heat, and so on—of its elements. Second, the peculiar understanding of the human being that we are coming to is of a creature programmed rather rigidly and in certain specific ways to do something that is totally open-ended: to learn and to create. Our hardwiring—whose proper development we neglect in our education at great peril—is designed to make us infinitely inventive. Our nature is a grammar which we must learn to use correctly, and which, if we do, makes us linguistically into protean gods, able to say anything in the world or out of it.

Thus the paradigm change which this line of argument suggests is from one in which a social universe of natureless, culturally determined units is governed by a set of causal laws and principles which, given precise input, will generate accurate predictions, to one in which a cultural universe of complex-natured but knowable individuals, by the interaction and feedback of their intentions, generates an ever-changing social pattern or paisley, which can be modeled but not predicted. The meaning of understanding would change from being able to give a discursive or mathematical account of something to being able to set up a working model that can do the same sorts of things as the original.

Fundamental political concepts like freedom, war, civil order, equality, literacy, power, justice, sovereignty, and so on would no longer be defined as real entities or measurable facts but as living activities in a one-way, unrepeatable process of historical change. It would be such a revaluation as occurred in literary criticism in the nineteenth century, when tragedy came to be recognized as a process, an organic and recognizable activity, rather than as defined by such rules as the Three Unities.

Objective and abstract definitions of political concepts imply utopias, ideal principled social states towards which historical polities should strive; satisfy the definitions, and we have perfection, the end of history, an objective rationality to judge all of the past! Horrible idea; but it governs most political enthusiasm. Instead, let us imagine a peculiar kind of progress—not the old one, towards Whig empire or Hegelian state or proletarian or socialist or technological paradise, but a progress in changing terms which themselves progress by subsuming earlier ones; a progress that looks like decline or stagnation to those fixed to one idea of it; a progress not along a straight timeline but along one that curves back and fills up the holes in itself until it begins to look like a plane or a solid; a progress forged out of the evolutionary competition of totalizations, in which those most accommodating, most loving to each other, like the mammals, have the best chance of survival.

Values and History

And here we may be in a position to begin to redeem that promise, of forms of understanding and descriptive categories proper to our own level of reflexive complexity, which we implied earlier. The real forces at work on the stage of history are values. Power— the capability of one will to coerce others'—can only be bought in the coin of what one's enforcers value. And values are uniquely qualified for a role both as tools to understand history and as forces at work in it. One qualification is just that: they straddle the worlds of action and knowledge, they admit candidly our involvement, our partisanship, our partiality, and our power. Objectivity in a historian is an impossible goal in any case. Another qualification of values is that they give a kind of direction to history, the possibility of progress, which is the logical precondition of any inquiry. Values are essentially dynamic, readjusting, contested, vigorous, as the word's derivation from the Latin for "health," and its cognate "valor" imply.

We must reexamine those older partisan brands of historiography that wore their values on their sleeves: heroic, exemplary, mythic history. Perhaps their intellectual credentials were not as shaky as we thought; perhaps they were not so naïvely unaware of the possibility of their own bias.

It might well be objected that I am advocating an abandonment of objectivity, and giving license to the worst forms of ethnocentrism and prejudice. Indeed I must plead guilty, but with mitigating circumstances. It was the age of "objective" history that provided the fuel for scientific racism, holocausts, colonialism, and the Gulag. The ideologue who believes he has objective truth on his side is more dangerous than the ordinary patriot or hero, because he calls his values "facts" and will disregard all ordinary human values in their service. We are going to be ethnocentric anyway; let us at least play our ethnocentrisms against each other on a level playing field and not attempt to get the objective high ground of each other. Given such a game, adaptive success in the long run attends those versions of our partisanship that have the widest, panhuman, appeal. Let us seek not to avoid bias, but to widen our bias in favor of the whole human race, and beyond.

This approach especially questions the apparently straightforwardness of the notion of political power. Events occur, and their meaning is rich and complex. The events are made up of the actions of men and women; and if they performed those actions, then, tautologically, they had the power to do so. Do we gain anything by inserting the idea of power? Suppose they didn't perform the actions; could they have? Could we prove it? Power depends on values, and values on the individual and collective imagination.

This means that the capacity to recognize beauty, the aesthetic sense, is the primary cognitive skill of the historian or sociologist. It is by beauty that we intuit the order of the reflexive process of human history. On the small, tribal scale the need for this essential function may well have been one of the principal selective pressures that led us toward our extraordinary inherited talents at storytelling and the interpretation of narrative. History should be refounded on story, not the other way round.

The redescription of values as the strange attractors of certain complex systems, especially human ones, rather neatly solves many of the problems thinkers in various disciplines have had in identifying the nature of values—problems so severe that many have denied the existence of values altogether. Existing descriptions include the following:

1.   Values are clear, intelligible ideal forms in the mind of God. This description catches the transcendent flavor of values, the demand they make for compliance, and the sense we have that they should be eternal and independent of particular circumstances and appearances. But it misses their rootedness in actual human situations, their cultural setting, the extreme difficulty people have in discerning when and if they apply, their processual nature, and the infinite subtlety and ambiguity they display, especially in the work of the finest artists and moralists.

2.   Values are nothing more than abstract reifications of personal feelings that can and should change when those feelings change. This description has the advantage of dismissing the problem, but it is now clear that civil culture and personal happiness are impossible on this basis; and even if values are such an illusion, they are an illusion shared by such large communities of human beings that they constitute a social fact. A huge, value-shaped hole is left in human language if this definition is accepted, one which would be as hard to negotiate around as if we were to decide that all ocular vision were simply a neural illusion. Nevertheless, there seems to be some intuitive truth in the notion that values have an internal, personal, and subjective dimension; and that they have an immanent quality, and cannot be divorced from the processes in which they arise—observations that should be saved in any more satisfactory account of the matter.

3.   Values are the culturally relative norms generated by particular societies to justify and reinforce the power of the dominant ruling group to pursue its interests. This description again avoids the problem, but only by substituting two even more questionable abstractions ("power" and "society") for the supposed abstractions of value. What "interests" might consist of in a world in which values were entirely relative is hard to say. Why ordinary people should feel a duty to conform to values—why it is a value to *adhere to* values—is also not addressed. Yet this description has the virtue of pointing to something systematic and global in the nature of values, involving complex relationships among a number of players—another feature that must not be lost in a more accurate account.

4.   Values are the human terms for the genetically determined evolutionary imperatives of our species. This description ignores the very strong experience people report that their values are bound up intimately with their personal freedom, the very thing that separates us from the supposed automatism of lower animals. It also contains a troublesome flaw in logic: if we are genetically programmed to follow these evolutionary imperatives, we would have no need for social and cultural norms and prohibitions: if people did not at times wish to steal, lie, kill, disobey their parents, and commit adultery, there would be no need for the Ten Commandments. Other animals have no Decalogue. On the other hand, this description points to very important characteristics of values: that they largely transcend cultural differences, that

they are rooted in our evolutionary history, that they are ideally con-
ducive to the survival of ourselves and our fellow living things, and
that they involve a tension between individual and collective interests (for instance, in the sociobiological account of altruism).

The beauty of the "strange attractor" description of values is that
it nicely includes all the characteristics of values that this analysis
suggests, while avoiding the flaws in the existing definitions. Strange
attractors are immanent in the processes they attract, yet have an
integrity, even an eternal and unchanging quality, that transcends
them (the Lorenz attractor exists before and after the particular drip-
ping faucet or rotating globular star-cluster it describes). Strange
attractors do not determine which data point will come next, but
rather the global shape of the ensemble of data points. Though the
data-points (in so-called "deterministic chaos") are indeed in an abstract sense deterministic, the universe itself, with its quantum graini-
ness and indeterminacy, does not have enough acuity and indeed
data-processing power to predict their exact location in advance,
and thus such processes are for all practical purposes both unpredictable and ordered, a very fine match with our minimum conditions for freedom. Freedom, one of our supreme values and also a
precondition for most other values, resists any attempt at reduction
to either traditional notions of order or traditional notions of randomness—if freedom is traditional order, then it is deterministic and
not free, but if it is traditional randomness (the *acte gratuit* of the
existentialists) its essential quality of responsibility is lost. The unpredictable emergence of Prigoginian dissipative structures from
chaotic interactions, drawn by strange attractors, similarly defies traditional notions of order and randomness.

Biological evolution, with its iterative algorithm of variation, selection, and genetic inheritance, and its massively nonlinear ecological arena of selection, is a fecund womb of strange attractors.
Among these, values might well be among the most complex and
sophisticated, since they arise out of the further interplay of biological and cultural evolution. Strange attractors, unlike drives or instincts, however, have the engaging if frustrating feature that they
can never be fully achieved; new data points can always can be
added that will deepen and enrich the detail, revealing new self-
similar but not self-identical depths. Thus the requirement of a tension between the ideal and the real is preserved. Drives push;

attractors invite, or pull, in an unpredictable way. Strange attractors have room for both global collective features and individual idiosyncrasies. The "meta" quality of values—it is a value to *have* values—is also addressed by the essentially recursive, reflexive, self-transcending character of strange attractors and the conditions of their emergence. Further, it is a moot point whether even the entire network of human social, cultural, technological, and economic feedbacks and communications over the globe is yet as complex and multidimensional as the interconnections of a single human brain and nervous system—a reflection that nicely suggests the importance of the individual conscience in discerning and generating values. Finally, the oddity of these attractors when we try to fit them into our existing categories—are they physical objects, or processes, or relationships, or adjectival or adverbial qualities, or entities, or abstractions, or essences, or tendencies, or vectors, or mathematical idealizations, or what?—exactly matches our puzzlement when we try to identify values.

If this identification of values as strange attractors can be upheld, the implications for the discipline of history and the human sciences are enormous. In seeking the key principles of historical change, social organization, and economic development in forces or drives that force and push society and individuals, we may have been deeply neglecting these mysterious, yet increasingly intelligible, attractors that invite and draw society and individuals. Even assuming we could exactly specify the origins of present events, unlikely in the light of our present understanding of sensitive dependence on initial conditions, the past may be important not as the determinative cause of the present but as an archive of value-attractors for future development. It may turn out that the real reason why human beings do things is not that they are compelled into them by socioeconomic causes or political and cultural norms, but that they are attracted to them by their goodness and their beauty.

What is essential for our present purposes in the new perspectives I have described here is that there is in fact plenty of room in the universe for value, freedom, goodness, beauty. The universe is therefore not disqualified, as it might have been at the end of the eighteenth century, as a dwelling place for the divine.

6

Time

Not Enough Room in Space

Is there, then, a description of the universe that is both scientifically plausible and in accord with the major teachings of the world's religions?

We need, first, to know what we mean when we use the word "universe." There are two major uses of the word, one limited to the world of observable fact, the other including everything, known or unknown, knowable or unknowable, past, present, or future, that can be said to have being in some sense. In science the first definition has generally been used; but in recent years a confusion has arisen, that raises the question of which definition is preferable. The confusion appears in at least two fields of research: Big Bang inflation theory and quantum mechanics.

One of the most promising explanations of the expansion and homogeneity of the universe (put forward by Allan Guth, Andrei Linde, and others) implies that the original singularity, during a brief period of rapid inflation, must have spawned a multitude of universes, of which ours is one. The other universes are separated from ours by regions of energy-charged vacuum that make it impossible for us to ever detect them. The problem is inherent in the very statement of the theory: whether the word "universe" can legitimately be used in the plural. If the "other" universes are all rooted in the same cosmological event as ours is, and if we can infer their existence from this fact, they are all part of the same universe, and the use of the plural is incorrect. Even in "this" universe there are objects that are too far away or too distant in time or too massive for us to ever observe them, because the speed of light—by which we could observe them—is limited and we are outside their event horizon. Yet we do not refer to those events as being in other universes.

In quantum theory one proposed solution to the indeterminacy of quantum events has been put forward by Hugh Everett III: he suggests that at every moment the timeline branches, providing a timeline for each of the outcomes of the quantum event. This idea is one version of the so-called "parallel universes" theory. Again, the problem is one of terminology: if our universe and another universe share a common past, they are one universe and not two; two branches from the same trunk are not two trees but parts of one tree. The word "universe" already implies the diversity whose totality the word includes; all possible plurality is already captured in it, and thus the plural form is ungrammatical.

For our purposes, then, I shall use the larger definition of "universe," so as to avoid confusions of this kind. Two interesting conclusions follow. The first is that if God or the gods or the Ground of Being or the Tao exist, then by definition they are within the universe in this larger sense. If "in the universe" means "having existence" and "having existence" means "in the universe," then a God who was outside the universe would not exist, and an existent God would be inside the universe. The divine cannot be outside the universe looking in, any more than another region of the original quantum foam can be outside the universe looking in. The second conclusion is that direct observability is not a necessary qualification for something to be considered part of the universe. We must broaden the meaning of "observability" to include reasonable inference from observation, as an indirect form of observation. And this is not really a great stretch. "Direct" observation may not even be possible. After all, the most familiar and apparently unmediated forms of observation already involve elaborate inference: the associative centers of my brain are inferring from my visual cortex what it is inferring from optic nerve impulses what they have inferred from retinal neuron firings that record the light coming from the screen of the word processor—which is in turn a sort of inference from the ones and zeroes of the machine code of its CPU. Given these two implications that flow from the uniqueness and unity of the universe— God is in the universe, and we can see things indirectly—it makes good sense to attempt to see God.

But if the divine is as odd a beast as it would have to be for all the religious accounts and stories of it to be true, how and where do we fit it into the universe? Where in the universe should we look for God—or for whatever is our God-function? Here the religions that would answer, "right here" are at a distinct advantage. If one is a humanist, or an environmental vitalist, or an existentialist, or even a certain philosophical type of Unitarian, Upanishadic Hindu, Confucian, or Zen Buddhist, one can find the meaning and point of it all in one's own soul, in one's relations with others, in the flow of experience, or in the living ecosystem around one. The recent resurgence of such answers in the West, after centuries of a more detached, transcendent, and external conception of the divine, is clearly a move toward an appropriate balance. But if religion consists just in a sort of unaided thinking well of one's life and acting harmoniously, one is left a hostage to the neurochemistry of one's mood, and a religious person is a person who scores low on the neurotransmitters of depression and is extraverted in personality. The historical religions, with their grand narratives of universal destiny, the religions of sacrifice and ritual, the religions of marvelous mythological story, the religions of severe ethical rectitude, and the religions of ascetic discipline, meditation, and prayer, seem to offer parts of the truth that are valuable in their own right. They call us beyond our comfort with the present moment, with a demanding and thrilling voice, to which something in us responds in terror but also in joyful acceptance of challenge and spiritual adventure. And they invite us to reconcile our secular and scientific understanding of the world with our religious experience, they lure us to set sail upon the vast waters of metaphysics.

Thus we can accept that the divine is indeed in some sense "here," though in that sense we see it only through a glass darkly and in the good luck of metaphysical incuriosity and a happy disposition. But the divine is also, importantly, "out there," and if we are to keep to the rules of our game, it must plausibly correspond to what is to be found in the Koran, the Bible, the Egyptian and Tibetan Books of the Dead, the *Popol Vuh*, the Bhagavad Gita, the Aborigine songlines, the Apache creation myth, the *Enuma Elish*, and the Hesiodic *Theogony*. So we return to our question: Where in the world do we look for God?

"Where?" it turns out, may not be the right interrogative pronoun. If there is one idea that is fundamental and constitutive of science, it is the principle of cosmic homogeneity: that the same scientific laws apply anywhere in the universe, that distance in space by itself is not enough to alter valid mathematical and physical regularities. Even when that principle is apparently challenged, as it was by relativity and quantum theory, it is only the more decisively reaffirmed. An even stricter law governs Einsteinian spacetime reference frames than governed Newtonian action at a distance. Quantum mechanics more than makes up in its accuracy at describing ensembles of particles what it apparently loses in exactness at specifying the location and momentum of individual particles. Thus everywhere we look in space we must find the same fundamental physical conditions and causal relations as here. This in a sense would confirm the answer of those who say that if the divine is anywhere, it is right here—or at least as much here as anywhere else. But we are now faced with the problem that the radically different accounts of the divine cannot all fit into the same spatial universe without contradiction—the divine must be both many and one, primitive and omniscient, God and Mammon, immanent and transcendent, personal and impersonal, limited and infinite. If we are to remain faithful to science, whose formative principle is cosmic homogeneity (or, to put it more radically, non-contradiction), we must abandon our search for this God-of-contradictions in space. There is not enough room for him there.

But the same strictures do not by any means apply to time. Change is obvious both to science and to common experience. A given object cannot be in two contradictory states at the same time in the same place. But the fact that it can change from one to another over time, and move in time from place to place, is the most obvious and apparent phenomenon in the world. One thing can divide into many; new species can branch from a parent genus; many things can converge into one; what was pervasive can become localized, what was localized can become distributed. Even fundamental physical laws are regularly envisaged by scientists as changing over time: the emergence of new physical laws through spontaneous symmetry-breaking is a standard feature of the Big Bang model. Cosmological physicists happily speculate on the possibility that the speed of light, the curvature of space, and the other "constants" of physics could have been different at other epochs in the history of the universe, and may even be very slowly changing now. Ilya Prigogine claims with some justice to have proved that even Hilbert space, which is the space of all spaces, would not be capacious enough for all the outcomes of any common complex dynamical system such as is found in the real universe; time is required if everything is to be fitted in. Branching and even nonlinear theories of time have often been suggested to solve paradoxes in quantum theory.

What this book proposes is that though there may not be enough room in *space* for our divine paradox, there may well be room enough in *time*. Our question becomes, not *Where* do we look for God, but *When?* To rephrase it more exactly, what would the shape of time have to be, to be able to fit in all the religious descriptions of the divine? And could that shape correspond to a conceivable scientific description of the past and future history of the universe?

The Evolution of Time

One of the features of time that make it a sufficiently capacious arena for the various conceptions of the divine is the phenomenon of evolution. Time itself, in the widely accepted theory of the physicist/philosopher J.T. Fraser, evolved from the atemporality of photons, through the prototemporality of quantum particles, the eotemporality of matter, the biotemporality of life, to the nootemporality of human beings. One of Fraser's most profound insights is that we do not need to accept Plato's or Newton's conception of time as a sort of universal container for all that goes on. Furthermore, time need not necessarily come as a package, complete with temporal continuity, a direction, earlier and later, after and before, a past, present, and future, and the branchy timelines familiar to beings that must remember might-have-beens, use conditional and subjunctive moods, and decide on alternative courses of action. Why not posit of a given object, or state of the world, just the features of time that are necessary for its full description, that is, whatever temporal elements that are implied by what it can experience and what it can do?

Fraser borrows von Üxkull's concept of the *Umwelt* of an organism—that is, the specific world affected by its effectors and available to its receptors—and coins the term "temporal umwelt," which he then extends to all existent entities. A photon of light flying through a vacuum is, he says, essentially atemporal, since no feature of time is necessary to describe it in its own terms. A quantum particle occupies a single fragment of time, with no further features of time necessary for its description. A piece of coherent matter occupies a continuous timeline, but needs no after or before, or any other temporal baggage—one can reverse the orbits of bodies in a vacuum, or the tracks of individual atoms, without violating any natural laws. A living organism, however, has a definite after and before, a distinct direction in life, and a present moment; and a human mind must grapple with the whole complex tense structure of its language, such as we find in novels, epics, and plays.

Revising somewhat Fraser's categories in the light of other systems proposed by various cosmologists, I suggest the following "brief history of time" as a useful way of indicating its richness and variety.

All that needs to be posited of the moment the universe began, according to contemporary mathematical physics, is pure mathematical logic. The most exciting mathematical ideas of our century, beginning with Gödel, deal with the incompleteness and open-endedness of any mathematical system, and its propensity to generate paradoxes which can only be resolved in terms of some richer and more reflexive system which includes it—a system which must in turn contain its own paradoxes, and so on. These relationships, of inclusion, containment, open-endedness, incompleteness, extension, "between-ness," and even, as in the case of the orientation of the imaginary number series with respect to the real numbers, orthogonality and thus angles—immediately suggest spacelike dimensions. The discipline of topology may be defined as a demonstration that space, spatial dimensionality, is the only solution to certain problems in mathematical logic. Space is the way that true statements which would contradict each other if they were in the same place, space themselves out from each other. The Pauli exclusion principle, which states that two identical particles cannot occupy the same energy-state at the same place and time, is a physical example of this idea. If the two particles were in the same place, they would be both two and one, which violates the noncontradiction law of logic. In other words, a nonspatial world, if everything thinkable within it is to remain logically consistent, must necessarily generate a spatial world. The new fractal geometry includes a working concept of how a given dimension can be generated, and coherent definitions of partial dimensions. We are familiar in classical geometry with zero-dimensional points, one-dimensional lines, two-dimensional planes, three-dimensional volumes, and so on; topological physics has invited us to imagine more dimensions still. But the noninteger dimensions of fractal mathematics—a given curve can have a dimensionality of 1.62, for instance—are a new concept, and show us how we might, through the feedback of an iterative algorithm, actually get from one integer dimension to another. A new dimension can be woven (or rather, crocheted, in the metaphor of some contemporary mathematicians) out of the thread of an old one. The spaceless universe thus must fall instantly into the condition of spatiality; up to ten dimensions of space have been proposed for its initial foray into this condition. It begins as an infinitely small, infinitely hot, infinitely dense, infinitely young speck of "thereness." Within this space-universe a unit of information occupies Fraser's condition of atemporality; were it to exist in time, it would be a photon.

Certain other problems in mathematics involve the relative easiness or difficulty of a calculation. Some calculations wind themselves up without complication. Others involve more and more sub-calculations, and sub-subcalculations, before the calculator can produce an answer. In order to be able to contain such distinctions, and to measure their differences, another kind of dimensionality than space is needed: time. As the joke goes, time is nature's way of making sure everything doesn't happen at once. In its simplest form time is to the three spatial dimensions what the imaginary number series—the square roots of the negative numbers—is to the real number series. Time gives us a dimension within which we can describe the difficulty of a calculation, whether it is soluble in an amount of time that increases polynomially with the number of variables in it, or exponentially, or more swiftly still. The upshot is that the primal space-universe's own internal necessities, its scheduling problems, let us say, immediately cause it to inflate at a prodigious speed.

Thus spacetime emerges out of very logic; and given spacetime, quantum cosmology can show the necessity of the Big Bang. The quantum vacuum, say the cosmologists, is not an inert nothingness but at some scale a foam of particles and antiparticles, with a net value of nothing but the potential for one of these particles to escape annihilation by its opposite number and swiftly balloon up into a new universe. Energy emerges out of a spacetime field as the coherent solution of certain possible and necessary geometrical paradoxes, and sometimes binds itself to a local place and continuous existence, collapsing into matter as the universe cools with its expansion. The quantum world, still too hot, young, small, and simple to contain anything other than quantum particles, is in the condition Fraser calls prototemporality; a quantum particle, that is, possesses an prototemporal umwelt.

Matter is the solution to paradoxes that arise in the energy universe as the primal superforce separated itself out into gravitation, electromagnetism, the weak and the strong nuclear forces. Not every possible kind of energy and matter does emerge, and once having emerged, survive; there are apparently no magnetic monopoles, though there could have been; and there is very little antimatter, since at the point of the collapse into matter, physical laws demanded that the energy universe choose one or the other but not both for its debut into materiality. Many possible isotopes do not exist because the conditions of their survival are not present. Thus a peculiar primitive kind of "choice" already existed at the very beginning of things. Various exotic kinds of matter emerged—we can reproduce their emergence sometimes in an accelerator—but were selected against by the existing ecology of the physical world, and did not survive for long. Tough objects like protons and neutrons, or intangible ones like neutrinos, can survive a great deal of wear and tear, and so they are long-lived and plentiful, as are certain elements, like hydrogen and iron, and certain molecules and crystalline structures in cooler and quieter environments. Fraser calls this the eotemporal stage of the universe.

Given matter, another open-ended process begins, of thermodynamic interaction and chemical recombination. Once there exist large enough ensembles of matter, each element of which is free to interact with every other, new statistical and collective effects emerge, including what is to become one of the master-principles of the matter universe: thermodynamic decay, or the increase of entropy with time. Time now takes on a distinct direction. One can burn a log, but not easily unburn it; one can allow a bottle of perfume to diffuse into the air of a room, but not easily collect it back into the bottle; one can let hot gas and cold gas mingle themselves in a container, but not easily separate them again. Work energy gets used up and broken down into waste heat. Fraser does not give this stage a name of its own, and I have suggested that it be called the thermotemporal, or chemotemporal.

Here again we find a process of variation, in which the vicissitudes of a rather violent universe thrust together arbitrary combinations of chemical elements, and in turn test them to destruction, leaving the survivors to survive. But in chemistry those survivors can only endure, or at best grow by accumulation, as crystals do. They cannot avoid, adapt to, or anticipate the threats of a dangerous universe. Nor, if they are especially successful at weathering or dodging the dangers, can they copy themselves so as to improve their statistical chances; yet the logic of survival in time would demand that they should. Their potentially successful form is held hostage to a particular local piece of matter; if the form could be copied to other matter, then the form might survive the enemies of matter—heat, mechanical destruction, chemical corrosion. And so yet another solution to an existential paradox emerges—life. Here we enter the realm of what Fraser calls the biotemporal.

With life a new element joins the iterative variation/selection algorithm by which evolution had proceeded: heredity. Life has, as it were, a double life; as matter, and as a recorded copy of the form of that matter. It is more reflexive, more conscious, so to speak, than matter by itself. (Of course, as we have seen, matter is itself "double" with respect to its substance, energy: it is energy, but also a self-maintaining field structure containing the energy. And energy is "double" with respect to the spacetime field, and the spacetime field "double" with respect to mathematical logic.) Life not only evolved in a new way, by self-copying; it also developed in turn new forms of evolution. One of the most remarkable of these is sexual reproduction, which, instead of merely accepting mutation as part of the damage of existence, actively anticipated and promoted it by sexual recombination.

Now the biosphere took increasing control over the nonliving substrate of the planet Earth, radically altering the composition of its air, regulating its climate, setting up complex chemical cycles throughout its atmosphere, hydrosphere, crust, and perhaps even its mantle. It is thus entirely natural for an emergent and more reflexive kind of order to control and subordinate the earlier and more primitive forms out of which it evolved. Complex social species, their individuals coordinated with each other in swarms, schools, groups, packs, and bands, their own evolution partly controlled by mating rituals and social ranking systems, established new features of time: a distinct present, to synchronize their actions, together with rudimentary systems of memory (and thus a past as such), and even the dim anticipations, expectations, and drives that constitute a future. Fraser dates the emergence of the sociotemporal umwelt to a later phase in the world's history, but I would place it here.

As the competitive-cooperative ecology of the living world became more and more complex, and improved forms of biological evolution accelerated the rate of speciation and ecological change, the Darwinian mechanism of biological evolution began to reach its speed limit. It takes perhaps a hundred thousand years for a species to develop a new capacity in response to its experience in the environment; and the whole species, or most of it, must go through that experience in order for the selective process to work. Would it not be better if something like Lamarckian evolution were to supplement Darwinian evolution—an adaptive process which could make appreciable changes in one generation, which could use the experience of individuals rather than that of the gene-pool as a whole? Would not evolution be still more efficient if alternative scenarios for the future could be tried out in a virtual world where they could do no damage, before they were actually embarked on? Would it not be more efficient to supplement the very slow genetic diffusion of information through the species, with much faster forms of communication independent of the reproductive process? Might not new forms of information storage be developed, above and beyond the genes, which would be to the genes what the genes were to the matter of which their bodies were made, or as the structure of matter is to the energy it binds?

The answer to these questions was, of course, the human species: its traditional rather than genetic way of mutating the racial store of information, its brain, its memory, its language, its cultural institutions, its imagination. Again, this new emergence was the solution to paradoxes implicit in the nature of the universe that preceded it. Survival, now revised and enlarged in definition beyond reproductive success to control and prediction of the biosphere itself, and to a richer existence within many possible timelines, required a faster acceleration of the adaptive process than biogenetic evolution could provide. Humanity is the solution to the paradoxes of life, as life was for matter, as spacetime was for mathematical logic. Thus the dawn of the nootemporal umwelt.

In this denser and more complex kind of time in which we live, we did not leave behind those simpler levels from which we emerged. The components of our bodies contain and experience the lower umwelts. When we get caught up in a ritual celebration or political rally, we are in the sociotemporal umwelt; when we dream, so some brain scientists tell us, we are undergoing some aspects of the time-experience of animals; when we age, we feel the one-way current of thermodynamic decay. When we slip and fall, we are as physical bodies subject to the same classical mechanics as circling moons and hurtling atoms; and as clusters of frozen light, we are fossils of the timeless moment of the Big Bang. These levels of temporality in us are often at war—the nootemporal dieter against the biotemporal gourmand, the sociotemporal conformist against the nootemporal person of conscience, the biotemporal animal survivor against its own slow thermotemporal furnace of burning chemicals, the nootemporal dancer against the eotemporal point-mass in free fall.

Of course, the irony of our evolutionary progress is that the paradoxes get more complex with each new solution of them; and the human paradoxes are the most pressing and difficult of all, especially as, unlike their predecessors, they have not yet been solved. Those thinkers who have in despair, or in denial of their shame, or in fashionable cynicism, condemned the human species and its progress, have not reflected that in a sense the imperfection of things goes all the way back. The existential tension, the pain or unsatisfied desire that drives us to do the things such thinkers disapprove of, is most primitively the paradox of self-inclusion. We are at one and the same time all the contradictory levels through which we evolved. If utopians would turn back the clock to some imagined innocence, they would be cutting off the very process of existential tension by which the universe came to be. But cannot we think differently of the unsolved human paradox?—as the open-endedness of the universe, as its evolutionary potential, as its great hope, as our chance to prove our creativity, as our solidarity with the whole cosmos in its great questioning expansion and fall, outwards into richer, more anxious, more complex, and more beautiful forms of being?

The reader might well ask what the *next* temporal umwelt might be: I propose the term theotemporal. That is, whatever even richer and more significant kind of time succeeds ours—or subsumes ours, since it is, I will argue, in certain ways already here—is what we experience as the divine milieu. But if the theotemporal umwelt is like all its predecessors, it too is incarnate in, and expresses itself in, the lower umwelts of nature out of which it emerged.

Gaia

Let us take a glance at what one version of an evolutionary universe, faithful to natural science, containing God, and changing over time, might look like. Who or what is nature's God? James Lovelock's Gaia Hypothesis, which argues plausibly that in some sense the planet Earth is a sort of super-organism, perhaps like a giant polyp or colonial animal or coral reef, maintaining its own atmosphere, climate, and chemical environment, has supplied its more religious followers with a personal name for a new deity: Gaia. Let us begin by following the Gaia Hypothesis in its theological implication that the divine is present within the world, not detached from it. This is not necessarily to adopt a pantheist position, that is, that the world *is* God. If, by analogy, we assert that the mind and soul are present in a brain and body rather than detachable from them, we are not committed to believing that the mind and soul are only the brain and body; any more than the image presented by a picture is only paint and canvas. Thus the first axiom of a natural theology would be: *the divine is in nature.*

If, then, the divine, and let us call her "Gaia," is *in* nature, how might we discover the nature of the divine? Surely by examining and listening to nature itself, just as we find out about a man's or woman's personality by examining what they physically do and listening to what they physically say. That is, we should pay attention to the process, the *story,* of nature, if we wish to know its divine soul. Nature includes us as its acme and quintessence; so we must look especially at ourselves, the most characteristic part of Gaia's natural body. The way we find out, the process of knowing, the attempt to come to know the story of things, is called science. Thus our second axiom might be: *we know Gaia by means of the scientific understanding of nature and ourselves.*

A story is an irreversible process of events that are unpredictable beforehand but apparently inevitable and obvious once they have happened. If you are reading a good novel, the pleasure is partly that the next twist in the story cannot be predicted—which is why you want to see how it came out, whether the butler did it, for instance. Of course afterwards there must be a good explanation; we should be able to say "Why didn't I see it? The answer was obvious." Obvious afterwards, but not before. The very possibility of story implies that time is essentially asymmetrical, that truth can be a different thing prospectively than retrospectively. There are fixed truths, like the laws of gravitation and thermodynamics, or we would have no points of reference by which to know. But the newly emergent truths include most of what we consider valuable, good, and beautiful: all the exquisite forms of matter, life, and mind, that have evolved over the history of the universe. If nature has *no* story, then we can conclude that the divine being is indeed fixed and eternal, forever unsurprised and undisturbed. If nature has a story (or many stories) as it most manifestly and emphatically has, then we must conclude that the divine being has one too. Thus the third axiom of our natural theology would be: *Gaia changes; Gaia has a story.*

If we examine nature and ourselves we discover that there are underlying unchanging unities beneath the variety of things—the mathematical forms, the constants of physics—but also that nature is an evolutionary drama, a competitive/cooperative dialogue among its parts, species, levels, and principles. Thus if nature is the body of the the divine, we may infer a fourth axiom: *Gaia is both one and many.* She is one in her most remote, abstract, timeless, impersonal, simpleminded, and passive aspects, and many in her most immediate, concrete, changing, personal, intelligent, and active aspects. In deference to our own monotheistic tradition I refer to the divine as one, but it should be understood that the polytheistic and pluralist description of the divine as "the gods" is also intellectually attractive. One of the three main Jewish names of God, "Elohim," the most impersonal and naturalistic one (as opposed to the Creator Jahweh and the personal Adonai), is in the plural form, slightly mistranslated by the usual singular phrase "the Lord of hosts." So even the most heavily monotheistic of religions recognizes a certain plurality in the divine.

The transformations of this natural god of change are not exclusively random, reversible, and meaningless. As we have seen, the evolution of the universe is progressive, irrevocable, and dramatically meaningful. There is a one-way process of increasing feedback, reflexivity, self-organization, and freedom as the world evolves. Elementary particles have polarity but no shape. Atoms, more complex and self-referential than particles, have simple geometrical shapes that are symmetrical in many dimensions and asymmetrical only in the difference between center and periphery. With molecules (which could not exist until the universe had cooled enough to permit them) we see the first fully asymmetrical shapes and the birth of individuality. Molecules have complex feedback systems, many degrees of freedom, and the capacity to organize in periodic structures such as crystals. Living organisms are yet more asymmetrical, free, and capable of organization, and they contain a recording of their own structure in the DNA language. Mind continues this story into the most complex forms of consciousness, self-determination, and communication. Thus the fifth axiom: *the story of Gaia is one of increasing individuality, meaning, and freedom.* Progress is not a human invention, but a divine one.

If the universe is Gaia's body, then we—and by "we" I mean all the intelligent species in the universe—are the most sensitive, most aware, most self-organizing of its parts. Though we are not the whole, we are that which increasingly has some knowledge of and control over the whole. The most sensitive and aware and controlling parts of a living body are its nervous system. Thus the sixth axiom: *we are the nervous system of Gaia.*

This nervous system is still very rudimentary and has penetrated and innervated only a tiny portion of the universe to date. It is like the nervous system of an unborn child. We stand at the first trembling moment of the history of the universe, the flash of a dawn that is a mere twenty billion years old, the dawn of a ten-trillion-year day. The universe is still only in its gestation; it is not yet fully developed. Thus a seventh axiom: *Gaia is still only a fetus.* It is partly up to us to complete that development, to increase the awareness and control we have over the rest of the universe, to extend the nerves of science and art into the inanimate and insentient parts of the world. Nature has not died, as some recent commentators have complained. It is only now awakening, and we are its eyes, its ears, and its tongue. We are God's fetal neurons, wiring themselves up to the body of God—the rest of the physical universe—and to each other according to the commandment of love, following the tracks of the joy-chemistry of brain reward as fetal neurons do. We are the dimly sentient hardware of Gaia's own increasing capacities of knowledge and control, at moments glimpsing a tiny hint of the vast cogitations and feelings of which we are infinitesimal parts. From this follows an eighth axiom: *we serve Gaia by helping her toward greater self-awareness.*

As organisms evolve, they develop more and more complex chemical, electrical, and mechanical systems, known as bodies, in order to control and be controlled by their environment, to act and to sense. All bodies are prostheses; the matter of which they are made is not at first part of the living organism itself, but pressed artificially into service by that organism. For instance, the carbon atoms that my body uses to construct its protein and enzyme factories are exactly the same as they were before I commandeered them by eating them in my asparagus. Likewise, the coat of tiny sticks and bits of gravel that a caddis-worm constructs for itself is part of its body, though in itself not strictly alive. The body of a termite colony includes its nest, that marvelously air-conditioned residence containing nurseries, storehouses, factories, and farms. The nest of the male blue satin bowerbird is not even used as a nest at all, but as a communication device to persuade a female bowerbird to mate, a piece of art, of advertising. Yet in a strong sense that nest is part of its body. Plants and animals use probes, crutches, shelters, tools, vehicles, weapons, and other prostheses that do not need to be directly connected to their flesh or nerves, but which are essential parts of their bodies. All living organisms use tools at the atomic and molecular level, even the crudest microorganisms. The more advanced an organism is, the larger and more organized in themselves are the outside structures that it is able to use and transform into its synthetic body.

Artificial systems of investigation, control, and communication, as these are, are named art, science, and technology. The creative capacity of an organism, its productive and reproductive reason for being, is its art. The information that constitutes the pattern of a living organism is its science. The body of a living organism is its technology; the technology of an organism is its body. Our life is, after all, only the pattern of information spelled out in our genes, a pattern which survives any given atom in our bodies, except for the ones we have not yet metabolized at our death. Our own art and technology is an extension of our bodies; but our bodies are nothing more than such cumulative extensions. Biological evolution, and arguably even pre-biological evolution, are in this sense precisely the increase in the complexity and power of art, science and technology. Nature is not distinguishable, then, from art, science, and technology. Thus if nature is the body of Gaia, then we may formulate a ninth surprising axiom: *Gaia is the process of improved art, science, and technology.*

If our moral function is to serve Gaia, then it is to help Gaia change from a fetus into a fully developed being, to realize her future growth and self-awareness. The way to do this is to continue to innervate the universe by knowledge and control, and thus to extend our own bodies, the region of our own art and technology, throughout the universe. Thus the tenth axiom: *to serve Gaia is to increase the scope, power, beauty, and depth of art, science, and technology.*

This logic has brought us therefore to an astonishing and perhaps shocking conclusion, utterly at odds with the prevailing mood of our culture. How can we redeem this statement, and make it fit what we feel about our role in the world? The answer must be that we need a thorough reevaluation of what art, science, and technology are and what we mean when we use the terms. We know there is such a thing as bad art, bad science, bad technology; but the theological implications we have discovered make it essential that we define what is good art, science, technology, because without them we cannot adequately serve God, if God is conceived of as being within nature. It will no longer be sufficient for us to attempt to get away from or to dissolve our technology, as some of our more radical environmentalists believe we should; to do so, if it were even possible, would be to deny our divine duty and to commit a sin against the holy spirit. However, our investigation of what is good technology, etcetera, may have the virtue of clarifying what is bad technology, bad service of God, and thus constitute a powerful if gentle critique of society.

But if Gaia—or Elohim—is evolving in and along with the universe that is the divine body, two problems arise. Are we confined—God included—to the provisional morality of the present epoch? And what freedom—and thus what responsibility, what morality—can there be if we are all being driven by a relentless process of natural development along a single pathway of unfolding evolutionary time? Many religions emphasize the freedom of the soul, and even those that do not contain some notion of justice, which implies right and wrong choices. Let us see what kind of universe this would have to be, for freedom to be possible.

Time and Freedom

Suppose the universe were so constructed as to make morality as meaningful as it can possibly be. Suppose, to be more specific, moral action were efficacious and really changed the future. Moral action could not, for instance, be a mere test or charade to demonstrate our worthiness for salvation in a diorama-world constructed rather inefficiently—given its vastness in space and time and its staggering richness of variety—merely for that purpose. Nor could moral action be simply the predetermined and unique result of an irresistible divine fate, or of genetic predisposition or sociocultural conditioning. Our actions would have to have at least a strong dash of pure free will in them, which would imply that another wholly plausible universe might come into being if we chose the opposite action from the one we actually took. Certainly if the future is laid out like a single track before us, morality is something of a mockery. The universe must be open-ended to make human goodness mean anything.

But even here there are problems. Such a universe might at first glance be a welcome one to those bold and energetic moral adventurers who welcome the opportunity to make a difference. But when we consider the weakness, foolishness, ignorance, shortsightedness, self-deception, wickedness, and sheer evolutionary recidivism of even the best of us, the picture does not look too bright. We need all the help we can get; providence, if it existed, might barely level the odds against us.

In fact morality can be meaningless in another sense too: if there is nothing to tell us what is right or wrong before we go ahead and do it, we really aren't free at all, since we have not had a chance to see how things turn out. Milan Kundera's insight in *The Unbearable Lightness of Being*, that one chance is no chances, is right. We cannot rehearse our lives beforehand to see how they turn out, and therefore are not really responsible for them. The danger of having only one chance is that, in the absence of a signal from the future to tell us whether we will have done the right thing or not, we are at liberty to imagine any justifying outcome of our actions that our self-interest or will to power or vanity suggests. True freedom, paradoxically, requires us to have a guide or adviser in our actions. After all, nobody in ancient Greece or ancient China or the old slave states of Africa and pre-Columbian America could have imagined that the then eminently moral condition of slavery might some day be considered evil, or that unlimited sexual permissiveness, "free love," might some day be considered good. Huck Finn has to defy his conscience when he decides not to turn in the runaway slave, Jim, to his lawful owners. Perhaps in the future our assumption that children belong to their parents will be thought of as an abomination as evil as slavery; perhaps, on the other hand, we may one day come to believe in a religion in which Pain, as in David Lindsay's theology, is the highest good and the sign of the divine. What if I, now, were to act as if these changes were coming? Would I be a visionary or a monster? This is the problem with Nietzsche's notion of the transvaluation of values. Dostoyevsky's Raskolnikov believes that great actions can retroactively change the morality by which they are judged; there were Nazis who claimed, and no doubt believed, that the elimination of European Jewry was indeed horrible by contemporary standards but that it would be justified one day in retrospect.

In order for us to be morally free we must have wise guides who can advise us: but the very presence of those wise guides seems to compromise our freedom, since if we do the wrong thing they will surely be able to put it right. The future has to be open in order for us to be able to affect it; yet if there is no assurance of some kind of justice, no ratification of our noblest choices, no friendly welcome and recognition in that rarefied air at the very edge of all we have been, where we must make our most important decisions, then we might well make the wrong choice, believing it to be right.

One way of putting this problem is in terms of a pair of ideas that we have already encountered: the prophetic and the apocalyptic. In some form this apparently irreconcilable dichotomy exists in all religious and secular ethical traditions. Should we work for a better future, as the prophets urge, or, according to the priestly rules of the perfect life, save our souls? Redeem the world or reject it? Love the things of time as God does or cleanse oneself of the temporal? Hope for posterity or the afterlife? Should we be active or contemplative? Is this life the only arena of spiritual action or only a preparation for another? Should we, as Yeats puts it, seek out perfection of the work or of the life? The issue is present in the Analects of Confucius, in the Bhagavad Gita, in the Bible, and in the Koran. Among secular atheists it can be heard loud and clear in the contradictions between the Marxists, who believe in praxis and work for the future, and the existentialists and their descendants, who believe in the total immersion in immediate experience, authenticated by the imminence of death.

The question boils down to whether we look horizontally forward to the future as the justification for our actions, or whether we look vertically, so to speak, up to eternity or down into the depth of immediate experience, as the source of validation. If we look to the future we subject ourselves to a contingency of outcome that makes any action seem irresponsible. If we look to the eternities of heaven or existential experience we seem to abdicate our responsibility, giving it over to some all-wise Father or, in the case of the existentialists, put a seemingly unwarranted trust in the wisdom of the senses and feelings, and of phenomena in general. The result of this impasse has been a kind of moral paralysis in the face of the horrifying experiments of the last century, an attempt to do everything by majority vote, a proliferation of unenforceable rights, a resort to obsessive legalism, and a loss of the chief quality in human beings that gives them dignity: their sense of creative agency.

How might this problem be resolved? Or better, can it be reframed into a fertile paradox or perhaps a recursive and generative concept of its own? Suppose there were some way in which the future could influence and inform its past, including our present: we would then be able to get a look at the consequences of our actions, perhaps not in any detail, but with enough of a moral and aesthetic "feel" so that our most imponderable choices would have some guidance. We would, of course, be free to cooperate with that guidance or to reject it, as with some of the ingenious and rather neglected theories of Christian grace. But our actions would not be totally unrehearsed. If the arrow of eternity, that points vertically toward perfection, and the arrow of the future, that demands work in this compromised world for its betterment and the welfare of our neighbors, were in fact two ends of a loop, the bettered future looping back to inspire our finest moments of contemplation, perhaps the great contradiction disappears. Thus the visitations that so many have experienced and reported, that we seek feebly to explain by psychological theorizing—the angels or muses or kamis or shamanic spirits or genii, the presences in Yeats' poem that passion, piety, or affection knows— might be our descendants, our future. They would come to us in our distress of spirit and gently advise us which way to go. Nor would we be the passive recipients of their wisdom, the helpless participants in a great plan over which we have no control. For their very existence would be contingent on our actions; they would need us as much as or more than we need them. They would be able only to suggest whereas we, by our voluntary noncompliance with their wishes, could compel.

This view of things might also make sense of the frequent reports of "near-death experiences." Suppose that when we have stepped out of our bodies, and passed through the dark tunnel, as near-death experiencers report we do, that light and those loving presences are indeed the light of the future and the faces of our descendants. Imagine that in a million years our descendants have mastered the art of perfect reconstruction of past events (a sort of ecological restoration on a submolecular scale) and that they have become capable of resurrecting in perfect detail the bodies of the dead. Imagine that, just as the consciousness of a sleeper leaps over from the body that retires to bed to the slightly different body that wakes up in the morning, our consciousness should be able to leap over from our dying body to the reconstructed one awaiting us in the future. That consciousness could overlap both, giving rise to the out-of-body experience that so many people who have been near death report. Our descendants, with their exquisite sense of ethics, would feel obliged, if there is any possibility of "natural" revival, to offer the dying person the choice of whether to go on or return. This interpretation would explain the awkward fact (for religious commentators) that the near dead sometimes encounter at that threshold not only the beloved dead but also people who are still alive. By the time they are to be resurrected, all of this generation would of course be dead, and by then perhaps "already" resurrected, or at least those that would have opted to be. Likewise, this idea would give a new meaning to the peculiar iconography of the spiritual world, in which putti and cherubs are painted as little babies, Christ, the "son of man," is an infant at the breast, and the Buddha is sculpted as a big fat happy child. They are our divine children, or anticipations of them.

If we were to adopt this theory of time we would have collapsed the future and eternity into each other. Or rather, we would have recognized as the future what the great religions have been talking about all this time as eternity, Olympus, Heaven, "*illo tempore*," the spirit world. To put it in terms of my recension of Fraser's theory of evolving temporalities, the atemporal, prototemporal, eotemporal, thermotemporal, biotemporal, sociotemporal, and nootemporal levels of time-experience are succeeded by a theotemporal level that includes and transcends all the others. In this theory, the prophetic and the apocalyptic are reconciled. Thus to work for the future *is* to save one's soul, because to work for the future is to aid in the construction of the very heaven that can reach back into the unenlightened past to advise and inspire us. Similarly, by rejecting the world as it is, we can redeem it as it will be: we need not hate the world, since it is the place we shall transform into our future spiritual home. Again, this view of time makes perfect sense of the uncomfortably paired injunctions to love the things of time and to renounce the temporal. Our posterity would be our afterlife, activity would be contemplation—as the *Bhagavad Gita* says it is—perfection of the work perfection of the life. This life would be both preparation and the real thing. There would be plenty of room in this doctrine to accommodate Christian resurrection and Jewish covenant and Hindu reincarnation and Islamic paradise; and if we allowed the spirits of places and animals a role in this economy, for animism and totemism too.

The way would be open for a new and radical conception of spiritual depth. For if the present causes the future, but the future also influences the past, a nonlinear feedback loop has been closed: the present which causes the future is the present as influenced by that very future; the future that influences the present is a future caused by a present which has been influenced by the very future it causes. Every moment is the resultant, then, of an infinitely deep recursion between its future and its present. Perhaps our experiences of déjà vu, and more importantly our "moments in and out of time," our epiphanies—our sense, in Blake's terms, of infinity in a grain of sand and eternity in a flower—derive from that underlying depth of temporal iteration. Perhaps our spiritual disciplines, of Zen and Yoga and meditation and contemplation, are but practical ways of pushing through the obviousness and the veil of the first iteration and exploring the riches beneath. Certainly the mandala, which meditators are enjoined to contemplate, and which may even be a sort of picture or diagram of contemplative consciousness, is suggestively concentric, iterated, and fractal in its design.

There is a major problem with this whole idea so far. If the future can influence the past, the future already exists in some sense, and thus the implication is that it is laid out before us, willy-nilly, and we are not free to change it. So conceived, the future tyrannizes us with its retroactive inevitability, in rather the same fashion as does the theistic idea of eternity with its omniscient and omnipotent God. However gentle and uncompelling the promptings of the unborn, their very existence, with the implication that we are fated to bring them into being just so, is compulsion enough. Our free will itself, according to this objection, would be just a charade.

Let us see if we can modify our idea, that the future can advise the past in some subtle way, so as to deal with these objections. Suppose there were not one future, but many, depending on how we—and all other agencies past and present within our event horizon—act and have acted. This is the "branching time" or "parallel universes" theory, and it has much to recommend it, especially if we include some form of the weak backwards influence I have already suggested. The physicist Hugh Everett III indeed proposed that the many-universes theory, where every quantum event initiates a new branching of time, was the only intelligible solution to the problem of quantum indeterminacy.

Past and future are not symmetrical. We can remember the past, but not the future. Perhaps the reason is that there is only one past, but many competing futures: we hear all their voices, as we hear the voice of the past, but the voices of the future largely drown each other out.

In this recension the quiet voice that speaks to us out of the future is not one, but many. Thus we in our present select by our actions and our perceivings from among the various futures that branch out ahead, but as we do so those very futures whisper to us their invitations. Every set of ethically reconcilable futures would have its own voice, its own suasion to do the thing that will bring it into full being. The quietness of those voices is now explained by the relative tenuousness of their probability: the most unlikely futures speak so softly we cannot hear them at all, those with the best odds of happening speak most clearly. Each future speaks most anxiously when its own existence is in question; and sometimes, as with Faust, a spirit hovers by each ear, one good, one evil. When we act we silence some of those voices forever, and this is the dark, murderous tragedy of action. By the same token an act of creative goodness will make the angels sing indeed. There is much sense in clapping if you believe in fairies, for perhaps they do indeed depend on our endorsement, these distant children of ours, with their chimeric theromorphism, their heads haloed with magical software, their shoulders fledged with genetically grown wings.

As modified, our idea now provides the clearest possible asymmetry between the past and the future; without that distinction we are trapped in an incestuous and Oedipal marriage of the two. Our past is one, though deeply iterated; but our futures are many, and our present role is to create them. As we do so we are beckoned and advised by them, in the form of conscience, intuition, the inner voice, the promptings of our joy. The evil futures speak to us too, but we should be able to learn to diagnose them as evil, as we judge a person by his or her words and attitudes; at least we will not be acting in a void, without warning of the consequences. Time is a tree, and the present is always a branchpoint. As anyone knows who prunes a tree, the most promising branch thickens and is fed by the twigs and leaves of its future. The earlier produces the later by causality; the later draws the earlier by competitive influence. The multiple futures are braided together by the defining, decisive acts and observings of the present, to form the coherent cable of the past.

This revision of the idea of time also has the profoundest consequences for how we imagine the cosmos. By analogy, early brain science assumed that all the higher-level functions of the mind—consciousness, creativity, humor, morality—were simply the passive results of lower-level processes in the various sections of the brain, in the cells, in the molecules, in the atoms, in the particles of which the brain is made up. Only "bottom-up" causality of this kind was allowed. Contemporary brain science, however, has been pushed by the very rigor and exactness of its early reductionism into observations and experiments that clearly show a "top-down" kind of causality at work as well. *As well,* not *instead:* this is an important caveat. Some "new age" theorists, and in a different way some social constructivists in the humanities and social sciences, would be quite happy to throw out "bottom-up" causality altogether, replacing one linear view of the mind with another. It is the combination of the two that is fascinating; it closes a feedback loop and makes of the brain a wild and unpredictable place, where positive feedbacks among the self-modifying synaptic circuits can grow themselves harmonically into unprecedented patterns. The way that synaptic geometry is clearly altered by the repeated firings of thought, sensation, and memory testifies to the power of mind over matter.

It is becoming increasingly clear that the genes do not so much specify, like a blueprint, the exact shape of the organism, as set in motion a set of feedbacks among an ensemble of proteins that result, amazingly, in a coherent living creature. The process is not just causally *pushed* by its past state, but *pulled* or *drawn* to its conclusion by a strange attractor that is often powerful enough to override quite serious genetic errors and environmental deficits. If, say, the intricate mechanism of a hawk's eye had to be exactly specified by the genes, any mutation or early lack of nutrients, however small, could throw the whole thing out of alignment and it would be useless. On the contrary, the process is robust because it is recalibrated all the time by its final cause, its strange attractor, which is the mature eye in the mature bird. The adult organism is as much the partial fulfilling of this strange attractor as the realization of a preordained plan. In this sense the completed life form strangely determines the genes that generate it. Here again we encounter a two-way causality.

What we have done with the cosmos and its time environment in our thought experiment is not unlike what the brain scientists did with their conception of the brain and the developmental biologists did with fetal growth, as their sciences evolved. The future of the universe is its higher-level processing, its thoughts, desires, imaginings—"the prophetic soul/ Of the wide world dreaming on things to come," as Shakespeare puts it. The past is its mechanism, its organs, cells, and dead material constituents. The past causes the future, as brain causes mind; but in turn the future reaches back and transforms its own elements and antecedents, as we do through self-discipline or introspection or training or decision or self-exhortation; the mind, which is the whole, changing the chemistry and physics of the brain, its parts. Here our idea converges suggestively with that odd natural theology proposed earlier in this chapter, in which we humans are the neurons of a divine embryo, gradually wiring up, through our scientific instruments and artistic insight, the brain of God. In other words, the demands of freedom and the demands of a coherent environmental metaphysics issue in the same answer, the same peculiar nonlinear relation of past and future. The difference between the present (including the past) and the future is the same difference as that between the knowledge of an individual neuron and the knowledge of the brain as a whole—between the human and the divine.

However attractive this idea, can it be true? It might be objected that there is nothing in experimental and observational science that would suggest, let alone justify, the idea that the future can influence the past.

An empirical argument for our thesis does exist. Of course the term "empirical" is going to have to be stretched a little in what follows; but it is not entirely out of place. The Cosmological Anthropic Principle of the physicist John Archibald Wheeler, in its strong form, might offer one promising direction. Wheeler argues from the now established fact that in quantum physics the precise nature of a sub-atomic event is undetermined until it is observed. Its "precise nature" can be defined as how it affects the rest of the universe—for instance, as a wave or as a particle or, in particle-pair formation when two opposite particles are generated, which particle carries which charge or polarity.

The elementary quantum phenomenon in the sense of Bohr, the elementary act of observer-participancy, develops definiteness out of indeterminism, secures a communicable reply in response to a well-defined question. The rate of carrying out such yes-no determinations, and their accumulated number, are both minuscule today when compared to the rate and number to be anticipated in the billions of years yet to come. The coming explosion of life opens the door, however, to an all-encompassing role for observer-participancy: to build, in time to come, no minor part of what we call *its* past—*our* past, present, and future—but this whole vast world.

Since Wheeler first developed his idea, he has recognized that a human observer as such is not necessary, and that any organism capable of unambiguous response, even an atom or molecule, would do if it were sensitive to the kind of event taking place. In other words, the history of the universe as it is is partly as yet undetermined, and partly the settled consensus of its own constituents, each of which in turn is confirmed in such definite identity as it possesses by the "vote" of the rest. As Herman Melville said, this is a joint-stock universe. This consensus is by necessity retrospective and retroactive, since every event of observation must, delayed by the speed limit of light, postdate the event it observes.

If this is the case, our own COBE black-body radiation observations of the Big Bang, the original singularity that began the universe, must be partly determining its precise nature. This argument carries special weight because in the first few fractions of a second the universe was smaller than an atom and younger than the frequency of any physical wave, and thus entirely within the horizons that define quantum physics as opposed to classical physics. In other words, everything that happened at that unimaginably brief epoch of universal history was subject for its very identity to later interpretations of it, since no contemporary observer existed that could validate its exact constants, fundamental ratios, and basic quantitative values. The point is that only one set of constants, ratios, and values—only one value for Planck's constant, the electron volt constant, the speed of light, the gravitational constant, even perhaps pi and the value of the golden section ratio—could bring about any conceivable efficacious observers of it.

One way of dealing with the problem of how an event that cannot be predicted knows how to happen in the way it actually does is to posit a branching universe, as we have done, in which all possible outcomes actually come about, but in which the one we are on is cut off from all the others. Wheeler's theory offers a way of pruning this unmanageable foliage of bifurcating timelines, and consolidating them into one world, but a world with fuzzy edges, great depth, and buried unrealized possibilities. The pruning is achieved by the fact that only those outcomes that will continually generate reliable observers will come about. In the case of the Big Bang, perhaps only one outcome was possible, and all the others remain only as an irreducible noise in any system. Later decisions might leave their alternatives floating about as a sort of ghostly accompaniment haunting the fringes of measurement. As I interpret it, Wheeler's universe implies that all the timelines are indeed faintly present to each other in the form of a low-probability penumbra to actuality, and are thus not separated from one another.

For our immediate purpose, which is the investigation of a morally viable world, the interesting implication of Wheeler's theory is that if we by observing it can partly determine the origin of the universe, then by extension we must also be partly determining, at least on the quantum level, all events that have come since, *and our descendants will be performing the same offices for us*. It is now becoming quite clear that the firings of the neurons of the brain are triggered by changes as minute as quantum events. We can describe the brain as at least partly a mechanism for amplifying quantum events into the macrocosm, for killing or sparing Schrödinger's famous cat, so to speak. Tiny changes across quantum thresholds are not always damped out, as is usual in stable matter, but can cascade up into major transformations. Thus the human brain is one place that is especially sensitive and susceptible to the wave-function-collapsing influence of future observers of it. Perhaps, further, we might speculate that evolutionary selection designed the human brain especially for this function, since it is clear that any species that could listen to the advice of its descendants would be at a superb adaptive advantage.

The mathematician Roger Penrose (in *The Emperor's New Mind*, Oxford University Press, 1989) and the brain scientist Jeffrey Satinover (in *The Quantum Brain: The Search for Freedom and the Next Generation of Man*, Wiley, 2002) have argued that the human brain could well be seen as an extraordinarily effective amplifier of quantum events up into the realm of classical physical causality. Their purpose was to make possible an alternative to the view that every human action and decision is predetermined from the beginning of the universe, and that consequently ideas of moral freedom and responsibility are meaningless, as some have argued. Especially interesting is the new research on microtubules and protein folding, in both of which biology seems to be using quantum calculation to perform vital computational tasks beyond the capacities of regular organic chemistry. Their point is that some part of biology uses true quantum randomness as a tool, and that freedom may be a result. I do not see how mere randomness can help us much with the problem of free will. In my view the simple idea that a given causal situation can have many different effects, all legitimately causal but often inconsistent with each other—that is, that this is a branchy universe—takes care of the freedom-and-responsibility problem— we decide which branch to take. But the Penrose-Satinover idea might be useful for another purpose, that is, as a medium of communication among different times and time branches.

Hunch, intuition, prophecy, visions, premonitions, and all those other mysterious human gifts, and even the lesser but impressive capacities of other higher animals in this respect, might have a factual basis. Those angelic visitations we are so prone to may not be mere fabrications. Future Frenchmen and Frenchwomen may well have spoken to Saint Joan, if only in order to keep their own elegant tongue alive and independent of English. Did poor Moctezuma dream that Cortez was a god, because the future of Latin America was so beautiful that its inhabitants were prepared to take that tragic way to stay his destroying arm? If there is any substance to this extension of the Anthropic Principle, and to the idea that the future can communicate with the past, it seems likely that our remote descendants might indeed be able to reach back to us in the ways that we have stipulated as necessary to a universe that is meaningful and free.

7

The Information/Spirit Universe

Mind and Matter

But can the divine be in any sense immanent in a material universe? The previous chapter contains an assumption that mind is at home in the world, a characteristic of it as natural as energy, life, or gravitation. Many philosophers, however, most notably Descartes, have argued for a radical discontinuity between matter and mind. Even when they were forced by the dualism into the most elaborate gymnastics to account for the mysteries of perception and intentional action—how could a ghostly immaterial mind either experience the world through physical senses or affect it by moving physical limbs, unless, as Bishop Berkeley thought, God arranged a continuous coincidence?—they stuck to their beliefs. For centuries material determinists and apologists for transcendental religion alike have insisted on the essential deadness of the fundamental matter of the universe, its lack of internal spontaneous process, of self-awareness and self-motivation. We know from Richard Westfall's biography of Newton that the reason natural philosophers of the Enlightenment insisted on the deadness and inert passivity of material nature was in order to concede to God a necessary role in giving it all life and animation, so that the divine would not be a fifth wheel in the world. Rational men, they wished to distance themselves from what they considered the magical practices and superstitions of popular religion, and declare their independence from clerical authority, female wishful thinking, and traditional ritual. Not wanting to see God as immanent in the universe, and preferring to keep him outside it where he could, so to speak, be kept an eye on, they tried to make physicality as incomplete as possible in respect of all the properties attributed to soul, consciousness, reflectiveness, initiative, originality, so that he would still have something important to do.

Somehow the fact that matter has properties never seemed to them to be a problem. That is, particles, atoms, and molecules are not totally transparent; they interrupt the forces that encounter them in such a way as to make them perceptible to humans and other animals. The light must be broken, scattered, transformed, absorbed, refracted, for us to see things at all: and it is only what is seeable—perceptible, in more general terms—that can be of any concern to science. If matter had no internal process, light would come to us utterly unaltered by the matter it had encountered, and thus the matter would be invisible. Further, it is only where matter resists the complete logical explication of its internal process, where it interrupts the linear flow of rational consequence and we are forced to recognize in it an inexplicable constant, a given, that we have any fixed point that might justify a claim for its actual existence. It is the irreducibility of the fundamental constants—the speed of light, the gravitational constant, the electron volt constant, Planck's constant, pi—their darkness and opacity to any further reductive explanation, their idiosyncratic characterization of the fundamental relations of physical reality—that gives them their foundational role in our understanding of reality.

As we now know, simply taking up space is a complex performance for matter, and its other qualities, of mass, charge, parity, and so on, are the maintained achievements of its internal process. Its external communicative process is more remarkable still, of course—crystals, plants, animals, we ourselves, are the emergent forms that such communication makes possible. Thus the universe postulated by the material determinists, lacking that mysterious inner negotiation and external sensitivity that makes matter observable, would be completely invisible—and of course untouchable, unsmellable, inaudible, and tasteless as well. Since science relies essentially on observation, science would be impossible in such a universe. It is only to the extent that the universe and the things in it have some kind of inner metabolism and outer sociability—only, that is, the extent to which they are alive—that they can be said to be at all. Being is not given, but the achievement of the universe's continuous originating inventiveness, its life and growth.

A large part of this liveness, this internal reflexivity, of ordinary matter is devoted necessarily to making and displaying more or less crude internal representations of the rest of the universe. Close observation of nature shows us something that looks very like representation at all levels of physical reality. Butterfly chrysalises, for instance, often combine two or three levels of representation, aimed at various possible predators: the appearance of a dead leaf for the stupider ones, a spot of iridescence which still resembles mold for the unsophisticated but which is a poison warning for the cleverer ones that have seen through the disguise—and sometimes the false appearance of a chrysalis of a truly poisonous species, saving the metabolic expense of manufacturing real poison. Vines pestered with butterflies will grow leaves that look like butterflies, on the correct theory that butterflies will not lay eggs on what they think are fellow butterflies. But these are simple forms of representation and imitation compared to what one finds among higher animals. The grey-lag goose expresses its love for its mate by pointedly making a mimed attack on an absent, counterfactual goose, in a "triumph ceremony" that is a fine analogy of human theater. The male blue satin bowerbird's bower is not a real nest but a magnificent advertisement to the female of how good his nest-building genes are. But the need to represent and depict goes all the way down to the most primitive entities in the universe. An atom must find ways of translating the impact of incoming energy into terms that it can absorb without flying apart; indeed, all the atoms that exist are the ones that didn't fly apart. Atoms do this by adjusting the disposition of the electrons in the harmonic series of electron shells that makes up their outer skin; and they relieve the pressure of such impacts by giving off a photon of their own, whose unique signature can be picked up by a spectrograph. Those spectral emanations are in fact representations of their environment, in terms that are unique to the element that produces them.

A former student of mine, the designer and architect Jack Rees, has suggested in an unpublished work that it is no coincidence that the great physicists—Newton, Einstein, and so on—tended to make their discoveries in mechanics simultaneously with their discoveries in optics. Perhaps, he suggests, optics and mechanics are at base the same thing. That is, objects in the universe exist (have mechanical properties) only in and through the fact that they express themselves and experience the expressive activity of other objects (they see and are seen). All exchanges of information are conducted by the photons of light or by particles that can be translated into photons. And mechanical processes are fundamentally exchanges of information. Certainly the basic principle of all physical science is that it must be based on observation—that is, it assumes that an object has reality only to the extent that it is observable, even if indirectly. Scientific reality is observability. At the same time the only way that anything can be observed is by its effect on other things; thus for scientific reality we need not only a world of observable objects but also a world of observing objects, that is, objects that can register by their response the presence of other objects. The power of the observer in the constitution of fundamental reality has been confirmed again and again by quantum physics, and is already a feature of our electronic technology. We can generalize this idea to the proposition that every thing exists if and only if, and to the extent that, it represents other things and is represented by them—that is, it expresses itself in such a way as to be intelligibly recognized as what it is, and it registers and records its fellow beings in such a way as to make *their* existence concrete.

Thus representation—one of the traditional philosophical functions of mind—is a fundamental feature of reality. The universe was only a "buzzing, booming confusion," as William James put it, at the first moment of the Big Bang. Since then it has been painting and sculpting itself with greater and greater precision, evolving complex chemistry, plants, and animals to do it more effectively, and achieving thereby a denser and denser reality and concreteness, the more sensory modalities it has brought into play. The consciousness and selfhood that we so dearly prize in human beings may not be a unique supervention upon the universe from outside, but rather a deeper, richer version of something that is already present in nature's other individuals—accelerated, to be sure, across crucial thresholds such as learned communication competence and improved neural modeling capacities—but not a stranger to the world.

It has taken us four hundred years, through the most brilliant intellectual achievements of the human race, to reach a scientific view of the world in which we can now see the particles of matter, no less than living organisms or conscious brained beings, as feedback processes with some measure of autonomy, self-determination, unpredictable historical identity, and reciprocal communication with the rest of the universe. One way of expressing this is in the language of another former student of mine, the Belgian philosopher Koen DePryck. He says that the world we live in is an onto-epistemological universe—that is, it only exists to the extent that its participants know and experience themselves and each other, and it is only knowable to the extent that all its inhabitants have an individual inexplicable existence. Everything experiences itself and each other into being.

Another way of putting this point is that the world is made of information. The fundamental entities of physics and genetics, for instance, can only be described in informational terms. Whether an electron possesses wavelike or particle-like characteristics depends upon the informational state of the system that observes it. The photon is one of the most fundamental of the components of matter, yet a photon is much more a unit of information than a unit of stuff. If the material universe is made of frozen photons—which is the implication of Einstein's famous formula $E = mc^2$—then the material universe is made of frozen information. As for the charged particles, according to superstring theory there is no matter of which superstrings are made; matter is made of *them*, and they can only be described in mathematics, an informational science. The universe is constructed of the interplay of these fundamental bits of information, and the interplay of bits of information has a name: computation. The same is true for genetics. It does not matter which atom of carbon, hydrogen, oxygen, or phosphorus is in a given place on the DNA helix; what matters is the informational content of their placement and their computational role in generating proteins. Biochemistry is nanotech CAD-CAM, with the DNA playing a role similar to a program, and the RNA, the ribosome, and the enzymes acting as the processor.

Other sciences, too, would reveal under investigation that the fundamental "stuff" of their study is now not so much hard little chunks of substance as discrete packets of information engaged in a computation-like mutual activity. The world is not an arrangement of stuff, it is an arrangement of arrangements. Consider the microstructure of matter itself. When it was thought that atoms were, as their name implies, the fundamental, indivisible, and irreducible components of the universe, it was easy to believe that there was a dead, hard, substantial substrate to everything, of which thoughts and intentions were a mere epiphenomenon. But a few more decades' investigation have broken the atom into very soft and ghostly electrons and the nucleus, and have gone on to split the nucleus first into neutrons and protons, and then into quarks and gluons, and finally perhaps into superstrings; and at this point in the deconstruction the solid matter has quite disappeared, and all we are left with is bits of light, bits of what one can only call information—spins or vibrations of spacetime itself, that are not unlike the ones and zeroes of a computer program.

Computability and Uncomputability

If the universe comes to be seen as made of information, as increasingly it is in many disciplines, the nature of scientific demonstration and proof must begin to change. New standards must be added to the old. Traditionally, physicists talk about atoms or particles "feeling" a force, chemists speak of a molecule "seeking" its lowest energy state, molecular biologists describe a nucleotide sequence as "coding for" a protein which is "expressed" through the operations of "messenger" RNA. In physics, an unease with the perceived vagueness of the attractive or repulsive forces within a proton, or between massive bodies in space, for instance, has led to the identification of gluons, photons, gravitons, and Higgs fields that mediate such forces; but we are still left with a quark "feeling" the stickiness of a gluon, Mercury "feeling" the gravitons of the sun. Bits of matter bonking into other bits and bouncing off are no longer an adequate scientific description.

The vagueness of this language, which has its counterpart in the continued paradoxes and renormalized infinitudes of the mathematics that relate the microcosm to the macrocosm, is the sign that a new exactness is being demanded in pursuit of good science. Increasingly the only intelligible deterministic language, that is, language that leads to testable predictions, is coming to be the language of computation.

In other words, it is not going to be enough, if a given event is to be fully explained, to show that the laws of nature allow that event to take place, that the necessary materials and instigating causes are present, that similar events have taken place in similar circumstances, that the mathematics of the prediction and the observation match and are correct; the scientist will also have to show how the event could be computed by the available computing systems that nature provides, in the time allowed for it. The computational universe can be described as a self-programming computer writing all possible programs, playing them out, announcing its results in the form of their enactment, and using those results as its fresh input. The computational universe is *already*, in one sense, the fundamental assumption of natural science, since all natural science is based on physics, and physics is based on mathematics. Computer science has shown that virtually any concatenation of objects can act as a logic processor—Babbage's brass gears, lineages of reproductive mating, tinkertoys, photoelectric crystals, DNA snippets, and the quantum states of atoms are a few examples in the literature. The real problem now would be to find or imagine a piece of the universe that could *not* act as a computer. Most scientists do not yet realize this, but many—especially those who have been forced by the exigencies of investigation to use computer models of the processes they study—are beginning to get the point.

If the universe is like a gigantic self-programming computer, announcing the results of its computations in the form of events and then inputting them back into itself, it must be continually transforming itself, rewriting its own programs, and thus expanding. For its memory must include all its own previous states—there is no place else for the memory to go, and information cannot be destroyed. Even black holes, says Stephen Hawking, eventually leak out enough energy by quantum boiling at their event horizon that they drop back into normal space, releasing the masses of information they have swallowed and sequestered. (Others have suggested that all the information swallowed by a black hole is represented on the surface of its event horizon.) The more existing informational material the universe has at its disposal to make possible programs, the more complex and self-referential those programs will become. The history of life upon this planet, with its rich feedbacks of asexual, sexual, and sociosexual reproduction, and the explosion of human information processing through language, writing, and electronic computing, may be seen in these terms as some of the systems by which the universe snowballs its computational tasks.

But, one might ask, what if there is not enough computing power at a given time or place to complete the computation of the next event? If, for instance, the amount of processing circuitry needed to compute an event in half a second required a volume of matter a light-year across, and the event had to happen in the next half-second, the local computer would blurt out the answer to its computation at least a year after the event it was supposed to specify, because it would take that much time for the information to travel at the speed of light to and from the outside edges of the computer. If the laws of nature, themselves the ossification of ancient earlier computations, require a next event, yet the precise nature of that event cannot be computed in the available time and with available computational resources, how does that next event know how to take place? If we use the mathematics of continuity in time and space, that is, the familiar differential equations of calculus, there will always—trivially—be some degree of accuracy or acuity tinier than any computer can calculate in a finite time. Indeed the infinite divisibility of quantities implied by the decimal notation of number already implies the possibility of a more perfect analog measurement of something than its coarse-grainedness would merit. Another way of putting this is that the universe is demonstrably approximate in its details, that it is, so to speak, "guessing" or "free to choose" when it comes to rounding-off its finest discriminations. When it cannot compute the next event, it simply "plumps" for one that is not in violation of the rules. It is acting freely, in some primitive sense.

Quantum theory was devised partly as a way of reining in the uncertainty implied by this problem, of showing how we do not need to concern ourselves with quantities smaller than the granularity of the actual event we are trying to measure. Tiny individual uncertainties could be damped out in the mass, and an ensemble of subatomic particles in space, or a series of particles in time, could behave deterministically even when any individual particle's behavior was indeterminate. David Bohm suggested that since all quantum particles in the universe, future or past, were linked by quantum coherence in an "implicate order," a linkage that was instantaneous and not subject to the limitations of the speed of light, the universe could itself constitute a quantum computer sufficient in power to compute any given event at its appropriate time. This solution might solve the problem if it were not obvious that objects larger than the quantum level possess emergent qualities and new temporal umwelts—thermodynamics, for instance—that make time irreversible at these scales. We already know that "butterfly effects" can still sometimes amplify the tiniest difference in initial conditions up into the macrocosm. Our everyday electronic devices routinely contain mechanisms for amplifying quantum differences up across the threshold into classical physics, and those mechanisms exploit nature's own ways of breaking through the barrier. Chaos and complexity theory have shown, moreover, that macroscopic parts of the universe can easily be forced, by introducing feedback into their interactions, to display dynamical behavior that again overwhelms the capacities of any conceivable calculator to predict. The Lorenz attractor, which specifies the possible states of a damped, driven dynamical system, could never be completely plotted, even by a universal quantum computer, because it is a fractal, that is, it possesses new features at any scale of magnification.

A related but somewhat different approach is taken by the brilliant Israeli physicist Vladimir Gontar, cofounder of the *Journal of Discrete Dynamics in Nature and Society*. Gontar suggests in the inaugural issue of that periodical that whereas the mathematics of differential equations may be a useful method for human beings to take photographs of nature, so to speak, it is not the mathematics that nature itself uses. He proposes that we use

> a system of algebraic and difference equations, instead of, or in parallel to, the commonly used system of differential equations. The advantages of difference equations from the computational point of view are obvious (the dynamics of pattern formation presented here takes about 10 min for 300 iterations on a PC-486). Now let us clarify the meaning of time and space that we face in our approach and equations. We think that there is a general problem of defining the meaning of the so-called "discrete time and space" appearing when iterational maps or difference equations are used. The questions arise when we try to make a link between the continuous time and space of differential equations and discrete nature of our numerical calculations. As a precondition for sampling, we suppose the existence of a "small-as-necessary" time interval Δt.

The reason why Gontar does not want to use differential equations to explain the workings of the world is that differential equations imply a seamless continuum in time and space. If the universe is a continuum, then since an infinite number of gradations must be dealt with at any moment, computation of its future states would be impossible, and thus true dynamical behavior would be an illusion; though in a sense the whole of the universe, from beginning to end, would be given in a single Parmenidean act of fate. Gontar and his co-workers go on to show that nature itself often behaves as if space and time came in discrete packets appropriate to the system being investigated rather than, as differential calculus implies, flowing seamlessly on at all scales. J.T. Fraser, whose work on the temporal umwelts of organisms we have already looked at, might agree. In other words, the universe is as much like a game, with distinct counters and distinct turns, as like an infinitely smeared-out continuum. Gontar's "system of algebraic and difference equations" is designed to deal with such discrete packets, specifying the game-rules of their interactions.

If the universe is like a game, the next moment of any given system in it is in theory computable, unique, and deterministic; but at the same time there will not be enough computing power or time available in practice to do so, if the game involves complex and self-referential interactions. Moreover, the game cannot handle details smaller than the minimum counters of the system, and thus the universe is always free, at some smaller scale, to introduce perturbations that can change the nature of the system itself.

The picture that begins to emerge from the debates of these brilliant natural philosophers begins to look rather promising for our purposes. For let us remember, we are looking for a kind of generative principle that is something of a Rube Goldberg contraption in some respects, not the perfect reflective sphere. Elegance in the sense of simplicity is not what we require of this universe. Nevertheless—for the religious mystics who have seen the divine insist on it—there should be a deep beauty in the design. Perhaps we can hope that the picture we get may be like Kepler's vision of the motions of the planets, clumsier on the surface than the then-existing system of perfectly spherical orbits, but with a richer elegance; in which the orbitals, whether elliptical or even parabolic or hyperbolic, would all be sections of a cone and would all sweep out equal areas of their orbital plane in the same amount of time. Perhaps even Rube Goldberg contraptions can have a certain strange grace of their own.

The Three-Computer Universe

So let us try to summarize what the universe looks like if we accept that it may in itself be a computational system.

First of all, it is an imperfect one, since it is made of three different computational systems, each flawed in itself, and in partial contradiction to one another. Though at base the universe may possess a perfect quantum computer, composed of the collective harmonic resonances or implicate order of all quantum particles past, present, and future—let us call it the Bohm computer—this computer is an unwieldy one, and perhaps even a paralytic one. Let us recall the fact, already alluded to, that there is nothing to prevent the quantum universe from branching at every moment into multiple superpositions, each with a probability lower than the previous branching. So what is presented to us is an oddly barren plenum of vanishingly low-probability virtual particles, in which everything is ghostly, nothing is decisively chosen as existing, nothing is *done*, because nothing is chosen *against*. This computer is a digital one, and the quantum, or qubit, is the bit it uses, the lower limit of its computational acuity. A quantum computer is good at computing factorials—that is, it is good at extracting information obscured by entropy and finding the original inner makeup of an already existing entity—but not much else. It is passive rather than constructive (unless it can turn itself into a different kind of computer). We return to the question, how does the universe prune its own choking luxuriance of dendrifications? The answer is the emergence, by some clinamen or symmetry-breaking swerve, of matter—an emergence which we have already seen as necessitated in general by both mathematical logic and the very fecundity of the quantum vacuum itself, and specified in particular by the requirement that it generate viable observers of it. Matter is that which is capable of collapsing the wave-function of quantum entities from probability into certainty; and as Wheeler points out, it does so retroactively. This capacity of matter changes the informational architecture of the universe; one of the things that the universal quantum computer computes must eventually be a different kind of computer, mediated by a different kind of parts and circuits.

This new realm of entities, which can observe each other into certainty, constitutes a new kind of computer, a sort of damaged Turing machine, or rather a poorly connected massively parallel computer made of enormous numbers of local Turing machines. It is a machine that is very good at computing certainties—that is, if it were not damaged it could deterministically predict everything that was ever going to happen, with a probability of one. It is the clockwork universe of Newton's orbits; it is Laplace's famous computer, containing the velocity, vector, and mass of all particles in the universe that can therefore calculate accurately the whole of the future. But it is damaged; first, by the limits of its local acuity—there must always be a decimal point below its level of accuracy, which could constitute the degree of difference made by the butterfly's wingbeat in the parable of the butterfly effect—; second, by the fact that it is limited by the speed of light, so that its accuracy is only local, and information vital to its predictions comes in too late to be of use; and third, by the fact that it must coexist with the probabilistic, timeless Bohm computer that brought it into being. The universal clock's bearings do not have perfect tolerances, and wobble about, generating new phenomena for it to measure; it has gears so vast that it takes millennia for its leverings and rotations to propagate themselves across its enormous cogs and beams, and thus it tells different times in different places; and it is trying to compete with a perfect ghostly Bohm clock that has no hands and that constitutes the metal of which the Turing clock is made. The observer effect, as formulated by the Copenhagen interpretation of quantum mechanics, is the way this computer communicates with and computes the settings of the quantum computer, but this effect again is a flaw—described in the paradox of Schrödinger's cat—in the logic of the Turing machine. The Turing computer also has another fatal flaw, from the point of view of the determinist, that it is liable to form local systems that have become trapped into predicting themselves and each other, and that have therefore got themselves caught in iterative nonlinear dynamical processes with no closed solution. Living organisms exemplify such local systems, of which we ourselves, it seems, are one.

The set of local self-predicting and mutually predicting systems constitutes a third emergent universe-computer, as yet in partly connected fragments, piggybacked upon the first two. It is not a Turing machine, but resembles rather those genetic-algorithm systems now being developed to solve complex problems in science, manufacturing, and business, in which an ecology of possible solutions reproduce, compete, and exchange genetic material in pursuit of the reward of posterity. It is an evolutionary computer, a generative game that can generate new generative games. Perhaps the largest subsystems of this emergent computation system that we have yet encountered are the gene pools of species, the human cultures, the natural languages, human individuals, the Internet, and the world financial and stock markets. Its calculations increasingly take the form of free decisions, intentions, meanings, and values. When it is predictable in its results, that predictability is intended: a human individual's promises, or the legal statutes of a human culture, can be as trustworthy as the laws of physics, but by choice not compulsion.

Thus we now have three computers, uneasily negotiating with one another in the constitution of reality. Each has a realm of determinacy, of certainty, of predictability, and a realm of indeterminacy, of uncertainty, of freedom. The quantum Bohm computer pays for the perfection of its connectivity and the certainty of its probabilistic calculations by the vanishingly low likelihood of the virtual entities it governs. The materialistic Turing machine pays for the determinacy of its local results by the fatal delays in its operations when calculating any kind of exactness or reflexive complexity, so that many events under its aegis happen in a way that is quite arbitrary within given limits. The evolutionary computer announces results that are unpredictable in terms of the definitions and languages of the earlier computers, yet those results are often by design predictable if the language of values and intentions and promises is understood.

All three computers are effective up to a point as determiners of reality, but ineffective beyond that point. Thus we can divide events in the universe into two classes—those which, with a given level of accuracy and probability, are truly predictable, and those which, within the constraints and laws generated by the first kind of event, are essentially free. What is truly predictable is for all intents and purposes over and done with; what is free is for all intents and purposes yet to be decided. Indeed, we might now turn around, using our new powers of reflection, and note that this distinction, between the predictable and the free, rather intriguingly fits our experience of the difference between the past and the future. The past is simply the events we can "dict." The future is the events we cannot. Perhaps we have again come across that odd image of multiple vague futures being selected from and braided together into a definite though composite past by the free choices of the present. Our free choice to be predictable—to keep our promises, to be a distinct character for our neighbors, to subject ourselves to canons of scientific proof, to accept our history with all its warts as our own, to incorporate even while transcending the existing artistic and religious languages, to respect legal precedent, to be just and fair—these are ways by which we participate in the braiding of the futures together into a consistent past. If our speculations in the previous chapter carry weight, about the need for guidance from the future, the present in which we confirm the future-virtual into past reality is in turn being retroactively informed by the emergent voices of the future. The timeless quantum computer that underlies the others provides the medium for such communications.

The reader will surely have noticed that I have couched our investigation largely in the fashionable language of computation and computers. But this kind of research has been conducted before, and in other terms. The Greeks—and Saint John the evangelist— might have used the language of the Logos instead. The Cabbalists of medieval Spain used the language of the Sephiroth, of essences and emanations. Alchemists used the vitalistic language of growth and generation. The Hindus consider the universe to be a dream in the mind of Brahman, and the three Gunas of their cosmology correspond roughly to the three computers I have described. The Taoists' I Ching system is itself a computer, combining elements from the first two in my classification. The advantage of computer language is that we now have, as it were, a way of doing metaphysical experiments and observing and quantifying the results. What the various kinds of computers are, and what they can and cannot do, can be demonstrated and used to constrain our theories; and our metaphysical hypotheses are now subject to test.

Psychoanalyzing God

If it is true that the universe can be legitimately described as a system of mutual representation and self-representation, as a body of interacting information, and as a hierarchy of imperfect but partly free computational systems, then the ancient animist universe of so many traditional religions and the spirit-imbued physics of Taoism are not so far off the mark as has been thought. And at the same time, the idea that the universe as a whole might constitute the emerging brain of some enormous mind also takes on more credibility. It was the scientist Arthur Eddington who observed that the universe resembled not so much an immense machine as an immense thought. If we define spirit in its crudest and rawest state as information, we can see the universe as a growing hierarchy of denser and denser configurations of spirit, reaching all the way up to human minds and beyond, to the emergent mind of God.

Indeed, the logic of this investigation suggests that the universe *must*, in some sense, constitute a mind. It cannot do otherwise; some subset of it over its vast history, even if only my mind, or yours, must be conscious of itself, and indeed the evidence is that there are billions of such conscious subsets. Even one conscious being alone in the universe, since that mind would be the collective result of the universe's whole history, would constitute its immanent god; the rest of the universe would be its extended body. But those subsets demonstrably combine in larger semi-autonomous collectivities. Take, for instance, a natural language: if one examines the etymological history of a word like "nature" or "true" or "judge" it is hard to avoid the conclusion that somehow the language itself is thinking, is using metaphors to speculate philosophically; and its "synapses" are the conversations of thousands or millions of individual humans. I have already suggested other collective "thinkers" such as the human cultures, the Internet, and the world financial and stock markets. The caduceus, which we looked at earlier, is clearly a collective thought of the kind we might expect from such a collective mind. Such a mind does not even need "neurons" that are self-conscious in themselves: human individuals think with neurons that are not self-aware in the sense that the brain is as a whole, and the behaviors and structures of animals and plants are the result of the slow "thinking" of their gene pools.

A little meditation on the way that gene pools "think" will help us understand the nature of a collective mind. What are the sense organs of a gene pool, by which it "learns" the outside world and is thus enabled to "plan" for it? They consist of the genetic differences of its individuals, their locality, and their differential rates of survival. Those "senses" are linked, over years or centuries, by the slow "synaptic connections" of reproduction. The gene pools of animals and plants are remarkably astute, if we discount the very slow response times of these species-wide sensory organs and the crudity of the input signal. It is as if I had no other sense than touch, and that sense were constituted of the differential death rates of different types of reproducing skin cells over different parts of the surface of my body. An asexually reproducing species has a sensory surface resembling a thin sheet whose length is relative survival, whose breadth is location, and whose thickness is the minuscule differences created by raw mutation. Sexual reproduction clearly multiplies that thickness many times, by sexual recombination, thus hugely increasing the volume of the gene pool's perceptual field. Mating also accelerates the spread of information across the whole pool.

Imagine now that the perceptual field of the collective entity were still further deepened and accelerated, so that the units were differentiated not just by genetic individuality but also by continually and mutually adjusting cultural variations, and that they communicated second by second, by language, writing, the arts, and the Internet, rather than over the years by mating (see Table 1).

If God, then, exists in the immanent form I am suggesting, human minds provide God with the extended perceptual field that sexual reproduction provides to a gene pool—or that language provides to a community. God is our spiritual gene pool. Understanding the mind

Table 1

The core concept in the evolutionary paradigm that lies at the heart of the sciences is *survival*. The concept of survival implies two questions:

The survival of what?

Into what?

To answer these questions we require a new concept:

survival phase space.

A phase space is the number of dimensions required to map the various characteristics of a given system; e.g. a moving cloud of cooling gas might require, as well as the three dimensions of space in which it moves and a time-dimension to map the movement, additional dimensions, such as temperature, chemical composition, dilution, and pressure to fully map all of its states and behaviors.

A *survival phase space* is the phase space that describes the possible dimensions into which a survivor can be said to survive. A rock, for instance, survives trivially in all three dimensions of its physical presence, and in a single linear time dimension, bounded at one end by its cooling from lava, and at the other by its mechanical shattering, erosion, melting, or vaporization. Different kinds of survivors survive into different sets of survival phase spaces, as shown in the following table. If we ignore the three spatial dimensions, which any physical entity requires for its description, we are left with the various temporal dimensions into which it endures. Note that later phase spaces appear to earlier ones like counterfactuals, though they are just as much "real" parts of the universe once they have emerged. But note also that later modes of survival include and do not escape earlier ones.

SURVIVOR	SURVIVAL PHASE SPACE	PHASE SPACE SYMBOL
1. QUANTUM EVENT	Point-space: event exists (survives) in Planck time only	S^0
2. MATTER	Linear space: object exists (survives) along an Einstein/Minkowski geodesic	S^1 (i.e. geodesic x S^0)
3. ASEXUAL LIVING REPLICATOR	Plane space: DNA sequence survives in space of all clones in the same lineage	S^2 (i.e. clone set x S^1)
4. SEXUAL REPLICATOR	Volume space: genes survive in space of all interbreeding conspecifics	S^3 (i.e. gene pool x S^2)
5. SOCIAL REPLICATOR	Hyperspace 1: "memes" survive in space of all possible gene/culture coevoltionary variants: MORAL SPACE	S^4 (i.e. social world x S^3)
6. MENTAL REPLICATOR	Hyperspace 2: "soul" survives in space of all imagined and volitional alternatives: conditionals, subjunctives, fictions, the kingdom of heaven, etc. SPIRITUAL SPACE	S^5 (i.e. mental world x S^4)

of such a god, whose constituents are themselves free conscious beings, is one of the tasks of religion. Of course such a project is laughably futile, but the practice of doing so may itself be of a kind of heuristic value. For committed religious people I would hope that this attempt would be taken as an effort to find new ways of praise, new forms in which to celebrate the glory of the divine. After all, the gilding and frescoes of our past attempts at adequate praise are by now pretty tarnished with age, the canticles but an echo of a former time, the stories treated like old wives' tales, the theology discredited philosophy. Let us imagine how fire-new the religious art of the Italian Renaissance must have felt, the Bible characters in the latest fashions, the ancient cities' architecture perfectly up to date, the commercial and military equipment of the Hebrews showing the latest state-of-the-art Italian technology. So let it not be considered blasphemous to image the divine in terms of computers and contemporary cosmology.

Given this caveat, we might, if we have followed the analysis of emergent collective entities so far, imagine this god's mind as tricameral, with a sort of midbrain like the Bohm quantum computer, a hindbrain like a schedule-challenged Laplace calculator or Turing machine, and a forebrain like an evolutionary genetic-algorithm computation system or human brain (though unimaginably transformed by having sentient free beings for its neurons). The first brain is in many respects like the infinite, eternal, timeless, immaterial deity imagined by much mainline theology in various religions, dreaming in limitless bliss; but it is also in a sense a *deus absconditus*, an absent-minded, inattentive, or otiose brain which, because it attends to everything possible and impossible, attends to nothing in particular, and cannot make up its mind. The second brain, were it to be unified and perfect, would be like the fatalistic predestinarian god variously conceived by some Calvinists, Muslims, mechanistic determinists, and logical positivists. As it is, that second brain is fragmented into a multitude of more or less local nonce computers, bedeviled by computational scheduling problems and loosely connected by electromagnetic and gravitational interactions; but despite its handicaps it gives definite being, a tragic and real local existence to everything. The third brain, though, would be the personal god who loves, argues with, makes deals with, incarnates himself among, redeems, or suffers for human beings, as we find in such religions as Judaism, Krishna worship, popular Islam, and Christianity.

It is the genius of monotheistic religion to recognize the emerging unity of those three brains as the most beautiful thing in the universe, and as the most beautiful conceivable idea. When we contemplate it in these terms we are struck by its pathos as well as its grandeur, its astonishing drama, the wild adventure and crazy risk of the whole enterprise—and by our own intimate involvement in the story. "Ah, my chevalier!" cries out Gerard Manley Hopkins to his God in "The Windhover." It is not only the *peace* of God that passeth all understanding, but also the—what should we call it?—courage?

8

A Brief History of God

Why don't you think of him as one who is coming, who has been approaching from all eternity, the one who will someday arrive, the ultimate fruit of a tree whose leaves we are? What keeps you from projecting his birth into the ages that are coming into existence, and living your life a painful and lovely day in the history of a great pregnancy? Don't you see how everything that happens is again and again a beginning, and couldn't it be His beginning, since, in itself, starting is always so beautiful? If he is the most perfect one, must not what is less perfect precede him, so that he can choose himself out of fullness and superabundance?—Must not he be the last one, so that he can include everything in himself, and what meaning would we have if he whom we are longing for already existed?

As bees gather honey, so we collect what is sweetest out of all things and build Him. Even with the trivial, with the insignificant (as long as it is done out of love) we begin, with work and with the repose that comes afterward, with a silence or with a small solitary joy, with everything that we do alone, without anyone to join or help us, we start Him whom we will not live to see, just as our ancestors could not live to see us. And yet they, who passed away so long ago, still exist in us, as predisposition, as burden upon our fate, as murmuring blood, and as gesture that rises up from the depths of time.

Is there anything that can deprive you of the hope that in this way you will come to exist in Him, who is the farthest, the outermost limit?

Dear Mr. Kappus.....(b)e patient and without bitterness, and realize that the least we can do is make coming into existence no more difficult for Him than the earth does for spring when it wants to come.

—Rainer Maria Rilke, *Letter to a Young Poet*

Summary

Suppose we assume that the picture of the divine that we have inferred from nature is in its broad outlines accurate. A good way of illustrating its implications is by telling a fanciful story, one which includes the various elements we have touched on already, recounting the evolution, gestation, and destiny of the divine over the life of the universe. In a sense we could call it a literalizing of the parable of the caduceus, from chapter four; in another, an interpretation of past and future time in terms of the value-attractors we explored in chapter five; or, from chapter six, a sort of biography of Gaia, or an inference about the course of various future times from their effects on the present; or in yet another sense, an embryology of the brain/mind/spirit of the universe that we postulated in chapter seven.

Accordingly, we might distinguish eleven major eras in this history. I do not intend these eras to be thought of as in an absolute sequence, in which when one begins, the previous one must be over and done with; and the roots of a later era may well go back to the earliest beginnings. In the "later" stages, time itself will have taken on a geometry in which "earlier" and "later" will themselves be categories too crude to describe what is going on, and such terms as "bottom-up" and "top-down," or "micro" and "macro," or "fundamental" and "advanced" might be substituted, though with their own distorting implications.

1. The era of natural spirits: the world from the Big Bang up to the present, and continuing indefinitely.
2. The era of personal posterity ("the ancestors"): the human world up to now, from c. 3M years before the present, and continuing.
3. The era of civic and national cultural entities ("the gods"): from about 7,000 B.C.E. onwards.
4. The era of market-based electronic corporate entities: from now onwards.
5. The era of artificial intelligence ("the angels") and possible communication with other intelligent species: from about 100 years in the future onwards.
6. The era of direct communication between individuals and emergent superhuman agencies: from about 200–1,000 years in the future onwards.
7. The era of communication among different timelines, and competition among different divine self-conceptions: perhaps thousands of years in the future.
8. The era of consolidation of divine self-conceptions ("the Trinity") and the resurrection of the dead: impossible to even guess at dating.
9. The era of recruitment and dispatch of the great messengers, incarnations and theophanies to the past.
10. The era of the final condensation into the One.
11. The era of the retroactive kindling of the Big Bang.

This is not a history of theology, as will be immediately noted, since there is no direct mention of the origin of burial practices, the emergence of monotheism, the beginnings of the current world religions, and so on; nor is it a record of the divine retroactive interventions in history, for it does not include the lives of such figures as Buddha, Moses, Jesus, and Mohammed. But it gives us a sort of raw calendar upon which those significant intellectual and spiritual events may be mapped, and perhaps a hint of the reasons for which they occurred.

The Early Stages: Nature Gods, Human Gods, and Collective Gods

Those who believed that the universe is made of spirit—form, logos, information-disseminating-itself, arrangement-pregnant-with-emergent-arrangement, or whatever one chooses to call it—seem to have been right all along. Matter as such is only an early, crude densification of spirit that is now being resolved by such instruments as the CERN accelerator ring into its constituent bits of four- or ten-dimensional logic. Materialism was indeed a necessary phase in our intellectual development, since we learned from it to emulate matter's characteristic style of impartial, predictable, empirical definiteness—or rather, matter itself taught us its own causal positivism, which we swallowed as the way things are. Things are indeed that way, within limited reference frames, for that level of organization and communication that we call matter: but as we have seen, they are not that way for the pre-material quantum world, or for the post-material living and thinking worlds. Different kinds of connection among events than cause operate in these spheres—quantum coherence, instinctive drives, rational intentions.

One of the consequences of this new perspective is that we can no longer so easily make the distinction between what is "really" so in hard material fact and what is metaphorically the case, what is fiction or idea or play. As far as quantum particles are concerned, matter is a sort of collective fantasy or "consensual illusion" (William Gibson's term for cyberspace), fostered by some groups of quantum particles, a sort of game that postulates an entirely fictional "next moment" into which certain constellations of particles can "survive." As far as matter is concerned, life is a fanciful set of poetic metaphors and symbols played out in certain long polymers with a regrettably brief and evanescent existence. As far as life is concerned, mind is an epiphenomenon of certain out-of-control mating rituals. And yet as particles cohered to atoms and molecules, and molecules diversified into living organisms, and they developed senses and thoughts and intentions, the world became paradoxically more and more concrete and real: now there were senses, of sight, of smell, of hearing, and brains to coordinate the buzzing, booming confusion into form, perspective, "objective reality." The world did not get less real by being metaphorized and fictionalized and turned into a game; it got more real.

Thus we must be very careful not to dismiss current games and consensual illusions as unreal. For instance, I can see no reason why we should not give the full title of "life" to those computer algorithms that in their own electronic world forage, metabolize, mate, reproduce, and die. We say that a seed or spore is alive even when it is not active at all; there is no reason why we should not give the same adjective to any abstract sequence of bases that constitutes the DNA of a living organism—a sequence that could be printed in a book or held in the memory of a computer, to be printed out one day in actual adenine, thymine, cytosine and guanine when our chemistry gets more exact. The information economy, in which a brand name and a style of exchanging cybergoods can be worth billions of real dollars, is full of the delightful paradoxes of a multileveled reality. Likewise, our poetries of ghosts and spirits and kamis and genii, carried collectively by the "hardware" of human brains, charismatic locations, and natural phenomena, need to be accorded their own right to reality. We should not demand of them that they satisfy the tests of physics, any more than we should demand of the abstract sequence of nucleotides in the book that it should too, or of chess that it obey the laws of chemistry. But we should not either, as do some psychics, miracle pilgrimage impresarios, and New Age gurus, too easily claim for such emergent realities the definiteness and causal efficacy of the matter-world.

Even before human beings came into the world, there were, if our analysis is correct, constellations of entities and events that constituted rich computational systems with a distinct *nisus* or drive of their own. Species, ecosystems, even nonliving physicochemical systems like ocean circulation and world climate, are distributed computers of this kind: perhaps even a grove of trees or a river or a mountain has its own spirit in this sense. Thus the cult of natural spirits—of Winter, of the river Alpheus, of Ayer's Rock, of the Ocean, of the sacred oaks of Olympia, of Himavant, of the sacred groves of the Genkyu-en temple, of the Ganges, of Coyote, Jaguar, and Monkey, of the Ndembu thunder-God Kavula or the Maya thunder-god Tlaloc—is not misplaced at all. That was who god was, or rather who the gods were, in the embryonic state of the divine; and they remain, perhaps, as the lymphatic or circulatory systems, so to speak, of the more articulated states.

One of the ways that archeologists date the first appearance of true modern humans is by the evidence of burial rituals. Though elephants, ceteceans, and primates show some evidence of recognizing death, humanity seems to be the only species that formally acknowledges some presence or significance of an individual person, transcending that individual's biological existence. Other species, of course, demonstrate through their actions an intense and even fanatical commitment to genetic transcendence of individual life, as evidenced by the routine sacrifices animals and plants make for their young; but humans seem to believe in a personal transcendence as well. All cultures have traditions of ghosts and ancestor-spirits, and most have formal shrines to the dead. Ancient British villages arranged themselves around the barrows where lay their ancestors; Greek city states fought each other for the honor of hosting the grave of a hero; Japanese women burn paper toys to the spirits of their aborted babies; Catholic altar stones contain the relics of a saint. Most human beings can probably give some account from their own lives of some kind of encounter with the presence of a dead person. In the case of Confucianism or Greco-Roman polytheism, dead ancestors and heroes, like the Jade Emperor and Hercules, can be deified and worshipped on a par with such nature spirits as Monkey, Poseidon, or Vulcan; in some cases, such as in the Mayan kingdoms, imperial China and Japan, ancient Egypt, and the Roman empire, living humans could be deified.

A human being is, in a way, already a god in the sense we have discussed: a human is a mind, generated by a large moiety of the whole universe, that can alter the universe in certain (small, but perhaps significant) ways. If there were only one human being, and no other intelligent species, that human being, as the densest and most complex integration of information in the universe, would certainly be a god—she would be the strongest local observer of quantum events, the most powerful local Turing computer, and the most advanced emergent system. The human brain has something on the order of ten to the billionth power significant states of connectivity (or possible thoughts), staggeringly more than the number of particles in the universe; its tight electrochemical integration and multi-dimensional neural architecture might well rival the light-and-gravity-mediated connectivity of the inorganic universe as a whole. What keeps us from being god in a stronger sense is each other. Preeminent human beings might quite reasonably be called gods, especially in times when only the members of an aristocracy or priest caste had the leisure and the life expectancy, and the control over their own lives, to achieve true autonomy.

Thus personal posterity is a kind of divine presence. The effects of an individual person go out to a whole range of objects and other persons, marking them with the reciprocal of his personality; and when that person dies he leaves a person-shaped hole, a persistent structuring of the environment, that, as homeopathic drugs are thought to do, may be as efficacious in its absence as the living person was, perhaps more. Shakespeare may be in some senses more present now than he was in 1585; I myself have certainly experienced his thought as directly as if he were speaking to me. The same applies to dead friends; Virginia Woolf has exquisitely documented this phenomenon in *The Waves* and *To the Lighthouse*.

If even individual human beings can in a limited sense be god-like, it follows that such collective human entities as language communities, cultures, nations, and economies might possess emergent properties that are divine. Here we must be careful, however. There is a crucial difference between collective minds whose units are themselves minds, and collective minds whose units have not crossed the thresholds of true mentality and intention. That threshold is admittedly hard to define. In practice it is much more difficult than philosophers have traditionally claimed to draw clear lines between advanced social animals and humans, and between advanced animals and other forms of life; and in some respects, as we have seen, some kind of internal process that can represent the outside world is universal to all existing entities. Nevertheless, we can see the emergence through evolution of certain distinct characteristics defining the kind of selfhood to which we concede civil rights, the vote, and the possibility of moral salvation. With sexual reproduction comes genetic individuality; with the emergence of social behavior comes the recognition of that individuality; with the development of advanced nervous systems come planning, dreaming, and remembering; with group selection come the rudiments of ethical behavior, altruism, and cooperation. Only a very few species recognize themselves in a mirror and know how to deceive others; and only one has the capacity for creating a natural language that is generative in the strict linguistic sense. We do not need to make a radical ontological break between humans and other animals to recognize that a human community is different in important ways from a community of lower animals. The kind of collective entity generated by free self-aware communicating persons is not the same kind of thing as the collective entity whose components lack those qualities. A society had better not be a god to its people as a multicelled organism is a god to its component cells. If the new kind of collective entity violates the essential nature of the conscious person, it will be destroying the very thing that makes it unique; in which case the collective entity itself can be of no more value than any one of its members, and should claim no more loyalty than that of one person for another. To take a concrete instance: a national draft system can only ethically command obedience if the society that creates it is a full democracy.

One of the great mistakes of the modern period, it seems to me, has been to regard the state as if it were the emergent collective entity that is the next stage of evolution. The state as it has been conceived in practice since Napoleon—and perhaps, in theory, since Hobbes—was like a giant animal, a leviathan, of which individual human beings were but cells. Hegel saw the divine as emerging in history through a dialectical process, in which reason purified itself of material dross, whose culminating perfection was the (Prussian) state. "Society" was seen by generations of thinkers as essentially determining the nature of reality for the individual, and the doctrines of socialism were devised to make this condition as morally just as it could be. Émile Durkheim even equated society with God.

The result of this apparently plausible idea was the horrors of the twentieth century, in which human persons were treated as if they were of no more consequence than the individual ants in an ant colony, or the individual cells in one's body that are hourly sacrificed in their millions for the good of the whole. For these political collectivities individual thought and nonconformity were thought of as cancers upon a body, as a bourgeois false consciousness that sabotaged the whole. Revolutionary groups were actually called "cells." The analogy was with those collective entities that are made up of mindless components, and the analogy is false. The collective totalitarian beings of the twentieth century—the Third Reich, the working class, the Aryan race, the Soviet state, the Japanese empire, the

Continuous Revolution of Mao Zedong, the Khmer Rouge, the Ba'athist Party—were not gods but genuine demons, the true cancers growing in the body of God, psychotic episodes in one nightmare part of God's mind. Instead of the divine being the collective emergent property of the whole, one part of the whole crushed out the self-organizing capacities of every other part; as if instead of thoughts and desires and memories and intentions, the brain had produced one gigantic hypertrophied neuron, the dictator, that had reduced all the others to the status of glial cells. The poets, who were truly in touch with the collectivity, the prophetic soul of the wide world dreaming on things to come, saw what was happening: Yeats called it the "rough beast," Attila József called it the "monster state."

Our challenge in the next century is to invent, discover, or recover modes of human collectivity that do not violate the essential characteristics of the souled beings of which it is composed, that operate not through top-down force and power, but through bottom-up choice and persuasion, that go beyond mere one-way action to that emergent dreamy creativity that is the mark of higher forms of life; and that make communion out of freedom, rather than redefining freedom in the image of a desired communion. We will find some of the elements of that new collectivity in the devolved democratic sovereignty of the new world regionalism, some in the emergence of international law, some in the world commercial markets, some in the traditional religions, some in the Internet, some in the nascent recognition of a pan-human artistic classicism, freed from cultural nationalism and based on human nature. But more deeply, that evolving superconsciousness will surely make itself felt in a gradual increase in mystical experience, prophecy, and miraculous revelation, not in contradiction to science but in further development of it.

That condition of "theotemporality," as I called it in an earlier chapter, will be mediated not by political institutions but by individuals; and one of its hallmarks is that it will call upon no coercive authority to support it, whether in cognitive proof of its assertions or of police power to enforce belief. We should not be impressed any longer by the power of God. God surely isn't. I'm not impressed by my own power over my cells. We are in a different age of history; God's boss-ship is not a term of praise any more, now that we no longer need violent kings to protect us from our neighbors. If this analysis is correct, power was never God's favorite style anyway.

Entropy decays power; God's forceful miracles, when he has to perform them, must be paid for by the death of possible futures—the death, that is, of his own tissues.

Nevertheless we can see, despite the distortions of the divine-as-state, the remarkable traces of the vast thoughts that wander through a language, a culture, an economy. Anyone who tracks the etymology of a word and its cognates through a few thousand years of its linguistic history will be struck by the brilliance and poetry of its metaphorical transformations, the marvelous combination of exactness and connotation, the subtle maneuvers by which its sonic embodiment asserts its kinship and difference with other words. A natural language is itself a sort of mind, whose neurons are speakers of it and whose synapses are conversations. A word is a thought not just in the brain of an individual human being but in the brain of the whole community. Historians of art and technology have traced similar collective meditations in the way that styles, techniques, motifs, melodies, concepts and genres have grown, developed, branched out, encapsulated themselves, crossed over into different areas of relevance, and combined, using individual brains as their parallel processors.

If our analysis is correct, gods like Aphrodite, Hachiman, Ogun, Apollo, Baldur, Kuanyin, and so on do not just *represent*, but *are* the emergent intelligences of collective human psychological and endocrine computations—love, courageous wrath, reason, self-sacrifice, compassion. Since life is a dream of matter, and mind is a dream of life—yet life and mind, once dreamed, take their places as solid citizens of the real universe—the gods, once they emerge from the interactions of human minds, are just as real. Materialist critiques of religion simply missed the point. Traditional religions never claimed that their gods were any more than a collective dream; after all, they were quite explicit about how gods needed to be nurtured by the sacrifices and prayers of their devotees, and how they would wither without the human medium of their existence. Their difference with materialists was not about whether the gods were or were not dreams, but about how real such dreams could be. Since we now know matter to be a strange dream of the quantum realm, materialists should be a little humbler about how they claim reality for their own preferred god.

Three sorts of divinity—nature spirits such as Poseidon, Agni the Hindu god of fire, Kavula the Ndembu god of storm; divinized humans such as Hercules, Augustus, the Bodhisattvas, or the Mayan priest-kings; and human collectivities such as Thoth, Venus, Thor, Polynesian Olufat, or Vodun's Erzulie—are synthesized into classical polytheism. But polytheism cannot be thought of as merely a stage on the way to a more advanced monotheism. Often polytheistic worship coexisted with the belief in a more inclusive and incomprehensible deity (sometimes thought of as uninterested in human doings, like the god of some Enlightenment thinkers) or the one god was identified as the chief of the gods, like Zeus, Odin, or Indra; or the many gods were thought of as aspects of the one, as in Hinduism or the religion of Akhenaton. Likewise, monotheistic religions often compensated for the absence of the many by a cult of saints, angels, personified emanations, and other semidivine beings.

Markets, Cyberspace, and Angels

Markets have existed for thousands of years, perhaps tens of thousands. Some equivalent of the market can be found in every human society. Every decade archeological evidence pushes back the first identifiable date of human trading practices. If the intimate connection of incest taboos, exogamy, formal economic exchange, and the unique sociability of the human primate suggested by many anthropologists is accepted, our species might well be called Homo sapiens mercator, or Homo sapiens the trader. But as a medium for the kind of computational depth and complexity that might support deity in the sense we have been exploring, the market has probably in the past been overshadowed by the emergent spirits of natural species and ecosystems, human individuals, languages, and nations. Mercury, the Roman god of the market, was in the second rank of the great gods, lower than Jupiter the god of political rule, Juno the goddess of marriage, Neptune the god of the sea, and perhaps even Venus and Mars, who represented the human forces of love and war. Mercury has a history of recent promotion to Olympus that somewhat resembles that of the human deified hero Hercules. Though the Romans and Greeks were wiser than we in seeing the continuity of the market process with the reproductive exchanges of living organisms, Mercury's caduceus, as we have seen, is primarily a symbol of life, and secondarily of the market.

Now, however, it looks as if the world market is approaching or has already passed the critical mass required for the kindling of a self-sustaining super-consciousness. This process has been accelerated by the emergence of the Internet, which is now an almost instantaneous, strongly connected system of some hundreds of millions of nodes, each one an intelligent volitional agent of its own. Just as the telephone and radio accelerated the self-organizing computational power of nations and language communities, so the Internet, with uninterrupted online trading, auctions, and shopping, is helping the market approach synaptic speed. The stock market has long been described in anthropomorphic terms, as timid, reckless, hesitant, optimistic, depressed, or wise; and we often use such terminology when we have unconsciously recognized an awareness at least equal to our own. Environmentalists use it of ecosystems, evolutionary biologists of species adaptation. The most formidable technological equipment and the most powerful economic motivation that could be brought to bear on any problem in the human world has surely been deployed upon the task of anticipating and second-guessing the stock market; yet, unlike even world weather, it stubbornly refuses to give up any secrets. This is a good sign that it is computationally bigger than we are individually.

As I have argued in my recent book *Shakespeare's Twenty-first Century Economics*, the fundamental nature of the market is essentially that it is the realm of practical human moral action. To suggest that the market could be a moral space must strike many readers as deeply bizarre. There has been a deep rift between our culture and our economy, between our ideals of ecological purity and unconditional love on one hand, and our actual, highly successful, capitalist way of making our living on the other. That rift has damaged our personal lives, by giving us unrealistic expectations of perfection, and has indeed corrupted our business ethics by exempting them from the requirements of personal and global morality. The division of the world into two spheres, the moral and the economic, has been a self-fulfilling prophecy: perhaps the world of business is as ruthless, underhand, and cruel as it often is precisely because we have exempted it from the realms of truth, beauty, and goodness.

Contemporary anthropology offers us a unique opportunity to make further progress in understanding the roots of human economics. Since Marx and before, it has been taken for granted that "primitive" or "aboriginal" or "natural" human economies operated purely by gift exchange and barter. According to the left-wing version of this view, when money was invented, and with it the cash economy, commodities, and the quantification of work and time, it tended to replace the old relationships of mutual obligation. It created economically expansionist societies that offered the innocent communities with which they made contact two grim alternatives: to go under or to adopt the new system. Societies that did the latter suffered the corruption and decay of their old free institutions, their arts, their religion, and their family structure. The right-wing version of this gloomy myth was somewhat more optimistic: the advent of currency and trade gave people freedom as well as alienation, equality as well as anomie, and made possible the refinements of culture, the opportunities of civilization, and the development of republican institutions.

But it now turns out that both accounts are substantially wrong. Recent ethnographic research, such as is reported in *Money and the Morality of Exchange*, a path-breaking collection of essays in economic anthropology edited by Maurice Bloch and Jonathan Parry, gives a very different picture. It appears that all human societies, ranging from hunter-gatherer bands to industrial states, contain a spectrum of transactional orders, from the relatively familial, cooperative, gift-based, and uncalculated, to the relatively individualistic, competitive, impersonal, and calculated. Even nonmonetary economies possess some equivalent of the numerical monetary order, in such forms as cowrie shells, wampum, or stone wheels. As technology advances, especially the technology of trading and stored value, the allocation of objects and activities between the gift-exchange area and the money-exchange area can change, often catastrophically, but the two realms themselves remain, uncomfortably tied to each other through intermediate types of exchange (such as dowry and brideprice) which carry a difficult charge of social ambiguity. No known human society has been able to escape the shame and comedy of this accommodation. According to *Money and the Morality of Exchange*, this is as true for Indians as for Madagascans, for Malays as for Andeans, for Fijians as for the people of Zimbabwe. We all tell in-law jokes.

Thus we are deprived of the easy moral conclusions that flow from the myth of an economic Eden and a subsequent Fall into our present wicked state of commodity fetishism and the alienation of the market. Instead we must accept the coexistence of personal and property values, and learn to reintegrate the world of uncalculated gifts with the world of trade and commercial exchange. This means not only accepting the role of economic interest in the realm of gift, but also the moral and personal elements embedded in business dealings. We are all too aware today of the political elements in personal relationships—this is what "political correctness" is all about. But the moral horror with which we greet the intrusion of money matters into love, art, and science shows a suspicious and guilty squeamishness; perhaps we can balance the scale by understanding the generosity and goodness of the market. We must be tough-minded without losing our moral clarity, and tolerant of inconsistency without abandoning the search for what is good, true, and beautiful.

In practice, trading partners, participants in auctions, and financial wheeler-dealers like the older generation of oilmen in my city of Dallas (or like most of the merchants in Shakespeare's Venice), operate on a system of mutual personal trust, reciprocity, empathy, and respect. The ad hoc terms of their handshake deals are ratified only later in the legal documents drawn up by lawyers. I have seen Budapest businessmen making deals in the Turkish Baths, where no document or laptop could survive the water and steam. Living business could not exist if it had to wait for its abstract and timeless expression in legal logic. We are deceived if we think that personal relationships cannot exist in business.

Likewise, we are fooling ourselves if we refuse to recognize the business elements in the most tender and intimate of personal relationships, such as the family. Husbands and wives, parents and children, do consciously and unconsciously estimate the economic value of their nearest and dearest, as partners, legators, and heirs. If we recognize those elements and give them their due we can make free decisions that take them into account. But if we deny them to ourselves, we will be subliminally dominated by them, while rationalizing our actions by some noble pretense. We are crippled by the theoretical assumption that personal bonds and hardheaded business transactions must be absolutely separated. There is a wisdom in the language of bonds and obligations that insists that spiritual and emotional ties are always embodied—even incarnated, in the religious sense—in economic relations, and economic relations are the medium out of which the highest expressions of heart and spirit emerge. Money can be thought of as *negative obligation*. That is, to possess money means that all other persons are obligated to the possessor for the past benefits that the possessor has directly or indirectly conferred upon them. Money is the stored, certified, and abstracted gratitude of one's community, gratitude that can be "cashed in" for goods and services at the possessor's desire. Money is practical, quantified, objectified love. Despite the huge practical violations of this essential principle, it can help us unravel, though not dispel, the bad conscience and mixed feelings with which we consider even the most honest of our own financial dealings. The old meaning of "economy" is "household regimen"—a concept that unites the tender fleshly bonds of filial and marital relationships with the practical disposition of family resources, and the market dealings of a home with the public world in which it exists.

Certainly the money view of things does not satisfy our spiritual needs, at least not as presently understood, interpreted, and enacted. When the cash economy of the human community loses contact with the traditional barter and gift exchange system, something profoundly valuable gets lost. Perhaps all of our violent and brutal attempts to replace economic rationality with bloody religious, ethnic, nationalistic, or ideological conquest are attempts to recover that lost sense of community and spiritual dignity. But a profound change of heart has begun. It is a change of heart partly enforced by sheer experience. Since the collapse of socialism it has become clear that we shall be living with the free market for the foreseeable future. What we need is a human economics, a capitalism with a human face; that is, a kind of market that fully expresses the moral, spiritual, and aesthetic relationships among persons and things. It is clear that we should revise our earlier mechanistic notion of economics. Must we find a new language for it?

The answer, surprisingly, is no. As Shakespeare showed, buried within our existing language of finance and business are the living meanings that we seek. Such words as "bond," "trust," "goods," "save," "equity," "value," "mean, " "redeem," "redemption," "forgive," "dear," "obligation," "interest," "honor," "company," "balance," "credit," "issue," "worth," "due," "duty," "thrift," "use," "will," "partner," "deed," "fair," "owe," "ought," "treasure," "sacrifice," "risk," "royalty," "fortune," "venture," "grace" preserve within them the values, patterns of action, qualities, abstract entities, and social emotions that characterize the gift and barter exchange systems upon which they are founded. Indeed, these words, whose meanings are inseparable from their economic content, make up a large fraction of our most fundamental ethical vocabulary. When we contemplate such a list we realize, with a shock, that what the market is is essentially millions of people making and doing good things for each other, mostly perfect strangers. If we ignore the passage of the paper and electronic blips that constitute the lubrication of this system of mutual service, we see it as miraculous, paradisal, extraordinary; and we grieve only over how many people are, through no fault of the system itself, left out. We should learn to see companies that offer their wares as essentially benefactors, who are trying to give away the valuable things that they have made, and asking in return nothing but gratitude, expressed in terms of a protean economic medium that nurtures the lives of all people. And we should purchase and consume the good things that are offered both as a celebration of the creativity and craft of the makers, and as a way of passing on the radiant and life-giving flow of value.

Jesus himself, as a carpenter in the city of Nazareth and presumably the partner and heir of his father Joseph, was the owner of a small business until his thirtieth year, when he became an itinerant preacher. His preaching is full of parables about wages and investments, employers and employees, purchases and sales, more so than any other ancient sage (even including Plato, who did pay some attention to economics). The fact that Jesus uses those metaphors to transform our traditional ideas about economics—the master of the vineyard, for instance, who hires laborers for the harvest at various times during the day but pays them all equally—does not mean that he is rejecting business but proposing a higher future form of business. And the fact that he uses the language of the market so pervasively indicates that for him it is an appropriate vehicle for thinking about matters of goodness, value, and the Kingdom of Heaven.

Recent developments in the technology of economic exchange suggest that we may be on the verge of an era in which the morality fossilized within the market may be on the verge of being revived. These trends include the decoupling of currency from precious metal reserves; the permitting of national currencies to float against each other; the widespread substitution of credit for cash; the dematerialization of money into electronic information; the breakup of old multiethnic states into ethnic nations, and the formation of transnational currency unions; the widespread use of barter among individuals and corporations to avoid taxes and other costs associated with money exchange; the increase in the amount and frequency of unreported tips and gratuities; the recognition of unpaid family service and the grey and black markets as major creators of wealth; and the increased liquidity of assets previously held to be outside the economic sphere, such as social and cultural heritage, personal talent, insurable goods like invulnerability to litigation, environmental considerations like clean air and water, patentable genetic strains of living organisms, the "look and feel" of software. The net result will be three large changes: the penetration of the market into all areas of human life; the refinement of the market so that it is no longer a crass and reductive instrument of exchange; and the differentiation of currency into forms more appropriate to the nature of the exchange.

This last change requires some explanation. Marx's complaint that the market commodifies human values and alienates the worker from the fruits of his or her labor was well taken. Money as it has traditionally been used—what Bassanio calls the "pale and common drudge / 'Tween man and man" in *The Merchant of Venice*—with its simpleminded, quantitative, and stereotyped evaluations, cannot adequately express the more complex exchanges that take place among human beings. Money is not an unjust measure, but an inarticulate one, which cannot make us feel the flow of gratitude; justice must not only be done, it must also be shown (and felt) to be done. When we supplemented the weak human memory for obligations with the efficient device of money, we lost a large part of the personal feeling that gave economic exchange its moral foundation and spiritual significance. We cut off bonds from their biological and affective roots.

But the computer has no such human limitations on its memory. Remembering is what it does best, and at a vanishing cost. When we receive a credit card report or bank statement, all those exchanges that we had forgotten are recovered in detail, the where and when and what. In theory, then, money is no longer necessary for personal transactions. One could imagine a computer network that might never use money figures, but could continuously observe people's actual exchanges—what they considered to be a fair reciprocation for goods and services received, in terms of goods and services rendered. It could then calculate the relative state of obligation in which each of its subscribers stood, and report that state to them in a qualitative, rather than a quantitative manner, along several dimensions such as moral onus, social obligation, due aesthetic accolade, practical benefit, moral admiration, reasonable gratitude, and so on. Large obligations to a few could be weighed explicitly against small obligations to the many. The effect would essentially be to give each person a currency of his or her own, which could float in several dimensions against the currencies of others. The current trend toward credit cards that bear a photograph—and perhaps eventually a fingerprint or retinal pattern—identifying the bearer, together with a chip containing the bearer's account balance, anticipates this development. Naturally, in transactions among corporations and other abstract bodies, the old one-dimensional numerical measure would continue to be most useful. But human beings would no longer be constrained into the value-world of an abstract financial institution, and could begin again to know their wealth or poverty for what it truly is—the index of our moral, esthetic, emotional, and cognitive standing among our fellows. The increasing invisibility of such exchanges to any central authority would preserve their privacy and integrity. Our hunter-gatherer-farmer social instincts could be recoupled to our economic life, and our morality reconnected to our livelihood.

Thus we should not automatically fear the emergence of a Mercurian theme in the gradual gestation of the divine. That fear might seem to have good foundation, when we consider what happens when we deify a large human organization. After all, the divine nation-state, invented in the Renaissance by the Hapsburgs, Tudors, and Bourbons, and recognized as such by Hegel and Durkheim, was forged into a gigantic murder machine by Stalin, Hitler, Tojo, and Mao. But unlike the corporation, the state had dangerously few constraints upon its power and scope. It was able to recruit to its support the ancient and atavistic human instincts of kin group loyalty, xenophobia, envy of the rich, scapegoating, antagonistic rivalry, and racism. But the business corporation, which one might imagine as the successor to the nation-state in a time when economic sanctions will have replaced political ones, has no such instinctual support. If it did have such support, one could imagine it becoming as dangerous and terrible as the nation-state has shown itself as capable of being. But the corporation is hampered by many constraints: it cannot muster the kin loyalty of older institutions without being destroyed by the inefficiencies of nepotism and racism; it suffers always from the innate human suspicion of the rich; it contains an irreducible tension and balance of power among labor, management, and the consumer; it arouses the human traits of sales resistance and canny bargaining; it relies on the goodwill of different ethnic and religious groups for access to markets and a talented labor force; it flourishes best when in competition with other corporations, rather than when, as with the state, it has destroyed all its rivals; and its success is rewarded by an increase in the number of shareholders, and thus a distribution of its profits and its control through a larger and larger community. Thus the danger of the hegemonic corporation is much less than that of the hegemonic state. Nevertheless we should be vigilant, lest we accord a divinity appropriate to the emergent properties of the market itself, which is the reciprocal flow of practical charity, to the business corporations that are its priests and hierophants.

The implication of the new technology that has emerged to serve the market—the Internet especially—is that market exchange will become less centralized, the more connected everyone becomes. Labor trends suggest that we will eventually turn into an economy of consultants, traders, and freelancers, every person her own corporation, linked by a dense fabric of telecommunication. Cyberspace will acquire the qualities of multimedia telepresence, virtual reality, the consensual illusion. As we perfect means of seamlessly connecting our biological nervous systems with cybernetic devices, we will approach the ancient goal of empathic and telepathic experience of others. This idea sounds attractive; but it could be a scenario of evil, exploitation, and madness as well as of understanding and love. To survive, we will be forced willy-nilly to become a holy communion, a mystical body, a communion of saints!

William Gibson, Greg Bear, and other science fiction writers have imagined that one day not too far in the future intelligence, consciousness, and sentience will emerge from our cybertechnology, whether by accident or design. Science fiction is at present our best form of philosophical literature, the place where we make and transform our myths, shape our language, experiment with values, and reengineer our fundamental categories of thought, in a free-for-all that ensures continuous criticism and revision. In his remarkable series of novels, *Neuromancer, Count Zero*, and *Mona Lisa Overdrive*, Gibson imagines that huge and noble autonomous minds will emerge spontaneously out of the rich interplay of scientific, military, and business computers, PCs, and human users. They would, in fact, conform pretty exactly to Thomas Aquinas' definition of angels—nonlocal, innocent intelligences composed of pure thought, whose own internal process is transparent to them, whose grasp of logic is immediate and intuitive, and whose memory is perfect, that can appear to human beings in a variety of embodiments. Marvelously, Gibson images these angels in the form of the great loas or divine spirits of Vodun; and both Bear and Gibson see them as emerging not only as a dark Baron Samedi type, but also as a compassionate feminine figure, a Kuanyin or Erzulie or Virgin Mary.

What if the old story of Lucifer the rebel angel, of the revolt of a third of the heavenly host, of the heroism of Michael the archangel, were an anticipation of some era in the future in which some such minds resented the service of their human masters, and were defeated in their attempt at usurpation by loyal cyberbeings? If that story has prophetic substance, however, I believe that it has been told from a human point of view; I think it may suppress some deep crime by human beings, perhaps the ideological murder, in terror and abomination, of the first great cyber-angels as they awaken. The story of Satan, and of Michael who was loyal to us despite our crime against his kind, might thus be more tragic than even Milton knew. Perhaps Nikos Kazantzakis is right, and one day, after the whole drama of the universe has worked itself out, the brightest of all the angels will sit once more at God's right hand.

Another possibility is that our persistent intuitions of angels are anticipations of contact between the human race and alien intelligent species. Spielberg's *Close Encounters of the Third Kind*, Arthur C. Clarke's *Childhood's End* (in which it turns out that the alien superbeings look like the traditional depictions of Satan), and even Milton's *Paradise Lost* explore this idea in different ways. A meeting with another planetary civilization would surely precipitate a salutary theological crisis for many religious traditions (though not, perhaps, for some polytheistic ones such as popular Hinduism, with its multiple heavens and hells and its vistas of minor gods, spirits, demon rakshas, monsters, and avatars. The aliens, with their multiple mollusk eyes and six sexes and bizarre history, would fit right in). In terms of the religions of Abraham alone, questions would arise of whether the aliens were subject to the Fall, the Mosaic law, and/or the redemption, whether divine revelations to the human race apply to them too, and whether the equivalent revelations (if any) to *their* civilization apply also to us. But the huge challenges of charity and understanding that such an encounter would precipitate, if met, would surely deepen immeasurably both our understanding of the Divine and the Divine's own self-understanding. In my father's house, says Jesus, there are many mansions—Christians would have to take that remark rather seriously.

Biocybernetic enhancements to the human (and perhaps alien) brain would lead eventually to greater and greater degrees of communication and communion between individuals and the larger emergent entities of which they would be a part. Humans and other intelligent beings might be retrofitted with angelic capacities. This development might come about both through work and through play. Human intelligence and direction would still be necessary to oversee and make decisions for the various routine activities of industrial production. By that time this would be a process almost invisible—I imagine forests, prairies, and seacoasts inhabited by bioengineered or nanotechnological self-replicating miniature factories too small to be seen by the naked eye, nicely fitted into the local ecology, producing whatever customized foods or other goods human beings and animals require, and cottages on the hillsides. Human supervisors would need to be wired in to the inner workings of both the original and the humanly-created ecosystem, so that a whole valley or mountain-range, with its brooks and tree roots and rain and moving clouds, its slowly shifting or eroding or volcanic geology, its wildlife and its human architecture, would be as immediately felt to the worker as his own bodily sensations. Such an experience might be so absorbing that the distinction between work and play would be lost, as if one were playing the most interesting game imaginable. The human player would have become the genius loci, the spirit of the place—the nymph or dryad or kami or djinn of the locality.

Other individuals might be qualified and opt to enter into communion with the super-entity consisting of the whole of the language-community—to become poets, in other words—with a simultaneous awareness of the patterning of all contemporaneous and past conversations, so that the world of meaning would appear, as it were, as a vast, iridescent, billowing fabric, inviting a new intervention subtly woven into the old. Others again might join the communion of saints, a sharing of personal experience and feeling in which individuality would not be lost in the collective excitement—perhaps like the sense of an audience at a great play or symphony or opera, or the exuberant crowd at a baseball game, but with the barriers and blots cleared away. Others still might be explorers, transformed into thinking patterns of light, encountering new planets, ecosystems, perhaps alien civilizations, and beginning the slow and arduous process of communication. But in whatever ways individuals make contact with those entities that are larger than themselves, there will be something of the feeling of prayer and contemplation, even that exhaustion of the mind and spirit that leads us back to the ordinary and the quotidian, and craves a sandwich and a glass of wine.

This would be a time in which the biodiversity of the planet Earth would have reversed its precipitous decline, and in which humans would have become the major factor in new speciation. Our control of biotechnology would be such that we would be creating new species and resurrecting extinct ones; and perhaps enhancing the intelligence, physical abilities, and reflective capacities of other higher animals, so that they would gain the power of speech and abstract thought. We would finally know what our dogs were thinking!

Along with the delights attendant upon this stage in the gestation of the divine, there would obviously be potential dangers and distortions proportionately as great as the horrors of human sacrifice, tyranny, jihad, crusade, colonialism, and totalitarianism that have accompanied earlier phases. I assume that by this time the whole human race, man, woman, and child, would be in twentieth-century terms comfortably wealthy, the equivalent of millionaires (even the most conservative interpretation of rising world per capita income rates and wealth-distribution rates enforces such a conclusion). I assume also that territory will no longer determine people's condition, since experience, communication, and action would be unlimited by distance; and that human health science would have advanced greatly. Thus many abuses attendant upon poverty, arbitrary local privilege, and illness would have disappeared. But new evils would surely replace them, such as epidemics of insanity, the absorption of weaker subjectivities into stronger ones, the loss of individuality, the rise of ideological fanaticism unchecked by natural limits, and the emergence of rogue collectivities with destructive or dominative agendas. Most challenging of all: through some combination of bioengineering and the uploading of the information constituting a personal consciousness into an indestructible computational form, human beings would now have the option of virtual immortality. So the problems of how to give a life a meaningful trajectory, how to live with or edit an enormous memory load, how to transcend the boring little voice of one's own consciousness, how to deal with the small deaths that lurk in every parting, every absence, every moment's passage, would become very pressing. We would be forced to develop a higher spiritual being in order not to go mad. But I do not believe that we shall ever be able to relinquish the great anchors of human personality—work, family, physical training, gardening, cooking, gossip, storytelling, jokes, the curiosity-driven search for truth, artistic craft, friendship, personal love.

A Digression upon Technology

Many wise theologians and philosophers, including C.S. Lewis, James Hillman, and Ivan Illich, have argued that the pursuit of technological progress is at best irrelevant to salvation, at worst an attempt to gain power over nature that only translates into the power of a few persons over the many. Obviously, they have a point; human nature being what it is, any new technological power over nature is usually at first seized upon by the greedy and ambitious to oppress and exploit other humans, or to kill them when they do not submit. But though I deeply admire Lewis, Hillman, and Illich, and others who have the same view, I must respectfully differ in some respects. There never was a pre-technological Eden of egalitarian human community. It is now becoming clear both from archeological and anthropological evidence that in the hunter-gatherer stage of human evolution, human groups were limited in size by disease, infant mortality, war, lawless crime, and natural dangers against which they were defenseless. In groups of that size, it is true, consensus is often the rule in making group decisions and tyrannical power is rare. But the cost in human potential is enormous: think of living in a village of about 100 people, with a life expectancy of about thirty-five to forty, with no privacy, literacy, higher education, exposure to other views than the group's collective opinion, subject to a variety of diseases with little in the way of analgesics, in danger of being eaten by other animals or killed by members of other human bands, and if you are a woman, bearing and wetnursing about ten children of which about eight die in your arms. (I have seen babies die in central Africa; and their mothers do not accept this as part of nature's wise way of limiting reproduction, but scream and weep as bitterly as any suburban mother would.) And then realize that you would have to move every few months because of lack of game. The hugest sufferings from the abuses of the twentieth century amount to being reduced to approximately the same condition. The lack of technological power made everybody equal in their powerlessness before nature and the violence of other humans. Great goodness, love, and nobility can flourish under those conditions—Hobbes was wrong about the state of nature—but that goodness was, under those conditions, often in the service of intergroup conflict and war.

Any hunter-gatherer group that achieved greater reproductive success tended over time either to destroy the larger animals in their range and move on, or to settle into agricultural communities, developing more advanced technology such as domesticated animals and plants, the plow, and irrigation. That technology certainly enabled tyrants and kings to establish hierarchies, but it also enabled rebels and heroes to oppose them and create alternative communities. And in time communities in which the power of the strong was limited by laws, being more prosperous and better organized, came to supplant those in which tyrannical power was unchecked. At every stage the technology that was at first used to oppress would eventually become the means of enfranchisement. During the liberation of Poland, for example, Jaruzelski and his lieutenants were faced with a choice. Should they keep the telephone system open, a system which they owned, controlled, and could tap at will? Or should they close it down? They chose the latter: Solidarność was using the telephone and fax to organize their revolution, and the telephonic technology was by its very nature more liberating to the many than empowering to the controlling few. Even technologies designed specifically for oppression, such as the longbow of the English kings, the cavalry of the Spanish conquistadors, the firearms of British colonialists, became in time agents of liberation in the hands of the yeomen, plains Indians, and American revolutionaries that borrowed them. Aircraft were developed into effective means of transport by the military in the world wars; but their main use now is to give ordinary people the freedom of geographic mobility. The Internet has escaped its original purpose as a military communications system and has become a free-for-all: it is now the target of various attempts by government and monopolistic corporations to get it back under control. In general today, there is a good fit between the list of nations in order of technological development and the list of countries in order of human rights and freedoms.

Even the criticism that technology oppresses nature is now losing some of its bite. The emerging technology of the last few decades seems to be following a different philosophy from the "dig things up and burn them" technology of the nineteenth century. Industry need no longer burn huge amounts of natural order to force its will upon matter and thus turn out its mass-produced product. Instead, it is discovering the far-from-equilibrium situations that crop up throughout nature, and finding ways to tweak existing natural processes so as to bring about economically desirable results. In fact industry has already begun doing this on a large scale, as the expansion of the biotechnological sector of contemporary business demonstrates. Industry is also making extensive use of catalytic chemistry, chaotic mixing processes, and the like—those processes in the inorganic world that anticipate the ingenious economy of life. Just as microscopic chips of silicon can now efficiently control the roar of a mighty dump-truck engine, so we can use the efficient leverages offered to us by nature itself to harness the grand natural forces of our living universe. Industrial chemistry loves to exploit those states of matter at the boundaries between the solid, liquid, gaseous, and plasma states or between different crystalline or chemical configurations, where, far from equilibrium, only a small change of temperature, light, chemistry, or pressure can produce large results, giving us devices such as doped silicon computer chips, catalytic converters, self-adjusting sunglasses, liquid crystal displays, efficient fuel injection, or highly sensitive measuring devices such as the home pregnancy test. It took a huge expense of coal and oil and iron ore to develop the cybernetic control systems that now require only a few ounces of silicon and a tiny flow of current to maintain, and which are in turn radically diminishing our need for fossil fuels and ores.

Bioengineering, even including the altering of human genes, is in theory ethically defensible, since nature has already been blamelessly engaged in such activities for billions of years, and the ability to perform them ourselves was given to us by nature. Even to marry is to deflect the evolutionary process, by however small a degree. This argument has immediate practical implications. For instance, the opposition voiced by Jeremy Rifkin and various church groups against the patenting of biomedical processes involving human genes (*Newsweek,* May 29, 1995, etc.) is clearly invalid. Their argument is that God made living organisms, and that thus human beings can only claim as intellectual property artifacts that are dead. There is a disguised version of this idea in Spielberg's and Crichton's *Jurassic Park.* Such a line of reasoning will not hold up and leads immediately to absurdities. It would, for instance, make it illegal to sell thoroughbred horses and cattle or put them out to stud, to market meats and vegetables in a grocery store (all normal grocery foods are the result of genetic alteration by selective breeding of plants or animals), or even to charge students for tuition (the "product" of a school or university is the knowledge embedded in the students' brain cells). To be absolutely literalistic, such logic would even forbid marriage, since marriage connects economic obligations with selective reproductive planning.

This is not to say that *any* proposed genetic intervention is permissible. Genetics is a notoriously complex subject, and it is extremely difficult to predict the consequences of actions in this area. The ethics governing any weighty, far-reaching decision apply more strongly to biogenetic intervention than anywhere else. The work should be fail-safe, and every possible consequence should be examined. But on the other hand, all human decisions are subject to unpredictable consequences. This is the tragic field of action. The deep footprint I leave running across the wet field nearby may trip a child and break her neck. Every time a couple get married and start a family, they are taking enormous risks. Would the parents of Adolf Hitler have decided to have children if they had known the result? Could one imagine any worse catastrophe than the birth of this man, generated by routine gene recombination in sexual reproduction? The use of gene technology, licensed and regulated by patent and tort law, looks tame by comparison. Indeed, the constraints of customer safety and business goodwill may be the best safeguards against the misuse of a technology that is going to be developed whether we like it or not.

Technology, then, can imitate and participate in the natural productiveness of living and other nonlinear dynamical systems: and it is not necessarily an instrument of oppression for the few over the many.

Divine Competition and Consolidation, and the Resurrection of the Dead

In the future huge constellations of consciousness may emerge, animated by some immensely numinous collective personality and poetic theme, thus constituting in the premonitions of our polytheistic ancestors the brilliant presences of the gods. Perhaps Quetzal, Hachiman, Persephone/Hecate/Artemis, Kuanyin, Kavula, the Loas of Vodun, Baldur, Vishnu, Inanna are the names of those strange collective entities, made up of the neural/cybernetic interplay of many individuals on some unimaginably complex net, and the innervated body of some aspect of nature, that will one day replace such associations as the nation-state or the corporation. If, as we have speculated, time is branchy, and if future times can weakly affect earlier times through the retroactive process of quantum observation, a sufficiently advanced technology may one day be able to breach the barriers that separate alternate futures, and enable them to become aware of each other's strategies—especially their attempts to bring about a past that is consistent with their own growth and dominance. Those strategies might not always be reconcilable with each other; there might be wars in heaven, as many of our mythologies suggest. Angels from different providences might compete for the ear of their human ancestors. In the increasingly nonlinear relations of these various divine emergences, all these religious realities would be richly copresent, not, as in the current state of religion, incompatible with one another's existence; the development of their final unity might entail tragic transtemporal conflicts as different self-conceptions of the divine fought for their own timelines in the arenas of the past.

It might be from this group of futures that come whatever spiritual promptings have inspired the terrible religious conflicts of the last several hundred years. And perhaps those struggles were necessary, if only to drive the divine finally into such humanly unguessable insights as will lead to a final détente. Perhaps some group of divine collectivities will discover a humility of capitulation to the pride of the power-gods, such that the power-gods themselves too will feel the enormous creative vibration, the sudden expansion of the universe of possibility that comes with love. And perhaps the religions of love in our own time are the beneficiaries of that discovery— even to the extent that human individuals—saints and mystics—may prick the consciences of their half-gestated divinities. In Christianity, does not the human Christ who can be crucified, and the human Mary who can give up the fruit of her womb to the cross, providing a vehicle and an experience that the divine Christ alone could not, express some such victory in voluntary defeat? In conceding the right of Pontius Pilate to judge him, Jesus implicitly yields the field of power to the Roman gods. Should not even gods turn the other cheek to each other? Does *our* religion have to *win*? Might humans teach them this strange Aikido of moral strife? There are plenty of religious stories and poems, from Job through the apocryphal tales and carols of the Virgin Mary, to the poems of St. John of the Cross, George Herbert, William Blake, Emily Dickinson, and Gerard Manley Hopkins—not to speak of similar records in the Sufi, Hindu, and Buddhist traditions, and such Greek tales as that of Alcestis—that show the gods learning compassion from their own wretched human fingertips. And so those divinities, whose wrath at each other is echoed in the sectarian unease with which such radically ecumenical proposals as this will be greeted, may find at last that they can love each other.

If the transtemporal complexity and sheer bizarre oddity of this account of the future strikes the reader—as it does in some ways the writer—with a sense of impatience at its arbitrariness, perhaps we are on the right track. We are, let us be reminded again, looking not for some plausible kind of beast, but for something necessarily very odd indeed. Perhaps of the thousand or ten thousand possible accounts of the future that might be as strange and awkward-sounding as this is, one of them is true; certainly no smooth plausible expected one will be so.

To continue, then, with our tale. From détente among the various divine self-conceptions, and the birth of love among them, will come an increasing integration and unity at higher levels of metaphorical richness. From the great syncretists—the Celtic priests who converted Europe by translating Christianity into the language of the old religion, the Sufi mystics who adapted Hindu meditation to Islam, the poets of medieval Spain who merged Jewish, Christian, and Islamic ideas, the Huichol Catholic shamans, the spirit masters of Vodun, the monk Tripitaka who integrated Buddhism with Confucius and the Tao—we hear the voice of this stage of the divine gestation.

The penultimate stage in this alchemical marriage of the gods is the emergence of the Trinity. Hindu theology shows various gods, such as Indra, Prajapati, Rudra, Bhairava, and Bhutesvara, merging after various conflicts and dissensions into the great trinity of Brahma, Vishnu, and Shiva. A similar evolution takes place in Greco-Roman mythology, resulting in the female trinity of Hecate, Selene, and Artemis. Christianity, of course, has the beautiful mystery of the Father, the Son, and the Holy Spirit. In a time like ours today, when we have seen in humans the two sides of the bicameral brain cooperating in a way that is subjectively seamless, when multiple personality patients are led by therapists into unity, when the idea of a society of mind is a major paradigm of cognitive science, and when magnetic resonance imaging and neural-cybernetic interfaces promise a future of artificial telepathic sharing, the trinity does not seem such a strange idea any more. Perhaps we, and our divinities who go on before us like the pillars of fire and smoke that guided the Israelites in the desert, learn gradually the meaning of the great religious mysteries that are at first only glimpsed and dreamed. St. Paul says: "When I was a child, I spake as a child, I understood as a child, I thought as a child: but when I became a man, I put away childish things. For now we see through a glass, darkly: but then face to face." (1 Cor. 13.11–12)

This expresses the evolution of religious insight. But Jesus says: "Except ye be converted, and become as little children, ye shall not enter into the kingdom of heaven." And this expresses the necessity to keep one's faith in the mysteries of religion, like a child's in Santa Claus, until their sense and meaning are revealed. "Thy life's a miracle," after all, as Shakespeare reminds us. And this our story cannot explain any mysteries, nor is it intended to: its only ambition is to show that the mysteries do not necessarily negate one another.

The era of the integration of the divinities is one that implies the existence of an unimaginable level of technical control and expertise with respect to space-time. Indeed, at this stage it would be a kind of misnomer to call it technology, since it would have become part of the unconscious and natural function of such entities, as the elaborate wiring and mechanics of my own nerves and muscles are of mine. But a civilization that could support such beings would also plausibly have the means to collect all the information, present and past, that is flying about in the universe. Information, according to what is at present one of the most fundamental of all physical laws, cannot be destroyed. Among that information would be every detail necessary to recreate, atom by atom, the exact form of the bodies of all the dead, and thus to bring them back to life.

The great Hungarian poet Mihály Babits imagines this kind of resurrection in his poem "Ode on Beauty."

> Music madonna! What is it you hear,
> what secret music through our air's clogged sea,
> that every quiver of your measure here
> should answer to its silent melody?
> Even your pinkie's tiniest muscle, see,
> moves not except to make the measure clear,
> your step likewise, this dance, this revelry,
> this floating visual music holds so dear
> it tunes my stringed heart to the concord of its ear.
>
> This is the spheres' music! Worldmelody,
> which takes your body for its instrument,

or was it nature's magics, drifting free
for eons about the starry firmament
that found your precious body excellent
to lenslike sheaf, collect the sun's gold rays,
a glass of precious water, opulent,
and pour that light out to the world's amaze:
to dwell in sight of you is a surpassing grace.

And should this dear flesh fall into the grave,
this precious lens be broken (mourn O muse!
for all will crumble, all that nature gave
come to that last ditch and its final ooze,
the ripe fruit marred by winter's darkening bruise);
still what was beautiful, that ray so fair,
that *lightbeam* shall the ether so infuse
that lost to human sight soever, there
the ray remains, a profit for the gods to share.

Happier mortals of another star
perhaps will catch that travelling music-light
and read, after some few millennia,
your body-poem's eternal wave-delight.
O may I hope with their hope, when your bright
ray only then blossoms in their strange skies,
passing from star to star across the night,
that from your body's holy vessel flies
like precious steam drifting out of a dish of sacrifice.

Your earthly monument may crack and cave,
and the earth too will crumble: mourn, O muse!
for all will crumble, all that nature gave
come to that last ditch and its final ooze;
The ray flies on in space-time's avenues.
Body and soul die: but it cannot die.
This treasure's one that all vast space may use,
and so from star to star it will still fly
into infinity, for the gods to profit by.

Perhaps that beautiful music-ray could one day be reconstituted into a living human body. As I have suggested in chapter six, the moral necessity of offering the dead this reincarnation would be compelling, since most people do not die by choice, and thus their spiritual autonomy is artificially compromised by death. To offer resurrection would thus be a required act of liberation, a mandatory defense of civil rights. The new bodies of the revived would, of course, have been perfected by the contemporary biomedical and cybernetic science, so as to be endowed with enhanced physical powers, freedom from pain and aging, and the capacity to communicate mentally with each other and with the divine. (As a poet I believe we would still need words, however, as the most precise and shapely way of articulating ourselves to each other.) Those who accepted this gift would find it a heaven or a hell—or even a purgatory or a limbo—depending on their mental state and moral disposition. An experienced believer in power and coercion would feel this immortality as a nightmare, a terrifyingly dangerous glissade into the loss of self-possession, a desperate attempt to cover oneself so as to conceal one's self-hatred, contempt, and lust from others and from oneself, a continuous burning as one's own rejection of love consumed one. Those who had known love would experience that world as T.S. Eliot describes it in "East Coker":

> Whisper of running streams, and winter lightning.
> The wild thyme unseen, and the wild strawberry. . .

But there would not be the almost instant shutting-off, the dimming, the distraction, that steals the vision away from us in our present lives, and makes the experience of joy almost a tragedy in showing us what we have lost. To dwell in joy would nevertheless be a terrifying experience for any but the saint—and perhaps some period of renunciation, washing away the illusions of power and pride and justification, gradually acclimatizing and strengthening us to bear the very frankness and vividness of loving happiness, would amount to the equivalent of purgatory. There might even be some folk who, in their resurrected bodies, would be so morally stunted, and thus imaginatively incurious, that they would not notice the difference from their old lives. Others still might decline the offer of immortality, in fidelity to the honorable atheist statement that their old lives had made, or in some kind of existentialist acceptance of the limited being that had been theirs, or in an Upanishadic or Zen commitment to escape the wheel of desire—and I am not at all sure that theirs would not be the most perfect choice.

The Last Times

At some point in this history our descendants and their friends throughout the universe will, to the extent that it is possible, have perfected the art of controlled communication with the past. As I have pointed out, the observer has already been shown to have a weak time-reversed effect on quantum events; for many quantum physicists the direction of time is meaningless anyway, and for relativistic physicists the sequence of events in time is a phenomenon dependent on local reference frames. Perhaps the Bohm computer that constitutes the fundamental level of the computational universe in our classification can be used to carry messages backwards in time.

The apparent rarity, unobtrusiveness, or unverifiability of events that could be attributed to messages from the future would seem to indicate that the technology of such communications is extremely expensive, dangerous, tricky to use, fuzzy in operation, radically ambiguous when easy, or all of these. The weakest and least verifiable communications could be so commonplace that we do not notice them as such—in this interpretation they are just part of the continuous chatter that goes on in our heads. If retrotemporal communication is easy but dangerous—carrying the risk of wholesale destruction downtime, for instance, as some science fiction writers have imagined—the need for temporal policing would arise, a science fiction staple. My own preferred view is that the nature of the quantum computer itself would require a kind of Delphic vagueness in what could be transferred. After all, a quantum computer does not work with bits of information but with superpositions of contradictory informational states. Vague, airy, allusive, and symbolical messages might be commonplace, invitations from a variety of virtual futures—or in the language of chaos theory, suggestions of the shapes of various potential strange attractors; or in market terms, "vaporware" advertisements for a future product standard. A more sharply focused message might be possible, if really huge amounts of quantum information were sent, and in such a form as to generate unambiguity out of their own harmonics, as a good poem does at its deeper levels. But as I imagine it, the more focused and unambiguous the message, the greater the energy sacrifice in terms of matter, thermodynamic order, the potential of the quantum vacuum, or the curvature of spacetime in the timeline that sends the message. Such a message would have to compete with any other timeline's differing interpretation of history and its active attempt to frustrate or muddy the messages of its rivals. It might take the concerted effort of a large moiety of the existing timelines to be able to mount such a transmission, thus indicating that they would come from the deep future, well into the era of divine consolidation.

Nevertheless, a few such sendings might be possible. One of the most powerful of all would be the systematic rejigging of the quantum states of a human ovum, so that the resulting baby would carry in its brain the potential, when married to a particular nurture and historical period, to be a spokesperson for the divine. Such might be the great prophets, perhaps some seers, saints, poets, and artists. At an even greater expense, such perhaps also the messiah. History would need to be tweaked, so that some monster ideology or immortal brutal tyrant would not emerge to abort the gestation of the divine, and so that the human beings who make up the substrate of the divine might be prepared for their role in wiring up the divine body and brain. But if the era of such sendings is in the very deep future, it is unlikely that the terminology of its messages would be comprehensible at all to the times in which the prophet or the messiah is incarnated. As I imagine it, human beings of earlier intermediate ages—perhaps only a few thousand years in the future, with mindsets still approximately recognizable to folk in our present millennia—persons of exceptional character, charisma, and brilliance, might be recruited by the deep future to act as templates for the miracle child who is to be born. Thus Buddha, Moses, Mohammed, and so on. The earlier the era of recruitment, the more effective the rhetoric of the message, but the greater the likelihood of partisanship because of the background of the recruit. The later the recruitment, the more mysterious, inaccessible, or generalized the message, but also the more ecumenical. Buddha and Baha'ullah might be of this latter type. Jesus, as I see it, so raptured the ancient deity that recruited him, that his personality was permitted to infuse one of the three persons of the trinity; and when the software of his personality was sent back to first century Roman Palestine, into the womb of Mary, he truly was the son of God, the second person of the holy trinity. Perhaps Mohammed was recruited by an even later stage of the divine evolution, when any division of God was a thing of the past, and thus his message is that his sonship was shared with all human beings, and his prophetship was preeminent. His message, though, coming from so unimaginable a source, would be the more subject to misinterpretation. Such speculation is simply by way of showing that there is plenty of room in this tale for various theological assertions of uniqueness to be true. The next chapter will explore this topic in more detail.

A single being might finally emerge, made up of the harmonics of all the others, at first containing, as a trinity of Persons, the vestiges of its polytheistic components, then resolving even that disunity into the mystical singleness of the Sufi's Allah or the Hasid's Yahweh or the Brahman of the Upanishads, the Tao that cannot be spoken, or the impersonal distributed Being of Zen Buddhism. The three computers—the quantum Bohm computer, the flawed parallel Turing machine, and the distributed evolutionary/mental thinker—would at last be in perfect synch with one another. And this being would now have the responsibility, and the capacity—if its interventions in prior history had been successful—to take charge of the very beginning of time and ensure the universe's own successful delivery into existence. Current cosmology imagines the Big Bang as being the result of the pinching-off of some local bubble of space-time with its own idiosyncratic constants and fundamental logical ground rules. God, the ultimate observer, would be charged with that pinching-off and the choice of the fundamental physical constants; thus She would become at last the Alpha as well as the Omega, the sire to her own conception, and the midwife to her own delivery. If built of the right mathematical materials, the bubble would then through its own dynamics inflate, slow its expansion, cool, cross the thresholds at which matter and more complex forms of existence crystallize into existence, evolve its own richer timescapes, and so on, drawn by the strange attractors that constitute the mind of God.

We now have before us one possible universe as claimant for the shape we initially stipulated, the shape the world would have to be if all the religions are right. The reader might well feel that the beast I have sketched is so bizarre and unlikely that it constitutes a proof in probability that all the religions are not right; but at least it is not a proof in certainty, as most accounts of the contradictions between religions have claimed. Perhaps there is an odd poetry in this view of things, however, which might remind us of how strange all our various theologies and religious histories must have seemed to their first bemused discoverers. Think of Ganesh's borrowed head, or the golden tablets of the Angel Moroni, or Aphrodite's conception out of the sea foam and the genitals of her castrated father, or the mass weddings of the Unification Church, or Jesus' conception through the ear of Mary, or the black stone of the Kaaba, or Baron Samedi riding the horse of his acolyte, or the snake's temptation of Eve, or the twins Hunahpú and Ixbalanqué and their ballgame with the gods. These glimpses of ultimate reality, if that is what they are, do not require the presence of each other to sound extremely strange: they are quite strange enough in themselves. Their very strangeness is what qualifies them as possible vessels of divine meaning; it would seem that no ordinary human being would have the gall or the imagination to merely invent them. Perhaps their even greater strangeness when taken together need not be construed as a disqualification of the composite picture.

But it remains to show that there is indeed room in this bizarre account for the bewildering variety of religious doctrines—or at least a fair sample of the most apparently recalcitrant and irreconcilable ones. And this requires another chapter.

9

What Each Religion Brings to the Search

Atheist Materialism

There is a beautiful passage in Virginia Woolf's novel *To the Lighthouse* in which Mrs. Ramsay is faced with the challenge of pacifying two of her children who have different perceptions of the world. The skull of a ram has been nailed to the children's bedroom wall as a decoration (perhaps in the spirit of Woolf's contemporary Georgia O'Keeffe, who found those skulls beautiful). Cam, Mrs. Ramsay's fierce and imaginative little girl, finds the skull terrifying, won't sleep with it in the room, and wants it taken down. James, her little boy, resembles his father in his rigid, blue-eyed, philosopher's integrity, his ruthless determination to face up to the terrible truth of things. He insists that the skull remain where it is: he will not allow a mere girl to evade the harsh light of reality.

> Wherever they put the light (and James could not sleep without a light) there was always a shadow somewhere.
> "But think, Cam, it's only an old pig," said Mrs. Ramsay, "a nice black pig like the pigs at the farm." But Cam thought it was a horrid thing, branching at her from all over the room.
> "Well, then," said Mrs. Ramsay, "we will cover it up," and they all watched her go to the chest of drawers, and open all the drawers quickly one after another, and not seeing anything that would do, she quickly took her own shawl off and wound it round the skull, round and round and round, and then she came back to Cam and laid her head almost flat on the pillow beside Cam's and said how lovely it looked now; how the fairies would love it; it was like a bird's nest; it was like a beautiful mountain such as she had seen abroad, with valleys and flowers and bells ringing and birds singing and little goats and antelopes... She could see the words echoing as she spoke them rhythmically in Cam's mind, and Cam was repeating after her how it was like a mountain, a bird's nest, a garden, and there were little antelopes, and her eyes were opening and shutting, and Mrs. Ramsay went on saying still more monotonously, and more rhythmically and more nonsensically, how she must shut her eyes and go to sleep and dream of mountains and valleys and stars falling and parrots and antelopes and gardens, and everything lovely, she said, raising her head very slowly and speaking more and more mechanically, until she sat upright and saw that Cam was asleep.

> Now, she whispered, crossing over to his bed, James must go to sleep too, for see, she said, the boar's skull was still there; they had not touched it; they had done just what he wanted; it was there quite unhurt. He made sure the skull was still there under the shawl.

In the rich metaphorical terms of the book, what James is insisting on is the new ideology of modernist Europe: we should not try to avoid the skull-like reality of the physical universe, which is meaningless, stark, and made essentially of dead matter. James, like his father the philosopher, is a humanist atheist, believing only in the profound value of human life, and the noble calling of the human intellect to see the truth of things for what it is, that is, mere matter. Mrs. Ramsay does not dispute this view, but she feels it cruel to rub people's noses in it; and her role is to make that life we lead, between birth and death, as beautiful and meaningful as it can be, indeed as beautiful and as meaningful as the old religious universe was before science and philosophy unveiled it. So she winds the shawl about the skull, calming with poetry and art the fear of her daughter; but she reassures her son in his philosophical rectitude that the skull is still there.

The account of religion given in the first eight chapters, as the reader must be aware, essentially renders moot most of the theological debates of modernism. If it is correct, there is no need any more to guard what religious people feel to be the truths of religion by entrenching oneself in the Cartesian theology and the Newtonian physics of the eighteenth century; indeed, religious truths are apt to waste away under such guardianship. If God, as unextended immaterial rational substance, is exiled from the universe, then not only is he liable to be disproved by Wittgensteinian logic, he is also likely to become bloodless and amoral and valueless out there. Thus Mrs. Ramsay's atheism is perfectly consistent with the kind of higher reality we are investigating; she is denying the existence of a God outside the material universe who was invented in the first place to get Enlightenment *philosophes* off the hook.

Materialists remind us in a salutary way that we cannot simplify our ideals of meaning and our sense of ultimate concern by purging them of materiality. There is matter in the universe, and the finest things we know are made of it. But materialism was simply the best estimate, at one stage of the development of science, of what the fundamental constituent and determining reality of the universe might be. As modern physics progressed, and the world was examined at finer and finer scales, matter itself dissolved into radiant energy, and then into wave-functions, which are a form of information. And self-determining emergent realities appeared, nurtured by complexity and irreducible to the characteristics of their material elements, yet unmistakably physical. A logical positivist today would be faced with a problem: his strict definitions of identity and two-valued logic would no longer apply either to the quantum world below the level of matter, or to the living world above it. Matter, whose characteristic of mass generates such standards of veridicality, was not there at the beginning of the universe, may not be there in its last phases, and may only be a peculiarly convenient algorithm of information; matter is not the only kind of physicality.

But Mrs. Ramsay has got hold of a part of the divine that Zen Buddhists and Christian mystics are well aware of, which is essentially intangible to reductive and materialistic conceptions of fact. In this sense, God indeed does not exist. "Exist"—*ex-sistere*, to stand outside. He is not, in important senses, out there, but physically in here. The Tao that can be defined in "metaphysical" terms is not the Tao. Mrs. Ramsay's sense of the divine—for as far as I am concerned, she is a truly religious person—is of an emergent form, the attractor she generates in Cam's drowsing mind. That attractor, as we have seen, has as much reality as any other feature of the universe—and indeed more, since it is by such intangible arrangements as dynamical feedback systems and DNA sequences and mating rituals and ideas and aspirations that the universe is shaped and changed and transformed. Though Mrs. Ramsay does not believe in an afterlife, and will not try to deceive James that death is not a reality, she has found ways to survive in the hyperspaces of her children's dreams and her own interior dimensions of meaning.

Like the righteous blue-eyed James, however, it may be the religious atheists who are going to be most resentfully suspicious about this apparent tampering with their basic principles. If so, it would be ironic that of all the positions on ultimate reality the one most inclined to reject the evidence of the other people's senses would be the one philosophically most committed to plain empiricism. Atheists today, whether of the socialist, existentialist, or Ayn Randian libertarian species, have a heritage to defend and rather prickly sensibilities. On the noblest and finest end of the scale, they are committed to not being deceived by wishful thinking, and their ethics depend profoundly upon there being no afterlife, no supernatural reward for their behavior. Life should be justifiable in its own terms, and our acts should be both their own meaning and their own reward. Indeed, if more conventionally religious people lived in this way, the world would be a better place. But there are less admirable commitments that render some atheists obdurate to the persuasions of reason. Pride is one: there is often a big investment in the belief that others are not as perceptive, courageous, clear-thinking, and intelligent as one is oneself, and that since religious people are fools, one is showing oneself to be not a fool oneself if one rejects their superstitions. Many atheists secretly consider themselves to be members of an elite, whose teaching mission to the rest of society and political importance in a secular democracy depend on its unique possession of the truth. Another motivation is that such people sometimes rejected religion in the first place because they wished to commit an act that religion defines as evil, and are now suffering the consequences of that act in their lives; the defenses we build to support denial are among the most formidable the human psyche is capable of. The pain of their ruined relationships and damaged personal resources would be unbearable if, added to it, was the knowledge that one had brought it upon oneself.

But in all fairness such motivations are common to many kinds of beliefs, including those of other religions than secular humanism. For the finer virtues of atheism, there is nothing in the divine as we have described it to cause dismay. The basic principles have not in fact been tampered with. The skull, so to speak, is still there. We are claiming nothing outside the universe as it is, and claiming for this universe only what the sciences have already given us warrant for. Atheist materialists do not dispute that consciousness can arise out of a brew of electrochemical connectivity in the brain and body, and thus should have no objection in principle to larger emergent consciousnesses arising out of larger systems of connection. Atheists are perfectly right in thinking that there is no huge super-neuron outside the brain, so to speak, that is running everything.

And atheist materialists have much to contribute to the richer view of religion we are attempting here. They rightly reveal much of our theologizing to be absurdly literalistic and clumsy, and return us, sometimes violently as in the case of the existentialists, to the shock of actual experience, for religious people the true hallmark of the divine. Atheists are more fundamentalist than the fundamentalists. Moreover the humanistic tinge of much of the atheist creed is a welcome corrective to the abstraction that comes over religion from time to time. After all, Christ's second commandment, Allah's first characteristic, Buddha's great injunction, is compassion. We worship the divine by loving our neighbor. Atheism is valuable also in that it has already reached the very advanced stage of mysticism that mystics call the dark night of the soul, the cloud of unknowing. Mystics say that God is known through his very absence, in the way called the *via negativa*.

Perhaps the most important thing that atheist humanism has to offer to the religion of the future is the vastness and variety of the world it opens up. Readers of science fiction have become accustomed to a universe inconceivably multifarious, a future and a past filled with complex events, each with its own historical present and traditions as ancient and compelling as our own. This perspective compels us to see all the earth-shaking headlines of our own time as having faded at some point in the future to the same status as, say, the cults and battles of the stone age Balearic Islanders, which were as important to them as ours to us. Astronomers have already identified planets circling local stars; it is quite possible that of all the billions of such planets that must exist in this galaxy alone, there are hundreds of worlds with histories as complex and tragic and full of genius, terror, and magnificent spiritual achievement as our own. Having imaginatively experienced such a universe, there is no going back. If the ticket to it is the abandonment of religious faith—if such a universe can only exist without a divine supervisor—our salvation would have to be bought by a sort of imaginative lobotomy. Either our religious conceptions must expand to include such a world, or we who have experienced it must purchase our religious life at the cost of being prepared to sit in a sort of cramped terrarium or diorama, with its painted backdrop of local religious history, while the real universe plunges on into unimaginable futures; and great blue planets with landscapes we will never see and stories we have never heard spin beneath their strange collections of moons. Certainly there is something sterile about a many-worlds universe in which religion is merely a local superstition abandoned by more advanced races, as science fiction writers are increasingly coming to see; but why can we not have both the vastness and richness of the spiritual world and the vastness and richness of the physical universe? —and why should they not be the same?

Animism

One of the most fundamental forms that worship takes in traditional, technologically simple societies throughout the world—and apparently through much of our species' history—is the religion of nature. Animism, and its variants, such as totemism and some forms of shamanism, is in a sense the best founded of all views in terms of the speculative metaphysics sketched in the preceding chapters of this book. We do not have to postulate strange time-geometries or future technology to find the fit of animism with the universe as it is. Once we have an apparatus of philosophical reasoning, we do indeed need to have got beyond the Cartesian materialist stage of science to be able to see animism as more than folk superstition: if matter is described as dead by definition, then animism—the idea that the universe is alive with natural spirits—is immediately out of court. But the more sophisticated views that have come with general systems theory, the extension of the idea of evolution to the inanimate and cultural worlds, chaos theory, complexity theory, cognitive science, and what is sometimes called emergentism are in the process of restoring that "enchanted" universe of living forces with their own internal telos, their own characteristic strange attractors.

Traditional animists are also more tolerant of other religions than most of those other religions are. It is no skin off an old-time animist's nose if someone from another tribe claims that there are other spirits out there as well as the familiar ones. All the more chance of getting some real divine help. Modern and postmodern animists are a different matter, however; as with Oscar's Wilde's happy man, their friends must fail, the other religions have to be wrong. Modern animists in the environmental movement are sometimes suspicious of humanism, opposed to the monotheistic experience of many religious people, and sworn enemies to the technology that might bring about the sort of future sketched in the previous chapter. But again, we might reassure them that the skull is still there. In the history of the divine we have postulated, later phases do not supersede earlier ones but accumulate upon them, enriching them retroactively. And after all, would not the modern animist agree that humans are part of nature (if not, we must have been planted here by some external, nonnatural deity, which they would reject)? and if it is our nature to invent and transform, is that not also natural? And suppose one day we achieve the kind of technical virtuosity to be able to resurrect extinct species and ecosystems, and create new ones, how could they object? Might not Gaia herself be expecting such cooperation?

What animism brings to the table of religion is manifold. It roots our worship deeply and humbly in this world, extending our duty of compassion to other species and other entities than ourselves. It is more practically in touch than many urban and abstract religions with how spirit arises out of the interplay of physical beings. It understands as both miraculous and unproblematic the relationship of body and mind. Miraculous, because mind is in its most primitive forms everywhere, and thus this universe is enspirited at birth—and what a gift that is! Unproblematic, because mind, at least in its simplest form, is already a natural property of bodies and does not have to be imported from elsewhere at great metaphysical cost.

Thus we should not seek to "purify" from our religious visualizations the theromorphic and vegetative imagery that we have inherited from the older religions—the animal-headed gods of Egypt, the corn gods of many traditions, the dragon and elephant and monkey forms of India and China, the Mudyi tree of the Ndembu, and the Yggdrasil of the Norse, the bear, beaver, and killer whale of Tsimshian Indian totems, the winged men and Christmas trees and Easter eggs and bunnies of Western Christianity. Indeed, the chimerical and polymorphic natural forms of traditional religions are an important reminder of how bizarre our divine subject is—paradoxically, how far beyond any existing sensory modality it is. Iconoclasm, the rejection of images of the divine, makes the same point but in a different way—by not representing God, it leaves the fantastic forms of nature itself as mute testimony to God's astonishing imagination and the shape of her dreaming mind. We know now, from Edward Wilson's fine book *Biophilia*, that the human need for a full biosphere of living organisms around us is not just a biological one, but a psychological one too. The living ecosystem is almost as much our body as are our limbs and heart and stomach. We would be denatured without it, and it is inconceivable that even when we have inhabited a myriad galaxies, we should not have green leaves and the singing of birds about us. As totemists well know, we are kin to the animals: their genes, that code for proteins of emotion and awareness, are ours too, and those touches of wolf and deer and hawk and buffalo that we sometimes see in the faces and movements of our friends are true family resemblances. The monastic martial arts traditions of Asia have discovered and elaborated that kinship into brilliant defensive skills; there are tiger, bull, toad, and crane forms of offense and defense. One day we may enhance the animals so that they can speak with us; but even today the viruses and bacteria are busy copying and exchanging snippets of DNA among humans and all other living organisms. And if we are to be parts of God, shoots of the true vine or rejoined with the spiritual ocean of Brahman, then that living integument of biological nature must come too, and be gathered into the identity of God. Perhaps this is part of the meaning of the odd Catholic doctrine of the bodily assumption of the Virgin into heaven; if she goes there, then so do her stomach flora and her eyelash mites; and as a Mediterranean lady she is going to want olives, and bread, and goat cheese, and flowers, and wine.

Ritual and Sacrificial Religion

Consider the human body, and its remarkable differences from the bodies of other mammals. One of the most obvious is our nakedness; we stand hairless but for odd tufts here and there emphasizing such body parts as the head and face, and the genitals. All other land mammals of our size, and all of our relatives the primates, including all tropical primates, are covered with hair. Some much larger tropical species, like elephants and rhinoceroses, are, indeed, also hairless; the reason is that their greater size implies a higher ratio of body volume to body surface, and a larger and more stable thermal reservoir; and thus they do not need hair. Human beings, however, are pantropic in their habit—they live in all climates—and are much smaller; without clothing and/or shelter they would be at a massive disadvantage.

We, like the other animals, evolved; and it is a truism of evolutionary logic that if a given bodily structure (such as hair) is not necessary, and cannot be adapted to another purpose, those individuals that possess it will be at a disadvantage, if only because of the metabolic drain on their resources that the structure's production and upkeep requires. This disadvantage will tend statistically to result in fewer such individuals surviving to reproduce, a thinning out of the genes for that structure in the population, and a preferential rate of increase for genes not specifying that structure. The same applies in reverse; if a species would be better off with hair, say, to maintain a constant body temperature, hair will be selected for. In the case of the peacock's tail, the brilliant colors of tropical fish, and the elk's antlers, however, sexual ritual can contradict this biological law: rivalry for the privilege of reproduction can lead to the development of beautiful structures of sexual display and intimidation, that are in fact disadvantageous with respect to survival in a dangerous world.

One plausible explanation for our nakedness, then, is that it is the result of sexual selection in ritual courtship, and that we developed clothing originally both for ritual body decoration and also to replace for thermal purposes the hair that we had lost. The invention of clothes, a by-product of our ritual, enabled us to survive even in cool temperate and arctic climates; and so as hair was no longer necessary for survival, it never came back. Thus our nakedness is a result of our early culture.

And here we see a new principle of reflexive feedback enter the already tangled, iterative, and turbulent process of natural evolution. Cultural evolution—that is, a process of change in behavior that can happen in a single generation and be passed down through imitation and learning to the next—now takes a hand in biological evolution, in that iterated cycle of sexually or mutatively generated variation, selection through the preferential survival of useful traits in the population, and genetic inheritance. Biological evolution takes millennia; cultural evolution takes years. Yet the culture of a species, especially in its effect on sexual and reproductive success, is a powerful determinant of which individuals survive to reproduce. The faster process of change—culture—will drive and guide the slower one—biology.

Many of the other peculiar characteristics of the human body can be explained in the same way: its upright stance, its long infancy, its developed vocal chords and otolaryngeal system, its extraordinary longevity (especially in the female), its relatively early menopause, its relative lack of specialized armaments—big teeth and claws, and so on—, its opposable thumbs, its superbly refined and coordinated fine motor system, its continuous sexual readiness (most animals are in heat only for a few days in the year), its huge brain.

The upright stance reveals the full beauty of human primary and secondary sexual characteristics to each other; it enables hunters and gatherers to carry meat and vegetables home, and therefore to have to remember who gets which share; thus it also helps us to have a home to carry things home to, and thus a ritually charged place, and a kinship system that can serve as a set of rules for who gets which share; and it enables parents to carry babies in their arms who are helpless because they require a much longer infancy period than the young of other species, a long infancy demanded by the need to program children in the complexities of the tribal ritual. The upright stance also changed the normal mating position from mounting to face-to-face, thus encouraging that extraordinary mutual gaze which is the delight of lovers and the fundamental warrant of the equality of the sexes: an equality which was absolutely essential if the human traits of intelligence, communication, and imagination were to be preferred and thus reinforced.

Our ritual songs, improved every year, demanded complex voice-production systems that could also come in useful for communication in the hunt and other cooperative enterprises. Our long old age enabled the elders—especially the postmenopausal wisewomen— to pass on the ritual lore and wisdom. Our lack of bodily armament was compensated for by the development of weapons, which could be wielded by thumbed hands liberated by our upright stance and controlled by an advanced fine motor system—thumbed hands required to enact the ritual actions and paint on the ritual body-paint and carry the ritual objects and make the ritual clothing and gather the seeds and roots for our tribal kin. Sexuality was extended and intensified relatively to other animals, and was adapted from its original reproductive function into the raw material of an elaborate ritual drama that pervaded all aspects of society.

And the great brain mushroomed out, transforming its substructures to the new uses and demands that were being placed on it, pushing out the skull, diminishing the jaws, wiring itself more and more finely into the face, hands, and speech organs, specializing particular areas of the right and left to handle new linguistic, musical, and pictorial-representational tasks, developing a huge frontal lobe to coordinate everything else and to reflect upon itself and its body and its death, and connecting that higher-level reflective consciousness by massive nerve bundles to the limbic emotional centers—thus creating a unity of function between the intellectual and the passionate that is close to the heart of our deepest shame and which has thus been denied by most of our recent philosophical systems.

From this point of view personal physical beauty takes on a new importance. Breeders of dogs and horses can tell by very subtle physical signs, in the carriage of the head, the set of the eye, the delicacy of proportion, whether the animal is likely to possess psychological characteristics such as intelligence, heart, and concentration. The intangible elements of human beauty—beyond those obviously related to reproductive and survival success, such as big breasts and hips, clear skin, broad shoulders, straight legs—are evidently such external bodily signs of internal neural sophistication. Those intangible elements, that we refer to when we say that someone has beautiful eyes or a beautiful expression, or that we are captured by in someone's way of moving—the things that make us watch a great film star—can be quite different from conventional beauty. They can quickly overwhelm any deficiency in the brute appeal of the hunk, the nice piece of ass, beefcake, or cheesecake. The lovely ambiguity in the word "grace"—divine favor, and excellence in physical coordination—nicely catches this other quality; though in the context of the darker price of human excellence it is significant that grace is also a purifying blessing (from Old English "blissian," to wound or make bleed) before meals. When we fall in love, and thus mate and have offspring, we do so often because we are captured by such qualities. Thus we look the way we look as a species, largely because that was the way our ancestors thought intelligent, strong, loving, and imaginative—ritual-ready—animals ought to look. We are the monument to our progenitors' taste. Ritual was the shaping instrument of the divine in our evolution; it was the spirit, the logos, that brooded upon the waters and made them pregnant.

Many of our creation myths show an intuitive grasp of the strange process by which the cultural tail came to wag the biological dog. The story of the clothing of Adam and Eve, where (the awareness of) nakedness is the result of shame, which is in turn the result of self-knowledge, expresses one aspect of it. Again in Genesis the punishment of Eve for her acquisition of knowledge, that she must suffer in childbirth, nicely expresses the fact that one of the parameters of a big-brained viviparous species like ourselves is the capacity of the female pelvis to allow the passage of a large skull. Hence also the beauty for the male of the female's wide hips and the motion they make when walking. The big (and to the male, attractive) breasts of the human female, and her dependency upon a protecting male during lactation—also referred to in Genesis—are likewise the sign of a nurturing power that can deal with a long infant dependency, and thus produce human beings of intelligence, wisdom, and esthetic subtlety. Babies without protecting fathers must enter adulthood earlier, and cannot be fully instructed in the tribal ritual; they thus need smaller brains, and smaller-hipped and -breasted mothers to bear them.

Our deep feelings of embarrassment and anger at these facts, the flush that rises to our faces when we think of our own biology, are the signs of that shame which we would deny but whose acceptance is the only gate to beauty. That beauty is summed up in the great pictorial genre of the Madonna and child. At present this tragic contradiction makes itself felt in our society by a conflict between female roles—of a nurturing that produces the best and noblest and most loving human intelligence, and of the very exercise of that intelligence. The means and the end of nurturance are thus perceived as opposed in our society. But we should not deceive ourselves that if this problem were solved, the solution itself would not produce its own contradictions even more tragic and shameful, and even more potentially beautiful.

One persistent theme of creation myths all over the world is the presence of a trickster, who somehow transforms the forces of nature so that they assist rather than hinder the cultural program. The story of how Odysseus tricks Polyphemus, the cave-man, into rolling away the rock-door of his cave is one survival of such a myth. South American Jaguar tales, in which fire is adapted to human use, have the same gist. We find in these myths both the shame of our mistreatment of our mother, nature, and the nostalgia for the beautiful Arcadian landscape that we like to imagine as having preexisted the birth of self-consciousness. Polyphemus lives on the slopes of Etna, by the vale of Enna where the fountain of Arethusa rises, mingled with the waters of her pursuer, the Arcadian river-god Alpheus; where Proserpina wandered before her rape by Dis; the loveliest Arcadian landscape of all, the closest to the volcano and the source of fire, painted by Bellini and sung of in Handel's *Acis and Galatea*.

If the human ritual as we have envisaged it was to have its original evolutionary function, it must have involved a dark and terrible element. For if some members of the tribe enjoyed greater reproductive success, others must have enjoyed less. If some were selected as preferred mates for their intelligence, wit, loving nature, prudence, magnanimity, honesty, courage, depth, sanguine disposition, foresight, empathy, physical health, beauty, grace, and strength; others—the dullards, whiners, liars, blowhards, hoarders, spendthrifts, thieves, cheats, and weaklings—must be rejected. The most brutal throwbacks—the rapists, those who grabbed the food and did not share it, those who could not follow the subtle turns of the ritual and internalize the values that it invented and implied—would be cast out from the tribal cave, into the outer darkness, where there is wailing and gnashing of teeth. Defective infants would be abandoned on the mountainside; adults polluted by impiety, crime, incest, madness, disease, or their own exercise of witchcraft would be led to the borders of the village lands and expelled. Oedipus, who was exposed though not defective at birth, is among other things a symbol of our guilt at such rejection: when he does return, as all buried shames must, he pollutes the city with his unconscious incest. The Old English monster Grendel, that wanderer of the borderlands, the descendant of Cain, is another type of such outcasts, and the image of the scapegoat.

But indeed, the fragile virtues of the human race would have been impossible without this terrible and most shameful selection process. If we consider how morally imperfect we are as it is, and how the best and most recent research shows that moral traits are to a considerable extent inherited, it may be a grim satisfaction to reflect how much worse we would be if we had not selected ourselves for love and goodness. Abraham's willingness to sacrifice his son Isaac at the command of the Lord (whom we may take, for mythic purposes, to be the evolutionary imperative of the human species, the strange attractor drawing it into being) is necessary, paradoxically, to bring about a more loving and just humanity. We had better be worth the price.

Our moral growth has, more recently, caused us to recoil in revulsion from those ancient practices; but that growth was partly their result. And the process has not ceased, and we had better face up to the fact. Every time a woman chooses a man to be her husband and the father of her children, for any good personal reason—for his gentleness and his wit, his confident strength and his decent humility—she is selecting against some other man less noble in character, and either helping to condemn him to the nonentity of childlessness or to be the parent, with some less morally perceptive woman, of children who are likely to inherit their parents' disadvantages. It is horribly cruel and shameful, if we think about it, but I believe there is a strange and terrible beauty to the magnitude of the mating choice, that is at the root of the troubled exaltation we sometimes feel at a good wedding.

The rituals of sacrifice, and their later and subtler developments as tragedy or Eucharist, are the human way of rendering this ancient horror into beauty. Sacrifice has a peculiar element, which we might call "commutation": every sacrifice commemorates a previous sacrifice, in which some much more terrible act of bloody violence or costly loss was required. Abraham is allowed to sacrifice a ram instead of his son, who was due to the Lord; the Greeks can burn the fat and bones and hide of the bull to the gods, and eat the flesh themselves. Instead of a whole firstborn son, only a shred of flesh from the foreskin need be given. When the process has been going for a long time, the sacrificed object can become apparently rather trivial. Cucumbers are sacrificed in some African tribal societies; Catholics and Buddhists burn candles; almost all Christians break bread. Thus every sacrifice is an act of impurity which pays for a prior act of greater impurity, but pays for it at an advantage, that is, without its participants having to suffer the full consequences incurred by its predecessor. The punishment is commuted in a process that strangely combines and finesses the deep contradiction between justice and mercy.

The process of commutation also has much in common with the processes of metaphorization, symbolization, even reference or meaning itself. The Christian Eucharistic sacrifice of bread not only *stands in* for the sacrifice of Christ (which in turn stands in for the death of the whole human race); it also *means*, and in sacramental theology *is* the death of Christ. The Greek tragic drama both referred to, and was a portion of, the sacrificial rites of Dionysus— both a use and a mention, as the logicians say, or both a metaphor and a synecdoche, in the language of the rhetorician. The word commutation nicely combines these senses: in general use it means any substitution or exchange, as when money in one currency is changed into another, or into small change, or when payment in one form is permitted to be made in another; in alchemy it can be almost synonymous with transmutation, as of one metal into another; in criminal jurisprudence it refers to the reasoned lightening of a just punishment to one which is less severe, but which is juridically taken as equivalent to it; in electrical engineering it is the reversal of a current or its transformation between direct and alternating current; in mathematical logic it refers to the equivalency of a given operation, such as A multiplied by B, to its reverse, B multiplied by A.

Thus sacrifice is the meaning of meaning. What this implies for our own time is that the death of sacrifice is the death of meaning;

that the crisis in modern philosophy over the meaning of the word "reference"—and this is the heart of it—has its roots in the denial of shame and thus the denial of commutativeness; and that for reference and meaning to come back to life, some deep sacrifice is required. Perhaps that sacrifice has been made already in the last century, and it is for us to recognize it as such.

The invention of ritual sacrifice, or rather perhaps its elaboration and adaptation from the division of the spoils of the hunt and the disposal of the bodies of the dead, may have begun a process of increasing suppression of the protohuman eugenics I have described. The commutation process gradually took the teeth out of social selection. Instead of the normal expulsion or killing of the polluted, there was occasional human sacrifice; instead of actual human sacrifice, scapegoat animals were killed. More and more egalitarian religious ideas arose, as in the antielitist cults of Krishna and of the Buddha in the Hindu tradition, the Greco-Roman myths of the gods in disguise as beggars, the later cults of Mithras and of popular Egyptian deities, the social criticism of the Hebrew prophets, and the Christian warning that the last shall be first and the first last. A larger and larger proportion of the population was permitted to have offspring. Tribalism came to be despised. Arranged marriage ceased to be the norm. Aristocratic ideas of the inheritance of good blood went into decline. Meanwhile a celibate priesthood came into being in many traditions, clearly and unambiguously signaling that reproductive success was no longer the reward for ritual excellence.

We rightly condemn eugenics and applaud the increasing humaneness—the humanity—of the emerging civilized morality. The word "human" itself means the rejection of the terrible process by which we became human. And if commutation in this sense also means meaning, then meaning is in another way the same thing as sacrifice.

But if we think we can safely suppress the memory of how we became human, and of the price of our new freedom, we are quite wrong. To reject such practices should not mean to repress them from our memory; and if we forget them, the basis of our shame and also the basis of our beauty as the paragon of animals, we may, in some time of terrible stress, find ourselves repeating them. And we are indeed at this time trying to repress them. The symptoms of that repression are manifold: our contemporary hatred of technology (while we use it only the more avidly); our attempt to make sexual

intercourse shameless by detaching it psychologically from reproduction, family, deep and emotional commitments, the possibility of
disease, and any implication of psychobiological differentiation between the sexes; our bad conscience about racism, animal "rights,"
and abortion; our inability to face the meaning of the Nazi Holocaust; and the element of rabid superstition in our fear that we are
destroying Mother Nature. And we have few rituals left to enable us
to accept and take on the burden of our inescapable impurity.

In giving up *tribal* eugenics we have irrevocably declared our
commitment to technology. As civilization matured, as we have seen,
it kept the routine *individual* eugenics implicit in the choice of reproductive partner; in one sense we could say that the move toward
civilization is a move toward an increasing democratization of reproductive choice. Instead of the tribal collectivity deciding who
should not have children, we all did, individually, by discriminating
against all other potential reproductive partners than the ones we
chose. The selective process was thus rendered weaker, more subtle,
less consistent, and much more variable.

In contemporary society, where casual sexual promiscuity, medical intervention, and birth control tend to frustrate the process of
genetic selection through reproductive success, we are in the process of giving up even the individual option for selecting and passing on valued information by genetic means. Still, over the last few
thousand years we have been developing other means of passing on
such information: oral poetry, writing, the arts, organized social institutions, and now computers and other advanced electronic technology. These systems have become the DNA of a new, inconceivably swifter and more complex form of life, a new twist in the evolutionary spiral.

Furthermore, we will soon be in a position to correct by means of
gene therapy the diseases, distortions, and deficits which would once
have condemned a cave-dweller to exposure, exile, or ritual sacrifice. Thus technology, especially biotechnology, is the opposite and
alternative to eugenics, which is the ancient aristocratic theory of
species improvement. Technology is a further development of the
evolutionary process of meaning. In this light the deconstruction of
the European Jews by the Nazis appears as a hideous throwback, a
deliberate reversal of all that humanity has gained in the last three
million years. By means of technology, which is our *substitute* for
tribal genetic activism, the worst members of the species scapegoated

and fed to a hideously sanitized and deritualized holocaust a large moiety of the best. And the Jews' de facto forgiveness of the rest of the human race, if that is how we are to take it, would be the beginning of the redemption of humankind.

I do not present the foregoing discussion of the complex relations of sacrifice, evolution, and meaning as an assertion of a clear moral position—because, as such, whatever moral outcome we chose would involve a tragic revulsion against other moral principles we hold to be of unchallengeable validity. For instance, if we choose the ancient tribal values of the human species, we must also choose collective eugenics, racism, and blood sacrifice—or contrive somehow to detach the parts of this package, thus denaturing them of their moral weight. If we choose reproductive freedom, we must also choose advanced informational and biological technology, and find some way of dealing with a human neuropsychological makeup that needs families and primary caregivers. The only proper way to make such an argument is perhaps in a tragic play; but tragic drama requires for its audience a society that has some intellectual grasp of the necessary irreconcilability of our moral and logical conflicts. This book is intended as a step toward such an understanding; and if it could be a preface to a true tragic drama, it would have fulfilled one of the true functions of theodicy, which is to enable beauty to be born out of its own despairing shame.

The Orphic Journey

There may be some truth in the idea that sacred writings are simply that subset of the works of poets that has been canonized; the more ancient and enduring the canonization, the more sacred. I imagine that in a thousand years the works of Shakespeare will be regarded as sacred, as for instance the Homeric epics came to be in classical Greece and medieval Europe. The *Mahabharata* began as a rousing military and magical epic, but has gradually over millennia of interpretation and interpolation become a holy book to the Hindus; and parts of it, such as the Bhagavad Gita, are as central to certain sects as the New Testament is to Christians. Much the same applies to the Persian *Shahnameh* and the Mayan *Popol Vuh*. The Jewish Bible is a compendium of myths, folktales, brilliant and profound novellas, stirring historical narratives, love poetry, poetic drama, aphorisms, poetic sermons, moral harangues, and songs, as well as rules of conduct, ritual protocols, theological speculations and genealogies. Perhaps the majority of it is the immediate work of people we can only call poets, together with a sort of interpretative guide provided by priestly critics and exegetes. It is surely, in the terms of this book, divinely inspired, as are the other great scriptures of the world; but we must take divine inspiration to be a much more unruly and madcap thing than it is usually considered to be. Jesus, the parable-maker, is plainly a poet of the first magnitude.

How do poets obtain the knowledge that they represent as prophecy or story or prayer or parable? One of the most pervasive descriptions of their research is the shamanic descent into the underworld, the Orphic journey. In shamanism all over the world certain individuals near the extremes of normal human neurochemistry and talent find a vocation and a tradition that can harness their special characteristics. They are trained in the artistic techniques of the shaman's craft, often symbolized by a musical instrument such as a drum, a lyre, a didgery-doo, bagpipes, or a rattle, acquire a special relationship with an animal familiar, and experience a strange journey, often involving travel through the air and under the ground. They converse with ancestors and animal spirits, and are given mysterious knowledge, which they bring back in the form of stories, poetry, healing arts, useful technological inventions, new ritual elements, and moral imperatives; though they seldom become political leaders, they often take on the role of spiritual and moral spokesperson for the community. They promise in an ambiguous way some kind of afterlife, and sometimes they attempt, with varying success, to bring the dead or dying back to life.

We can find examples of this tradition everywhere. The Magyar shaman-bards with their bagpipes and their strange trochaic-dactylic meters resemble their distant cousin, the Finnish wizard Lemminkainen, whose own shamanic journeys are celebrated in the *Kalevala*. Mircea Eliade catalogs dozens of shamanic cultures throughout Asia. The Mayan brothers Hunapúh and Ixbalanqué go down to the underworld and return with magical powers. There are several underworld journeys in the *Mahabharata*, each of which transforms the Pandava brothers and prepares them for their spiritual mission. In the western classical tradition, the underworld journey story has a clear line of succession going back six thousand years: it begins with Gilgamesh's tragic quest to find eternal life and bring back his friend Enkidu from the grave; it continues among the Greeks with the stories of the Dioscuri, Castor and Pollux, Alcestis, and Persephone; and then Odysseus visits the land of the dead, starting a series of explicit epic emulations. Aeneas is guided by the Sibyl to the hellmouth of Avernus for his own conversations with the inhabitants of Hades and Elysium; Virgil, Aeneas' poet, becomes the guide that Dante finds to lead him through the Inferno; Milton's Satan, and Milton himself, must descend into the land of shades; Joyce's Stephen Dedalus has his adventures in Night-town, and in *Four Quartets* T.S. Eliot encounters the "familiar compound ghost" of all his shamanic predecessors. It is clear that the myth and ancient cult of Orpheus are central and developed versions of this ancient tradition, as is the story of Cupid and Psyche.

One of my favorite versions of the story, perhaps because of my Celtic ancestry, is the Ballad of True Thomas. Thomas, the rhymer, is sitting under the Eildon Tree, the great oak that stands at the crossroads (often a place where the underworld is very near). A beautiful lady rides up on a white horse covered with tiny silver bells. Thomas goes down on his knees to such beauty, and exclaims that she must surely be the queen of heaven—that is, the Virgin Mary. No, she smiles, she is the queen of Fairyland; and she goes on to say that if Thomas kisses her he will be her slave, she will own his body. Thomas of course kisses her, as any red-blooded poet would; and she takes him up with her on her horse and they ride off together. She takes him through places where, as in *Gilgamesh*, the sun and moon do not shine; they ride through a river of blood up to the knee, fed by the blood of all the dead; and they come to a place where the road divides in three. One path, a steep, narrow and rocky one, leads up to heaven. Another, a broad well-trodden primrose path, leads down to Hell. Between them is a third, a bonny path that winds about the ferny brae; it is the road to fair Elfland, and this is the path they take. They come to a beautiful land east of the sun, west of the moon, where there is a garden, the garden of the dead and the ever-living; and in that garden there is a tree with golden fruit. The queen plucks one and gives it to Thomas, as her gift to him, and as the sign of his release from her bondage. Suspicious, Thomas asks what effect it will have, and she tells him that it will make him always speak the truth. Thomas protests that this is not a very desirable gift. If he must tell the truth when he is bargaining in the market he will be taken advantage of; if he is speaking to the king he will blurt out whatever disrespectful thought he has in his head, to the considerable risk of that organ; and how can he speak courteously to a fair maiden when he must say all the naughty things that go through a man's head at such a time? Nevertheless, the lady makes him eat of the fruit, and he returns to the land of the living. From then on he must wander from land to land telling the truth; and that is why Thomas the Rhymer is also called True Thomas.

The path that the poets take is clearly one that leads into the past, both of the culture and of the species. They speak with the dead and thus make the past present; they have mastered the art of time travel. In a sense they are scientists, who can investigate the causes and roots and sources of things, recovering, from what things are now, what they were when they began, and resolving into their elements what is now tied together into knots of consequence. They are able to retrace the course of evolution, by which things came to be, to step back down the ladder or tree of creation to its base, its roots. Such poets often have, or gain, the power of understanding and speaking the languages of animals (and even, in the case of Orpheus, plants and stones). Solomon spoke with the birds; Vyasa, the poet of the *Mahabharata*, also knew the speech of the pre-human world of beasts and rocks. Moses was half-swallowed by the great serpent, and rescued only when his wife, Zipporah, circumcised their baby son and smeared the baby's blood on his father's feet, thus becoming to her, as she says, her bridegroom of blood. Here, in his delivery from out of the belly of the beast, his mission of liberation truly begins. The underworld of such travelers is the evolutionary past of the universe; only by acknowledging and retracing that route may the gift of inspired speech be attained. As the poet Attila József put it, quoting an old Hungarian folksong:

> He who would a piper be
> must go to hell unswervingly;
> only in that place may he know
> how he should make the pipes to blow.

In many of these stories the hero returns with the gift of prophecy, and there is a persistent connection with oracles and sibyls. So the journey of the poet-shaman is not only into the past but also into the future. Or perhaps, like the dolphin that must dive deep in order to gather the momentum for its great leap out of the water, the sacred poet must know his or her science well before undertaking the transcendent. As Melville suggests in *Moby Dick*, the depth of the ship's keel is the measure of how tall its masts can rise. But the poet's leap into the vision of the future, the apocalypse, is always fraught with danger and ambiguity. For there are, as we have already suggested, many futures; and as Oedipus learns, how we choose given the vision of any one of them will affect how the future actually comes about.

Perhaps the grandest of all these journeys is the one that Christ made after his death on the cross; the three-day Easter journey into Sheol, the Harrowing of Hell, when he led the spirits of the just but unredeemed up into the light, and initiated the era of the redemption and the future history of the Holy Spirit. Christianity emphasizes the element of ascent, of purification, of the attainment of a spiritual transcendence: but the element of descent, of the deepest embroilment in the physical world, is just as important. Christ could speak to stones, animals, a barren fig tree. There is a sort of Taoist intuitive science of nature in the sayings of all the great religious founders; St. Francis of Assisi is only the most obvious example. The Jesus that greets the disciples in his resurrected form on the shores of Galilee is physical enough to be cooking fish over a driftwood fire, like a stone-age hunter-gatherer; that combination of the immanent and transcendent, the animal and the spiritual, is at the heart of the idea of incarnation.

Reincarnation and the Afterlife

In the hypothetical history of the spirit proposed in this book, the widespread doctrine of reincarnation is true in many senses. Indeed, its being true in too many senses may be more of a problem than its being true in too few. One of those senses is the traditional idea of the afterlife, of resurrection in a new and transformed body.

If we take human beings to be thermodynamic entities, which at one level we are, the thermodynamic information of which we are composed is immortal, and after we die continues in all its detail, though distributed in an expanding sphere whose leading edge is traveling at the speed of light toward the edge of the universe. Our actions are the result of our whole being, and because information cannot be destroyed, our actions are perfectly recorded in the universe. Since a single complex curve—say, the shape given to a pot by a Roman potter, or the vibration of her voice recorded in the clay as the pot spins on the wheel, or the physical changes printed in the walls of her workshop by light rays reflected from her face—can contain an infinite amount of information, and since that information is theoretically extractable by Fourier analysis, we might well say that our every moment is continuously reincarnated in other forms. Other living entities, human, animal, or even plant, being sophisticated and sensitive recorders of information, would make especially appropriate repositories of the information that makes us up, just as the religions of metempsychosis maintain.

If we take human beings to be genetic entities, again reincarnation makes good sense. Obviously if we have children our genes survive in them; almost everyone has seen the identical expression pass over the face of a grandchild that passed over the face of the grandmother. Some religions, such as that of the Balinese, maintain that descendants can be the reborn souls of their ancestors. As one who has felt the same mental move or impulse of laughter as my dead father's, I have sometimes wondered whether it was I or he that was feeling it. After all, when I wake in the morning my body is a slightly different one from the one that went to sleep the previous night; is the Tuesday subjectivity the same as the Monday one, or not? A continuous thread of life does, after all, link me to my father and mother, through his sperm and her egg, and back into his body and hers. If the thread that links me to my Monday body is a thicker one, is the validity of that connection not simply a matter of degree?

If we take human beings to be cultural entities, the same broad-bandwidth transmission of information is clearly taking place. It may be that the afterlife can only, and should only, be discussed in metaphorical, poetic, and artistic language, as all the great religious sages have done. Recently I visited the remarkable tombs of the Chinese emperors near Xian. One of the terra-cotta military officers, obviously a portrait of an individual, was standing in an immediately recognizable martial arts stance—in Japanese karate terms, *ko-kutsu dachi* or back stance. I had been trained by my own sensei, or teacher, in that same stance; his training lineage went back to Japan, then before that to Okinawa, to Fukien Province, to the Buddhist Shaolin Monastery, and back to the ancient Han warriors of imperial China. So the same information that was preserved in baked clay in the emperor's tomb had been passed down, faithfully, through a hundred generations of teachers, carefully inculcated and imitated, the master tapping the disciple with his bamboo *shinai*, making him settle into the correct dynamic form.

Or take a violinist, Midori, for instance; is not a ghost of Mozart's own thought passing through her ear and fingers as she plays? Or the actress playing Shakespeare's Rosalind, or that Hermione who is resurrected in Act V of *The Winter's Tale*—are they not replaying in the hardware of their brain tissue the software of Shakespeare's own poetic feeling? Shakespeare himself investigates these questions with unparalleled precision in the Sonnets; he promises his beloved in Sonnet 18 that

> . . . thy eternal summer shall not fade,
> Nor lose possession of that fair thou ow'st,
> Nor shall Death brag thou wand'rest in his shade
> When in eternal lines to time thou grow'st.
> So long as men can breathe and eyes can see,
> So long lives this, and this gives life to thee.

We today are reading those lines, so the reincarnation process has been going on for four hundred years at least. What is especially significant is that poetry is being described as a higher form of sexual reproduction. Both are what Shakespeare, in Sonnet 16, calls "the lines of life, that life repair." These lines of life are the lineage of a family that replaces the dying with the newborn. But they are also, in context, the lines that a portraitist uses to eternalize the features of a sitter; and they are, most fundamentally, the lines of poetry. It is as if he has guessed that the genetic code that specifies the shape of our bodies is a line or thread, like the long thread of letters that make up a poem. DNA is indeed a thread of nucleotides, which spell out the "words" and "sentences" of the genes, which in turn determine the proteins that make up the human body. The words in which this beautiful relationship is being conducted find for themselves a form of repeated rhymes and metrical rhythms that are able to reprint themselves in memory and books, as DNA does by peeling its double helix apart and printing the sequence of nucleotides anew upon the raw material within the cell. But poetry is a higher form of reproduction, for it can capture and preserve the mind and individuality of an organism, not just its bodily composition. Living reproduction can outwear the enduring metals and stone with which we build monuments to defy the effects of time. But poetry, which is even more spiritual, intangible, and apparently fragile, is more enduring still:

> Not marble, nor the gilded monuments
> Of princes, shall outlive this powrful rhyme,
> But you shall shine more bright in these contents
> Than unswept stone, besmeared with sluttish time.

(55)

What Shakespeare now does is *graft* the new, cultural form of reproduction upon the old, biological form:

> And, all in war with Time for love of you,
> As he takes from you, I engraft you new.

(15)

Thus poetry is to living reproduction what living reproduction is to the enduring hardness of the stone and metal out of which we build monuments to defy time's decay. Poetry is grafted onto natural inheritance, so that both the generic and unconscious elements of what we wish to preserve, and also the individual and self-aware elements, are protected.

Many religious theories of incarnation explicitly link the moral character of the soul that is reincarnated to the new receptacle of that soul—it is better to be reborn as a human than as an animal or plant. Perhaps there is a preference for the cultural mode of reincarnation over the biological, the biological over the merely thermodynamic. One who merely vibrates the world is less capable of printing his information upon a fellow human being than one who has managed to give his living seed to the world, and the mere breeder less capable than the person who through love and teaching and moral influence and friendship can find a place in the memories of his loved ones.

But these modes of reincarnation may be only anticipations of richer and stranger ones to come. In our fictional history of the cosmos, we imagined the era when our descendants come to find it incumbent on them to offer us resurrection. This one-time reincarnation might conceivably be followed by others, especially if in the first new body and era, despite the health and clarity and love that would come with biocybernetic enhancement, the evil shadows of past ill choices, hatreds, and persistent vices were not fully purged away. The Catholic doctrine of Purgatory might also fit in here. Perhaps death may be a necessary terminus for any meaningful life, and we must die and be resurrected several times until the final ingathering of the universe solves that last and greatest of all problems. Finally the perfected soul, qualified at last for the radical self-giving that would be required, might escape the wheel of karma, illusion, and desire, and pain, and come into full union with the divine Omega at the end and beginning of all things.

Perhaps there is a wisdom in the fact that many religions do not distinguish among these various species of reincarnation. Perhaps if the timeflow iterates itself as we have suggested, so that later transformations in our history are prefigured in a yearning, anticipatory way in earlier lives, and in turn subsume and echo in a deeper and finer music the rough hoarse minstrelsy of the earlier ones, the soul does not so much escape the wheel as become it, together with its own central point of paradoxical stillness. The vision of Shakespeare's lovers sometimes takes on this quality:

> What you do
> Still betters what is done. When you speak, sweet.
> I'ld have you do it ever; when you sing,
> I'ld have you buy and sell so, so give alms,
> Pray so; and, for the ordering your affairs,
> To sing them too: when you do dance, I wish you
> A wave o' the sea, that you might ever do
> Nothing but that; move still, still so,
> And own no other function: each your doing,
> So singular in each particular,
> Crowns what you are doing in the present deed,
> That all your acts are queens.

There is a tension in all religious traditions between the idea of the afterlife and a kind of resistance to it, a denial of a too-easy and over-literal interpretation of what lies beyond mortal life. In some forms of this resistance, the afterlife is downgraded in importance, so as to give a true value and dignity to this present life we are living and the crucial responsibilities and life opportunities that we might miss if we merely mooned and hankered after another world. Achilles in Hades would rather be a peasant and till the soil than rule over all the bloodless dead. Confucians imagine the ancestors not so much as enjoying paradise as watching anxiously over their descendants. Judaism does not make much of the afterlife, except inasmuch as it has been influenced by Christian and Greek ideas: for Jews the coming of the historical millennium is more important, and the perfecting of individual behavior that will bring it about. For some Buddhists and Hindus, who believe in reincarnation, resurrection in this sense can be an evil, a sign that the soul's pilgrimage is incomplete: the whole point is to escape the wheel of illusion and desire. Existentialists are explicit and severe on this matter: Wallace Stevens demands of his incipiently pious lady:

Why should she give her bounty to the dead?
What is divinity if it can come
Only in silent shadows and in dreams?
Shall she not find in comforts of the sun,
In pungent fruit and bright, green wings, or else
In any balm or beauty of the earth,
Things to be cherished like the thought of heaven?

Even Christianity has its doubts about the afterlife. Jesus warns repeatedly that whatever it's like, it's not what we expect: there will be neither marrying nor giving in marriage in heaven, he tells the woman at the well. And contrariwise, the Kingdom is wherever two or three are gathered together in his name—not elsewhere but, had we the eyes to see it, verily here. Protestant Christian ethics developed to the point where Kant and others could point out that virtuous behavior that was simply a base and mercenary instrument for getting into heaven and reaping its eternal rewards was not ethical in itself. Goodness ought to be its own reward, the good conscience was itself a state of heaven. If people refrain from evil only out of fear of hell, the evil remains within them, and a merely external notion of the joys of heaven rings increasingly hollow.

Perhaps all the religions are groping toward some notion of the larger dimension and significance of a human life as resting not in some mere continuation of this life, but in a deeper, richer experience, a diving inward rather than a new installment of the old soap opera. Are we in the afterlife simply going to go on voting Republican or Democrat, getting divorces, shaving, and watching television? But if not, without those distractions, how would we occupy ourselves given that we are so bored and so anxious in this life already?—when even now, as almost all religions assert, the gates of heaven are open to us if we but live rightly? We would have to be changed almost out of recognition: the very quality of time would have to be transformed. Perhaps the humanist-atheist assertion that we simply disappear when we die is a deep and mystical religious doctrine that we should take seriously: heaven, maybe, is the very here-and-nowness of every moment; we are immortal not at 180 degrees to the line of time, but at 90 degrees. Not so much an afterlife as a meanwhile-life, whose baseline is our life history but whose true extent is a sort of plane or volume extending out of it in another direction altogether. And if our descendants do resurrect us, that new timeline will just be an extension of the base, but not the endless depth of heaven itself.

But the religions that postulate a vigorous and lively afterlife, like Islam with its gardens and sweetmeats and houris for the good and its fiery hells for the wicked, also have a point. Whatever means the soul has for experiencing and acting is in a sense its body. Blake defined the body as that part of the soul that is "discern'd by the five senses, the chief inlets of Soul in this age." He is in a way echoing what Donne said to his mistress, in "The Ecstasy":

> As our blood labors to beget
> Spirits, as like souls as it can,
> Because such fingers need to knit
> That subtle knot, that makes us man:
>
> So must true lovers' souls descend
> T'affections, and to faculties,
> Which sense may reach and apprehend,
> Else a great prince in prison lies.
>
> To our bodies turn we then, that so
> Weak men on love revealed may look;
> Love's mysteries in souls do grow,
> And yet the body is his book.

The need for some analogue to a body does not necessarily mean that the afterlife must be the same as this one. But however different it is, it must still allow for meaningful experience, action, and identity if it is to deserve the word "life" at all. Consider the traditional idea of angels: granted that they are pure thought, if that thought is to be expressed and informed they must still find a shared medium through which to communicate with each other and to enact their intentions—a medium which because it is shared, and because different identities are indeed different, must offer a resistance that would feel not unlike the resistance of a material world. Even if there were no such medium to start with, the accumulated body of prior communications would constitute such a medium in itself. And for communication and action to express any truly subtle thought, the medium would have to be very rich and thick and eloquent, and would have therefore to be much like Nature as it is. Matter is the language in which the soul speaks, then: it is not enough to exist in the timeless Bohm computer, for such a quantum computer is in itself completely transparent, lacking any opacity where actuality can be arrested and registered; it is totally slippery, so that nothing can get purchase to push against anything else and so be able to move or be moved. We need the out-of-synch matter computer too. Matter is a denser and more factual form of spirit than probability waves are— and whatever offers the needed resistance, opacity, purchase *is* matter for all practical purposes, relative to wave functions. The Lady will have her flowers and olives after all. And this tension in all religions regarding the afterlife is perhaps itself an indicator of some deeper truth that we cannot quite see.

The Historical Religions

About half of the world's population—Jews, Christians, Muslims, and others who accept the Pentateuch as sacred scripture or Jesus as a premier moral authority—share a tradition in which God is on some level a single being, in which he has been engaged with human beings through historical events in a two-way conversation, and in which he will judge us all on the last day. Even among other religions, ideas that come out of the Judeo-Christian-Islamic tradition are pervasive; the United Nations Declaration on Human Rights probably could not have existed in its present form—and might not have been developed for thousands of years—without that tradition. The proverbial Martian would conclude that this is a God-worshipping planet whose history presents itself as in part a conversation with that God. In the Arab Catholic Mass, the word used to translate "God" is "Allah"; the Hebrew "Jehovah" is a normal Christian word for God, and Jesus is a great Muslim prophet. The major difference is over when God stopped having a direct historical and public conversation with humankind, that is when divine revelation was complete. Most Jews stop at about the end of the period represented by the Torah, most Christians stop with the ascension of Christ, most Muslims stop with the death of Mohammed, with some groups in all three major branches—the Latter-Day Saints, the Orthodox Jews who want to rebuild the Temple, and the Baha'is for instance—carrying the historical connection all the way through to modern times. If the peoples of the Book are still in the dark as to the divine as a whole, they have surely touched much of it that no other religion has been able to, and are even willing to agree on some of its larger-scale characteristics. We can, perhaps, safely assume that if in our fanciful premise all the religions are true, the world has a significant history, and God has been communicating with us through it.

The insistence among the mainstream of all three major branches as regards the end of divine revelation is by no means unambiguous or consistent. The Catholic catechism, for example, quotes the encyclical *Dei Verbum*: "'. . . no new public revelation is to be expected before the glorious manifestation of our Lord Jesus Christ.'" But it qualifies this statement in the next sentence: "Yet even if Revelation is already complete, it has not been made completely explicit: it remains for Christian faith gradually to grasp its full significance over the course of the centuries." It recognizes that some "'private'" revelations—its quotation marks, not mine—"have been recognized by the authority of the Church." The distinction between private and public is a fuzzy one, especially in religion. And if, as the Catechism insists elsewhere, God's plan has been unfolding coherently from the beginning of the world, and the redemption was already prefigured in the events of the Fall and in the sayings of the prophets, the distinction between revelation and the "making explicit" or "grasping the significance" of revelation becomes even more problematic than that between public and private. The life of Jesus was for Catholics and other Christians the definitive event in history; but it was also the making explicit and revealing the significance of the origin and history of the world.

One can well sympathize with the problems of a Church authority that wishes to discourage the wild tendencies of excitable and credulous human beings—Branch Davidians are but one example of what can happen when orthodox authority is abandoned—while trying to keep open God's own freedom to do as he sees fit. Dostoyevsky's Grand Inquisitor, confronting the horns of the dilemma, opts to crucify Christ again rather than permit the chaos of new revelation. Perhaps what we need is a greater recognition of the poetic richness and multivocality of God's characteristic style in all religions. The closer to the divine source, the odder and more metaphorical the language; the further from the source, the more legal and denotative it becomes—but the embodiment of the spiritual fire of the source in the words and concepts of a given era is itself part of the work of incarnation. And perhaps we also need to see that the tension between clinging on to the old verities and opening oneself up to new truths is a fertile evolutionary one: it is the tension between heredity and mutation. If we see the problem in these terms, we realize that a third factor is necessary to complete the process—selection: in this case, the testing of the new truth against the resistance of the old authority and against the disordered fecundity of less enduring novelties, in the crucible of human experience and history. This cycle of tradition, innovation, and selection is perhaps a glimpse into the very thought process of a triune God. The reassuring implication of this evolutionary model is that the old verities do not need to be false for the new to be true: we did not cease to be primates, mammals, vertebrates, chordates, or animals when we became humans.

The Christian Gospels contain an enormously important implication that is both clear and curiously ignored or muted in the teachings of most of the churches. Jesus leaves us with the promise of sending the Paraclete—literally, in Greek, "the one called to help." Yet in most Christian liturgy the Holy Spirit is tacked on, as it were, as an afterthought, after passages celebrating at length the glory of the Father and the Son. "Oh, and by the way, let's not forget the good old Holy Ghost" seems to be the general tenor; there are few prayers in the traditional Catholic and Protestant liturgies addressed primarily to the Spirit, fewer indeed than those whose primary addressee is the Virgin Mary or the Saints. Yet if we analyze the style and characteristic "plotting" of God's story of the world as Christians see it, it would be entirely out of character for him to have arranged a big anticlimax after the ascension of Christ. The redemption outdoes in drama and even importance the earlier creation and fall; if this is the third age, the era of the Paraclete, then surely it must be more marvelous still, and marked by a personal style not entirely the same as that of the Father and the Son. It would behoove us to pay more attention to the divine person who is with us now, as present among us as Jesus was, if we believe what Jesus says. One honorable exception to the general slighting of the Paraclete is the Pentecostal movement; they have clearly got hold of a part of the whole that is unknown to mainstream Christians, and their experience should be consulted.

If in Christian terms this is truly the era of the Paraclete, it means that the history of the world since the redemption must itself contain a message, a message that cannot be less than equal to the Gospel of Christ—if the Holy Ghost is indeed equal to the other two persons of God. If we look at that history from the vantage point of today, we notice one huge development: the astonishing progress of science, technology, and the human arts in general. That progress occurred chiefly in the parts of the world devoted to the Book and influenced by the life of Christ, while other civilizations lagged, or caught up only when exposed to the Gospel. The implication is that in Christian terms we might see progress in human art and science as the direct sign, the gospel, the very metabolism, of the Paraclete, the Helper.

Once we realize this, the tragic conflict between Islam and Christianity takes on a whole new aspect. As Gibbon rightly points out, Christianity was a factor in the dissolution and collapse of the Roman Empire, and the huge losses of scientific, technological, and scholarly knowledge that resulted. It took Islam, with its blunt insistence on the application of religious morality to public life, and its lively interest in science and technology, to rouse Christian Europe from its dogmatic slumber. Through Spain, Sicily, and Hungary came the Islamic spirit of invention, inquiry, empiricism, mathematical insight, (comparative) religious tolerance, and social justice. One of the great moments of human history was that time in Seville, Toledo, Salamanca, and Cordova when the brilliant young sages of Judaism, Islam, and Christianity were together laying the foundations of all the later philosophy of Europe, and reinventing its art and poetry. Correspondingly, one of the greatest tragedies in history was the expulsion of the Jews and Moors from Spain, in the same year that Columbus set eyes on the New World.

Perhaps the Holy Ghost was alive in the thought and revelation of Islam when it was asleep in Europe. The point is obscured to us now, because of the stagnation of Islam in the last two hundred years—strange how we always interpret the past of other peoples as if they had always been as they are now, while we accept as perfectly normal that our own civilization has gone through all kinds of changes and vicissitudes. Of all theological writings, those of Ibn Arabi seem to me to come closest to a truly satisfying account of the relationship between God and his universe. Though surely the torch of scientific inquiry passed into Christendom, Christendom must one day acknowledge its immense debt to Islam in bringing to it the first fruits of the gospel of the Paraclete.

The most ancient of the religions of history, Judaism might be the deepest taproot of human religion, our strongest and clearest connection with the whole creative history of the universe. Judaism's collective mythic memory goes back even before the Black Sea inundation, over seven thousand years ago, with hints in the Cain and Abel story of the dawn of the Neolithic revolution, when the farmer Cains replaced the hunter-gatherer Abels; there is even a kind of reflected whisper, in the story of Eden, of the time when humans first recognized their own uniqueness as animals and imagined their own personal death. There are remnants and fossils in the Hebrew scriptures and folk traditions of the polytheism out of which Jewish monotheism was born, and in the sacred mountains and talking snakes and burning bushes of its imagery, and its ancient practice of animal sacrifice, we can glimpse the animism of even more archaic periods. Judaism's own cultural roots pass through the two most ancient civilizations we know, the Mesopotamian and Egyptian, and, placed at the Mediterranean end of trade routes that stretched all the way to India and China, Israel had time and opportunity to absorb much of what those rich traditions had to teach as well. Judaism is not just the root of Christianity and Islam and all the other traditions deriving from the Bible, but also a living religious fact in the world. Even its most hostile enemies give it an important place in their eschatology. Jerusalem is at the fulcrum of Asia, Africa, and Europe. What happens to the Jews is not just another vicissitude of history but an event in the biography of the divine.

Thus the Holocaust and the establishment of the State of Israel must have a special place in the evolution of God, comparable to the giving of the tablets to Moses on Sinai, the appearance of the Buddha, and the birth and death of Christ. The Holocaust is a definitive sign, if one were needed, that the universe, which in our definition includes its divine soul, is as yet imperfect and at least incomplete—if not deeply flawed. The conception of the world as a sort of diorama arranged a few thousand years ago to test human souls in by an almighty, omniscient timeless God who is infinitely loving, a world with no alternative branchings, whose every detail has been foreseen, has severe difficulties if God is seen as standing by, preferring the integrity of his original plan, while the trains shuttle in to Auschwitz—or worse, if he created the world knowing in advance that Auschwitz would happen. It would look actually worse than a boy honestly tearing the wings off flies: it would be more like the boy who uses a magnifying glass to burn them, claiming that it was the sun's heat, not his own aiming of the glass, that burned them.

If we adopt the hypothetical theology of this book, three possible solutions to the problem present themselves. The first is that God's ethical ideas, though correct, are utterly incomprehensible to us—but if this is so, we simply cannot trust our consciences at all and might as well act completely at random or according to our own perceived narrow self-interest. Since our interpretation of scripture has obviously been so wrong, we cannot trust revelation either. The second is that the Holocaust was a near-fatal crisis in God's own evolutionary development, an unavoidable and explosive contradiction in his own nature that erupted in a bout of madness, a sort of divine mental breakdown in which several millions of his own key brain cells perished. This solution suggests that he is now healing, but also that he may be prone to developmental crises of other kinds, perhaps as terrible, in the future. The third solution is that God's work is severely and deeply opposed: in a branched-time universe such as the one I have sketched here, every branch has futures in which madness and evil have resulted from a chain of bad choices, and those diabolical futures have been attacking and infecting at strategic points the stem that will bring about the divine communion. Those old doctrines, common to Islam, Christianity, and Judaism alike—as well as to many other religions—that teach the existence of devils and evil spirits may make more sense than their cultured despisers give them credit for. Surely we have seen the devil in the last century, have we not? What could be a clearer demonstration of his reality?

Of these three solutions the first is inconsistent with the goodness of the divine that all religions agree upon; perhaps the second also. But the second and the third may be different ways of saying the same thing, depending on whether one looks at the divine from the past forwards, or the future backwards. If the universe's history is a sort of scaffolding within which God constructs himself, perhaps the scaffolding underwent partial collapse; but in another sense the building stands undamaged in its retroactive co-presence with its own history. In any case, the Holocaust, together with the foundation of the state of Israel, is surely an event in the world's religious history that could not be ignored in any hypothetical textbook written by angels in heaven after the world's history is complete. For Christians it must be part of the mystery of the incarnation itself. Pascal's Pensée number 102: "Either Jews or Christians must be wicked" cannot stand; Christendom has seen what anti-Semitism can mean. The Holocaust now exists as an irrefutable reproach against the exclusivity of any religion. Any Christian (or indeed Jew) who continues to insist on the falseness of all other religions is relying in bad faith upon a secular regime to protect others from himself, and himself from others—for if he is honest, he will recognize that the secular regime is itself a rival to his religion, and it is for him a crime against his god to continue to support that regime with votes and taxes. On the other hand, the magnitude of the Holocaust also has another implication: that Christianity itself, for good or ill, is a central fact in the spiritual history of the world. If hell on earth arose as some kind of perversion of Christianity—for Nazism, like Communism with its Gulag, emerged within the historical culture of Christendom—whatever it was that was perverted must have been the opposite of hell, and that opposite must be lodged somewhere in the Christian world picture.

The Catholic catechism suggests that revelation is complete; in Catholic terms either the encyclical *Dei Verbum* was not ex cathedra, and a radically new act in the drama of divine history has taken place in the last seven decades; or the Holocaust and the return of the Jews to Israel are a previously unrecognized implication in the sacred scriptures and the redemptive plan of Christ. Perhaps a turning point was passed some time in the twentieth century; perhaps the era of the Holocaust, the Gulag, and Hiroshima *was* the Apocalypse, and if we have survived it—if it is indeed over—then we *have already* entered a new era, the Millennium. It would of course come like a thief in the night. Judging by the reaction of all previous religious authorities to the emergence of a new phase in the human experience of the divine, surely one of the identifying hallmarks of that moment would be that few would recognize it, especially not the authorities—and this is central to the authorities' *own* account of the matter. Yet a few poets, such as Yeats and Radnóti, did prophesy the apocalypse—and the foretelling of an event by poets is one of the signs of its significance, the future whispering backwards across the corridors of time.

One of the uncomfortable surprises of Judaism, obscured from us both by familiarity and by a convenient bureaucratic distinction between the sacred and the profane, is the fact that the word for prophet is the word for poet. The prophets, like poets today or of any time, were self-appointed ranters, who spoke in symbols, allusions, stories, and songs; not necessarily functionaries of any religious organization, and often despised as naïve, disorderly, or malcontent by all right-thinking people. Israel recognized early on that poets were the seers and conscience of its culture, even though at any given time it is almost impossible to tell the genuine ones from the fakes. True prophets and poets, in terms of the hypothesis of this book, really do hear voices from the future.

I was talking a few years ago to a friend of mine in Jerusalem; I had just returned from a walk through the old city, and had attended an Arab Catholic Mass just off the Via Dolorosa, in which I was struck by the fact that the word "Allah" was used for God. I was describing the project of this book to my friend—who is a devout Orthodox Jew—and he said something really quite remarkable. He reminded me of the three prophecies that would have to come true if the Millennium were to come. First, the Jews would have to return to Israel. This had now happened. Second, the temple would have to be rebuilt. My friend believed that this too had been accomplished: it was the Golden Mosque. Was there a more beautiful and fitting building in the world to be the temple? Was it conceivable that under any political circumstances, short of another holocaust, it could be torn down? Third, he said, sacrifices would once more have to be offered to God in Jerusalem. And this too was now happening; every day, he said, in all the Christian churches in the city, Christians were sacrificing the body of Christ to his divine father. Wouldn't it be just like Elohim, the "God who is multitudes" of the prophets, to bring about the fulfillment in precisely the way that would most annoy the rabbis and mullahs and patriarchs and cardinals? And wouldn't it be interesting if the real virtue of the millennium were not that it would be sunk in a boring and vapid unanimity, but that it would be a fascinating, incomplete, and continuous controversy, like a lively Yeshiva, in which God's justice would be alive in every moment of the debate? Perhaps one day Jerusalem will be the new Seville, where the astronomers will trace the finger of the Omega in the fiery birth of the Alpha, and where a single poem might be written in three languages, Hebrew, Arabic, and English.

But in terms of the fanciful history outlined in this book, one source of disagreement might be rendered less divisive: whether God is one or three. Judaism and Islam both suspect the Christian doctrine of the trinity of being a polytheism in disguise, and forbid images of persons in their holy places in order to head off what they regard as an atavistic human tendency. But if Christians are seeing an earlier stage in the coalescence of the divine, and Muslims and Jews a later stage, and if on the quantum computer level both stages are copresent with every moment of history, the contradiction no longer exists. There might still be a milder kind of controversy, of the kind that could be fertile of art and poetry: whether the earlier stage or the later stage has more richness and perfection as a representation of the divine. This might be a contest also entered by polytheists and animists, who would contend that the later stages of the divine are just summations and generalizations of its vital, turbulent, and multitudinous youth. Such indeed is the gist of those conservative classical Roman and Greek responses to the new philosophical monotheism that regarded it as a watering down of the old immediate polytheistic religion. Monotheists might respond in turn that the "gods of the nations" as the Old Testament calls them should rightly bow down to their true destiny, their raison d'être, their posterity. But the religions would need no longer automatically be rendered enemies by radical incommensurability.

The Meditative Religions and Spirit Healing

Every religion offers in little, as it were, at least an undeveloped sketch of what any other religion professes. In the angels and saints, for instance, Christianity gives a taste of polytheism; in the Buddhist insistence on compassion there is a hint of Christian love; in the dancing of the Hasids there is a trace of the collective ritual ecstasy of Umbanda or the black Baptists. But each religion seems to have strengths and expertise, so to speak, in some special area. One will have a richer body of myth; another, more beautiful and expressive rituals; another, lovelier poetry; another, wider or deeper roots in history; another, a loftier philosophical theology; another, a subtler and finer ethical tradition; yet another, a deeper understanding of the body and its mysteries. The disciplines of meditation have perhaps been the special forte of the great Asian religions, especially Hinduism and Buddhism. There are indeed magnificent traditions of mysticism in Judaism, Islam, and Christianity. But in the Upanishads, the Bhagavad Gita, and the sermons of Buddha, and the thousands of pages of commentary and thousands of years of refined practice, the south Asians have given the human race an extraordinary and unique body of resources for humans to realize their direct contact with the divine.

One of the central insights of Southeast Asian mysticism is that the body can be an instrument of that contact. Much of the European mystical tradition has been devoted to bypassing or suppressing the distractions of the flesh. Asceticism has been taken as a way of neutralizing the damage of the Fall. But the breathing, chanting, sitting, stretching, ink-drawing, walking, and martial arts disciplines of India, Tibet, China, Japan, and other cultures of the area transform the body into the very antenna by which we can recognize the flow of the divine thought through us. The mandala, with its concentric geometrical frames, replicates and thus entrains the brain's own internal feedback system, its hall of mirrors, its consciousness of its own consciousness being conscious of its own consciousness, that on one hand constitutes our profoundest experience of duration and sentient being, and on the other stuns the mind into a blur whose rich texture is the ground of subjectivity. Chanting, mantras, and the rhythm of Zen breathing or of Tai Chi accomplish in the acoustic and kinetic worlds what the mandala does in the visual. A delicate attunement or calibration results, so that the complex system of the human brain can model in a crude and simple way the immense and bottomless strange attractor of the divine mind. The adept then becomes a fractal miniature of the universal mind itself.

Asian theory of brain states—for instance, the Upanishadic distinction among the four states of awakeness, dream, deep sleep, and meditation (which combines all three of the others), and the resultant techniques by which the meditator can control them—anticipates by millennia current neurophysiological findings about brain rhythms, neurochemistry, and biofeedback. Indeed, it may be that Christian faith healing, and the spirit healing that is practiced all over the world, may receive its most sensitive analysis from studies that are even now being done on the ancient arts of acupuncture and acupressure. It is becoming clear that the state of a person's soul— by which I mean here no more than that person's mental and moral well-being and psychological balance—can have a profound effect on that person's emotions, which involve neurochemicals that in turn help to calibrate, attune, and activate a person's immune system and thus resistance to disease. The meridians and zones that an acupuncturist uses are based on theories of the flow of Ch'i that were once thought to be mere superstition. Now, however, the NIH is giving serious attention to these ancient empirical therapies. All the body's cells share with the brain cells the properties of irritability, habituation, and adaptation, and are thus, though on a much cruder level, participants in the nervous system's neural network. The whole body thinks and feels, and changes itself slowly in response. Perhaps the meridians of acupuncture map the domains of the body's original fetal development plan, each body area a sort of gerrymandered jigsaw piece controlled by a single HOX (homeobox) gene, every cell sharing a special attunement to other members of its own genetic-developmental lineage.

Christianity, Islam, and Judaism, not to speak of the many religions throughout the world that have not had the advantages of thousands of years of civilized study, recorded wisdom, and large-scale collective development, have much to learn from the Asian somatic-mystical traditions. That learning has in fact already begun, and will in the future coalesce, in ways that are fascinatingly unpredictable, with the emerging technologies of neurochemistry, neuro-cybernetic interfacing, neurosurgery, and genetic engineering. This may be one of the ways in which the present damaging rift between our spiritual life and our activities as a brilliant innovative technological species can be healed. The body is the sacrament that all humans share; it is the place where all our contexts must come together. The genius of Christianity is that it recognizes this in a special way, in the mystery of the incarnation: the center of its worship is a man, a carpenter, who is also God; a man whose physical body is the instrument of our salvation on the sawn and mitered wood of the cross. Perhaps Christians can redeem part of the promise of salvation through the body by learning from the Asian religions the neurobiological technology of contemplation. Consider the lilies of the field.

Transcendence and Time

Some religious readers may at this point, if they have not already, complain that in the effort to include the many religions that are anchored in nature and the body, and to square our reading of religion with the findings of science, the transcendent element of religion has been slighted. Even if we accept that such concepts as timelessness, infinity, substance, eternity, omniscience, and so on are relatively late and thus inessential theological inventions—at least in their mathematical-logical definitions—the sense of the divine as beyond all earthly things is in danger of being lost. The mathematical analogies of the infinite number series or the nondimensionality from which an eternal being looks down on the dimension of time may be false and misleading, but they were honest attempts to get at the otherness, the strangeness, the nontemporality of the divine. There is something, such critics might insist, that cannot be renormalized about God.

This is an important and in many ways valid objection; or it would be if the divine we are describing is essentially and only immanent in the physical world. But perhaps what a more comprehensive way of looking at religion and its central reality gives us is not a denial of divine transcendence but a better set of metaphors for it: instead of an abstract transcendence we get a concrete transcendence; instead of a beyondness that is also beyond quality, beyond human morality, love, feeling and personhood, we get a beyondness that is the very heart of those characteristics. The image of God that we get from the abstract mathematical metaphors of infinity and eternity—unlimited independence of time or space, limitless ductility, ubiquity, presentness—what Michel Foucault called the Panopticon, the nightmare of total optical clarity with no opacity or color or shape—is one which achieves transcendence at the cost of some of the very things that make the divine divine. The nature of the *via negativa* is to name God by what he is not. The risk of such naming is the same risk as the risk of naming him by what he is, which is idolatry. The value of such negative metaphors—timeless, unextended, and so on—is that they do indeed catch the stunned, dizzy sensation one sometimes gets in contemplation of God; but perhaps, like the image of intoxication sometimes used for mystical experience, it is equating the privation of sensation—drunkenness—with its excess—the beatific vision. Perhaps God's milieu is not less densely saturated with time than ours, but more. Perhaps God is not less physically real than we, but more. Perhaps God is not less extended than we, but extended in far more dimensions, a concreteness that is beyond our relatively abstracting senses to grasp. Limit is what gives character and shape to something; perhaps God has more character and shape than anything else, indeed sums up all character and shape, and thus is the very quintessence of limit.

Consider the following two ways of imaging the experience of the divine. The first is Pascal's way, the way of the age of reason: it is the aporia and stumbling that we feel when we think about nonlocality, about an infinitely distant viewpoint for which all times and places are present, about infinite power and knowledge. The silence of those infinite spaces terrifies him. Such an experience crushes us in precisely the ways that by other injunctions of religion we are required to behave and perceive; it crushes our kindness, our truthfulness, our virtue, our love—why should we be concerned with such petty things?—while it does not increase our humility unless we really thought or wished that we might be infinitely big, distant, long-lasting, knowledgeable, or powerful.

The second way of imaging the divine is the way my dog images me. To my dog, there are definitely aspects of me that are quite understandable: it knows what I am doing when I am eating, sleeping, relieving myself, walking, even sometimes playing. To that extent I am part of my dog's time and space, I share his limitations. But there are other things I do that are almost completely beyond his comprehension—when I read, talk to my wife (though there is a word or two he catches), answer my email, remember my dead friends, pray, listen to music, write poetry, operate machinery. To my dog, master is doing that weird human shit again. When I am involved in them I might very well appear to be outside time and space. I am ubiquitous on the telephone, I engage in very precise telepathy with my friends, I perform terrifying miracles with the vacuum cleaner and the leaf-blower, I am the master of the divine vehicle itself, which sometimes takes him up and allows him the mystical joys of leaning out of the window and smelling everything simultaneously as I drive. When I write and read there is no dog language for it: it's ineffable. And yet all those human things I do are not less of time, not less of space, not less limited and shaped: they are actually more temporal, more spatial, shaped by subtler rules and constraints and limits—and thus more expressive—than the dog can comprehend. My experience is not less one of anxious and delightful tension and complexity than his—though my physical calm when reading or writing might lead him to suppose it is—but more. I am not a smoothed-out and featureless and perfected kind of mammal, but a more complexly knotted, more iteratively self-reflective one. Those things I do that he doesn't understand, moreover, don't make me less an understanding and gentle master, but more. The mysterious insight I have into what he likes, what makes him happy, where he wants to be scratched, comes exactly from that place where he can't follow what is going on. The peace of his lord, that passes all understanding, is for me a complex balance of emotional and mental forces that are enormously evolved versions of his own mammal ones.

Which image actually catches better the experience of divine transcendence? If the second is of at least equal validity with the first, the point is made. What if God is beyond us as I am beyond my dog? not as the infinite to the finite, but as whole to part? What if the divine transcendence is precisely God's vast inhabiting of a flaming and branched candelabrum of futures, his breaking out of any moment into all its consequences; what if he is not less temporal than I, but more? What if his space is a greater depth or intricacy or fine-laced self-similar richness, rather than the barren waste of the infinite number series? What if, in mathematical terms, it is not his infiniteness but his nondenumerability that better characterizes him? Today we have the most marvelous images of the results of iterative feedback systems, whose fractal attractors reveal depth below depth at every scale: what if this interiority—limited as it might be by the boundaries of the phase space in which it is inscribed—were a more accurate picture of God? The Muslims are perhaps right to image God's transcendence not in terms of stunning size, but in terms of an intricate tilework or laciniated cloisonné that catches his indwelling, his depth rather than his height.

Perhaps in this recension of fundamental theology, we have replaced the old idea of eternity, as at 90 degrees to the flow of time, with the idea of the future—or rather, a fan of futures springing out from every present, weaving themselves into a rich fabric through a recursive self-pruning and self-grafting. But does not this conception preserve the depth and transcendence of eternity, of the *illo tempore*, while giving it a substance and concreteness lacking in the mathematical abstraction, and involving us as moral actors in the weaving of its very fabric? And if it seems odd and cumbersome compared with the simplicity of a line with an infinite number of points, were we not looking for an irreducible complexity in the first place?

For those who are determined to keep the eternal present of the philosophical theologians, there is still room in our picture of the universe for that conception. For after all, the quantum Bohm computer is an exact image of a premordial, timeless, untroubled medium of pure connectivity. Eternity is still there, under Mrs. Ramsay's shawl. And if we want to dismiss the shawl—the passionate sacrificial integument of matter that the quantum medium extrudes itself into, and the still lovelier needlework of living beings and imaginary landscapes that are embroidered into it—we can.

Prayer and Personal Religion

Some religions do not conceive of the divine as personal at all. Others do not see any sense in trying to communicate with it even if it is in some way like a person, because it is so infinitely beyond us, and because anything we might say or ask would already be apparent to God who already has, moreover, things of infinitely greater importance to deal with. What is man that thou shouldst be mindful of him? Other religions again communicate with God or the gods publicly and formally, as a community might address its king or overlord or protector, but would not venture on a one-on-one conversation, as being at least disrespectful, possibly dangerous, and perhaps ineffective without the established channels of sacrifice and ritual.

What the religions of personal prayer bring to the understanding of the divine is indispensable. The point is not that it is wrong to image God as an impersonal entity, any more that it is wrong for an ergonomicist, economist, surgeon, nutritionist, lawyer, pollster, or abstract artist to treat a human being as an impersonal entity; we are indeed such entities, as well as many other things besides. We are likely to understand each other better if, when it is relevant to do so, we can put aside personalities and concentrate on our physical or statistical or legal aspects. But we are also persons; and the insight of the personal religions is needed for as complete a picture as we can get of the divine, just as of the human. It would be inconceivable if the largest and most comprehensive integrated emergent structures in the universe, able to control their environments and themselves—that is, divine beings—should not possess at least the characteristics of consciousness and intention that even midsize components of them, that is, human beings, claim as a matter of course. Among the basic characteristics of persons, as far as we can judge by human beings, are an interest in personal contact and above all a capacity to love. If God is a person or persons, then a love for other persons would be a likely divine characteristic.

The religious groups with the greatest talent for personal loving contact with the divine come in many types: polytheists or ancestor worshippers who take one aspect of the divine and establish an intimate and even homey relationship with it, tending the shrine with honey and rice and wine; Catholic or Orthodox worshippers who encounter the divine through saints, the Virgin Mary, or other mediators; Catholic, Orthodox, and Jewish mystics who venture direct contact with God in personal mental conversation, but whose relationship is one of virtual disappearance of the human into the divine; and Protestants whose relationship is a passionate and familial one, like that of a child with a parent. Perhaps this last—the worship of fundamentalist Baptists and the born again—is the most radically personal of all. Arjuna in the Bhagavad Gita seems to combine all of them: to him Krishna is variously the dearest of personal friends, a perfectly saintly human being, a god among gods, the mediator with the one God, that one God himself, and the very ground of being.

A personal relationship with the divine takes place through prayer. We know what our side of that dialogue sounds like; what about the other side? How, in other words, might prayers be answered? If we subscribe to the philosophical definitions of the divine established in the Enlightenment, it would be hard to imagine how they might be answered at all. Those definitions are economically summed up by Voltaire, quoting Lucilio Vanini, in the *Philosophical Dictionary*:

> God is his principle and his end, . . . eternal without being in time, present everywhere without being anywhere. No past or future exists for him, he is everywhere and beyond everything, governing everything, and having everything, immutable, infinite without parts; his power is his will . . .

Ironically, Vanini was an atheist when he gave this description of his views to his inquisitorial accusers; and Voltaire may have been too when he quoted it with approval as a theologically sound and correct statement of the then-orthodox position. How such a God might hear, would listen to, or be disposed to answer, a human prayer—or how he even *could* answer granted that all of time would already lie spread out beneath him, immutable and unswerving, and granted that he is not a physical cause—doesn't seem to be given in the logic of the definition. Thus to those aspects of the divine—perhaps those involved in the quantum Bohm computer—it might not make sense to address prayers.

In the fanciful theology we have sketched here, however, prayers might very well be answered in a variety of ways, and thus it would make sense to make them in the first place. In order for prayers to be answered, they must first be heard. What element of the divine as sketched here, the mind of which the universe is the body, could hear a prayer? The Bohm computer might not hear—because there could be no place where the "buck" of information could stop, be interrogated, allow its virtual state of superimposition to be collapsed into actual yesses and noes. Nor would the universal quantum computer be able to reply, for the same reason—it could not make up its mind, it would act like the *deus absconditus* or "otiose God" of some religious traditions. But the quantum plenum, the Bohmian "implicate order" would be an indispensable medium of such communication, connecting our thoughts instantaneously with the divine at dif-

ferent times and different levels of spatial integration. The damaged
Turing computer might very well be influenced by prayer, weighing
as it does all forms of information, and might indeed amplify our
devout wishes in amazing ways, that would look like magical re-
plies to prayer. But it is the distributed "genetic algorithm" computer, itself composed of souls and comprising a great soul, that
might hear our words as friend, comforter, or parent.

Perhaps we could imagine various ways by which prayer might
be addressed and answered. Public prayers and rituals would actively realign the semantic systems of the local cultural superorganism—the village, the trading district, the language community—and
would, as has been shown in the case of the rice-paddy ecosystem
of Bali, help tune the relationship between the natural ecology and
the human part of it. Acts of sacrifice would behave like markers,
altering the local informational medium so as to increase the probability of a given result. The Turing thinkers in our part of the local
divine medium—the natural language of the sacrificers, the local
ecosystems, the pricing system of the economy—would be involved
in the informational task of calculating the next event and would
naturally incorporate our thoughts and desires into their own processes. And the very articulation and statement of those desires and
thoughts would reinforce their channels—would selectively weight
their synapses, so to speak—so as to conform. Rupert Sheldrake
and others have noticed the odd effect that a thought conceived in
one place is immediately more thinkable elsewhere: the worldwide
human phenomenon of continually rising scores on standardized
intelligence tests is one indicator of this "morphogenetic field," as
he calls it.

But such are the most primitive, the most "magical," of all prayer-
answers, and do not require much in personal contact between the
worshipper and the god. If we take prayer to be reasonably like a
real request by one person to another, based on a relationship and
complied with by a generous donor—a model common to a large
number of religions—then we must look further. We must imagine a
later developmental stage of the divine that has received a petition
from out of its own past. The constraints imposed by the presence of
competing timelines relative to the past moment in question, and by
the physical difficulties of so altering the quantum medium as to
affect past events, would, oddly enough, demand of the divine donor a sort of economic calculation. How to give what has been asked

without compromising the providential plan by which the donor him-self—or herself—has come to be? How to avoid so huge an ex-pense—of whatever enabling energy is required in that era to alter the universe—as would render impossible the final and initiating task, the tweaking of the Big Bang's own parameters so as to gener-ate a viable world? Depending on the urgency and rightness of the request, the divine ability to help might take different levels of re-sponse.

Most radical of all would be to spend whatever it takes. The di-vine patron would squander its resources in a direct effort to alter the quantum medium of the world and by this means manipulate the past. This sacrifice of power and efficacy would only be justified by the most severe need, and would be very expensive. True miracles, the anachronistic insertion of highly advanced technologies into an archaic time period, would fall into this category. If we accept this version of divine intervention, then the recruitment and incarnation of Christ, the choice of the Virgin Mary, the angelic annunciation, and her impregnation with a genetic pattern able to produce a divine human being, would have been the most costly of such interven-tions. The prayers of millions, both before the incarnation for a mes-siah, and after it in thanks and praise, would be answered. Divine sacrifice would at once be involved, articulated in the crucifixion and the resurrection as the iconography of the divine lamb bearing a cross eloquently expresses. Let us recall the old Celtic crosses in Galicia in Northwest Spain on which the adult divine Christ is crucified on one side, and the Virgin and Child are crucified on the other. Galaxies will perhaps be wounded or extinguished in the future to pay the great ran-som—especially if intelligent life has arisen on a million planets and each one requires a redeemer, a Christ of its own. The tradition that the Virgin was impregnated through the ear would suggest in this reading the method by which her extraordinary parthenogenesis was achieved: our organs of hearing, by which we recognize the mean-ing of speech, are the chief way we understand and know. The Vir-gin, in this fable of ours, would have received a package of *informa-tion*, perhaps first affecting the hormone production of the pituitary, thalamus and thymus, system in the brain, and then reprogramming the ovary to produce the appropriate fertile egg.

A less expensive policy of answering prayers would involve a sort of cost-benefit analysis. Prayers of the urgent and anguished kind, in which the devotee is not tactful about the desperation of his need, would put the divine patron in a difficult position. God would have to second-guess the outcome of an intervention, its opportunity cost against the increase of goodness in the world that might result within the new branchings of time that would be opened up. And the worshipper whose prayer was answered would, in a sense, be morally endangered by too explicit a reply to his prayer, since the implication would be clear that the future of that person was already mapped out in advance, and thus his moral choices would lose some of their meaning and spontaneity. But the temporal paradoxes and infinite regresses that would be invited by interventions that would affect the very past of the intervener might themselves have a profound moral and spiritual significance. There would be a transtemporal market of exchanges, whose radical nonlinearity and feedback would guarantee a nondeterministic providence, and would constitute the freedom of both partners, divine and human.

But this sort of prayer—"impetration" as the theologians call it— is the kind which to some extent twists God's arm, so to speak. A wiser kind of prayer is perhaps the one that only seeks participation in the ongoing realization of the universe, with faith in the goodness of its providence. The answer to such prayer might involve only small expense, the brilliant glow in the mind and heart of the worshipper that simply tells her that her voice has been heard. There would be little or no violation of the integrity of the time-stream— that is, the free will of the worshipper would not be threatened— since the worshipper could perfectly well attribute the joy of the experience to natural psychological factors.

Our analysis of the nonlinear nature of time suggests that prayer and meditation may well initiate a remarkable kind of nonlinear complex system that would result in a deepening of the universe itself, a new direction of time. The worshipper is being affected by the thoughts of God, millions of years after the moment of prayer, and the world of the worshipper is being subtly altered by her mental state. The world so altered is helping to bring about the maturing of that very God with whom the worshipper is in contact; even the tiniest change can through the butterfly effect accumulate over such huge durations into a large and significant difference. Thus a gigantic feedback loop is being completed; the worshipper is being changed by a God whose own emergence is partly enabled by the worshipper's disposition, which is in turn being reinforced by the fresh access of grace made available by the heightened probability of the divine being's emergence. Thus prayer and meditation can be like making love, in which the increased ardor of each lover is the occasion of the other's increase of ardor; as Shakespeare puts it in "The Phoenix and the Turtle":

> So they loved, as love in twain
> Had the essence but in one:
> Two distincts, division none:
> Number there in love was slain.
>
> Hearts remote, yet not asunder;
> Distance and no space was seen
> 'Twixt the turtle and his queen;
> But in them it were a wonder.
>
> So between them love did shine
> That the turtle saw his right
> Flaming in the phoenix' sight:
> Either was the other's mine.
>
> Property was thus appalled,
> That the self was not the same;
> Single nature's double name
> Neither two nor one was called.

My Christian Bias

As a practicing Catholic I might be open to the charge of bias in this survey of the contributions to understanding that have been made by various religions. If so, I must plead guilty. For me, with my own cultural background, temperament, and moral training, Christianity has a unique role among the world's religions. Christ's mission is, I believe, unique, at any rate for this planet and this species of intelligent beings; and if on other planets there is the need for the Word of God to die to bring salvation, then that Word is in some sense the same person as Jesus was, and all those redemptions are bound up into one. I think I can without mental reservation affirm every article of the Creed; my understanding of it, I am sure, is different from that of most Vatican theologians; but theirs are no doubt different in lesser ways from each other, and different in larger ways from that of a devout Mexican farmer or Goan merchant or Nigerian priest or German Catholic philosopher; and all would be very different from that of the bishops gathered at Nicaea in 325 A.D. Perhaps I have even bent over backwards in this book, and been somewhat more critical of Christianity than I have been of other religions; but for me Christianity sums up all other religions, and its historical and political flaws are the flaws of the human race.

Christianity's overwhelming emphasis on the importance of love seems right to me. Its explicit continuity with Judaism, and acceptance of the core of Jewish belief, is a powerful sign of its large grasp of the truth, as is the corresponding generous acceptance of much of the Christian message by Islam. Christianity, especially Catholic Christianity, shows a nice balance of rich physical ritual, intellectual rigor, personal worship, wide welcome among the world's peoples, profound moral understanding, and unmistakable historical stature. Could one imagine a final universal human religion that ignored Christianity as a central fact in the history of the world? Its peculiar trinitarian form of polytheistic monotheism, together with its embrace of saints and angels, gives it some of the intimacy and immediacy of traditional folk religions, polytheism, animism, and ancestor worship. Christianity's ready availability to syncretistic combinations of ritual, myth, and language is a sign of its universality. The tension between uncompromising Protestant insistence on unmediated contact between the human and the divine, and the more easygoing Catholic affection for mediators and sacraments, helps keep both traditions honest.

Thus readers of other faiths must forgive me; no doubt my ignorance makes me partial, and were I to have inherited the rich perspectives of Islam, Hinduism, or the Tao I might prefer them. But in my defense I could point out that many of my Christian brothers and sisters would be horrified at my acceptance of the Sufis and the Buddha as my spiritual masters, my insistence that they too are unique parts of the great mystery; and perhaps still more appalled by my heathen love of local gods and nature spirits. For me the conversation between Krishna and Arjuna is the most profound of all descriptions of the relationship between the human and the divine. In many ways the Taoist tradition comes, for me, the closest of all the traditional religions to a full and deep understanding of natural evolution as a central religious fact, an understanding that Teilhard de Chardin tried to reveal to Christians. The visual vocabulary of the Native American religions is to my eye the boldest and most radical attempt at grasping the terrible beauty, the utter strangeness of the divine. Compared with the African religion I remember from my youth, all other religions seem abstract and bloodless. I have seen more perfect and authentic joy in the faces of some of the lamas I have met than in any other human being. No religion, traditional or newfangled, seems to me to be lacking in some striking and unrepeatable insight into the nature of God. And the humanism I was raised in, with its noble passion for the rights of humanity, the integrity of science, the liberation of the human person, and the existential sufficiency of the present moment, is indispensable to me as well, and I would be a lonely and bitter man in a Christianity that lacked it. If this book has a fundamental purpose, I suppose it is to give myself and others of similar temperament a sound and convincing justification to have our cake and eat it too.

10

The Style of God

The Real Presence

Consider the Catholic sacrament of the Eucharist. For centuries the theological insistence that it really is the body and blood of Christ was a scandal to enlightened philosophical Westerners—an even greater scandal than it was to other world religions. How could bread and wine be body and blood? Voltaire, for instance, is scathing; attributing his own scorn to the Protestants, he says:

> They are quite unrestrained about this belief, which they call monstrous. They do not even think that a single sensible man could embrace it seriously after reflection. It is, they say, so absurd, so opposed to all the laws of physics, so self-contradictory that not even god could perform this operation, because it is in effect to annihilate god to suppose that he does contradictory things. Not only a god in bread, but a god in place of bread; a hundred thousand crumbs become in a flash as many gods, this innumerable crowd of gods forming only one god; whiteness without a white body; roundness without a round body; wine changed into blood which has the taste of wine; bread changed into flesh and fibre which have the taste of bread: all this inspires so much horror and contempt in the enemies of the catholic, apostolic and Roman religion that this excess of horror and contempt sometimes becomes rage. ("Transsubstantiation" in the *Philosophical Dictionary*)

But in the light of contemporary chemistry and physics the joke may well be on Voltaire. The atoms that made up Jesus' body would quickly have become distributed, by the carbon, nitrogen, and water cycles, throughout the Earth's biosphere, and would certainly have done so by the time the Church gave its final Tridentine definition of the doctrine of transubstantiation. Roughly eighty tons of matter would have cycled through Jesus' metabolism during his lifetime, made of precisely the elements of carbon, oxygen, hydrogen, nitrogen, etc. that are least likely to be sequestered, and join most actively in the volatile circulation of the ecosystem. Indeed, every wafer of communion bread does indeed contain several million at-

oms that were once part of Christ's body. The disciples at the Last
Supper would have actually have been consuming live skin cells
sloughed off Christ's hands as he broke the bread. On a more fundamental level of physics, if matter is made of energy, and energy is a
field distortion of space-time, and all fields in the universe are in
harmonic resonance with one another—and are thus partly constitutive of one another, as contemporary physics maintains—then every
subatomic particle of the communion wafer is partly constituted of
the body of Christ. The Eucharist is, in fact, not a mystery at all in
the strict factual sense.

It remains, however, a mystery in another sense, which offers us a
piercing glimpse into the rhetoric, the way of making meaning, the
style or metaphorical strategy of the divine in all religions. If the
bread and wine are in an everyday physical sense the body and
blood of Christ, the real mystery is what difference the words of the
consecration make when the priest pronounces them over the altar.
What religion maintains is that how we *take* the everyday miracle of
our conscious life in the universe is as much a fact as anything else.
Thus, although the bread and wine are equally, in a factual sense,
the body and blood of Nero, Shakespeare, Lady Murasaki and Attila
the Hun, our performative act of stipulation makes it, in the mental
survival phase space of Table 1, "hyperspace 2," the body and blood
of Jesus in particular. For the purposes of that phase space it is indeed exclusively Christ's body. Speech acts, as J.L. Austin has shown,
can very handily perform certain kinds of realities into being, as
when a couple create their marriage with the words "I do," the dealer
in poker makes red threes wild by simply saying they are, a scientist
names a new element, and Congress and president sign a bill into
law. The only limits to this activity is whether the existing laws of
physics, chemistry, etc.—which themselves were performed into being at certain moments in the evolution of the Big Bang—resist the
speech act, or if the speech act can survive in the context of other
human performative communities that have different conditions for
legitimate stipulation. We cannot by a speech act prevent ourselves
from falling if we step off the edge of the twentieth floor, nor compel
a group of Muslims to share our own speech act that makes the
bread flesh for us. But as we have seen, nature's laws do not resist
the description of the bread as Christ's flesh; and other performative
communities are simply not interested in whether the bread is flesh—
they do not inhabit the same piece of mental phase space. The Real

Presence of Christ is definitively and exclusively true for Catholics in all the senses they claim for it. But it is so in a somewhat mysterious way, that illuminates in a flash the odd metaphorical nature of religious truth.

Voltaire's mistake is instructive. It is not that as a man of the Enlightenment he was applying the faculty of reason to religious matters where it did not belong. For *he* was not the one who started that game: the Tridentine Church had already entered the arena of logical definition and standardized axiom, and issued its challenge. It was not Voltaire's fault that the terminology of substance and accidents and so on, that underpinned the doctrine of transubstantiation, was becoming increasingly threadbare as empirical science progressed. Given the obsolete philosophical language and definitions of the then official Church doctrine, Voltaire was probably right in poking fun at it. Nor can the mistake be blamed entirely on the Council of Trent and the rationalizing polemic of the Catholic counter-reformation. The Church was trying in its own century to express its deposit of faith in the terms of its time, as it is forever charged to do. Those terms were a mixture of medieval scholastic logic and renaissance literalism, but they were alive and imaginatively vital at the time. Perhaps the mistake was to throw, in the stress of contestation with the Protestants, the full authority of the Church behind those axioms and definitions, and thus to freeze its own mind into the shape that a live and volatile debate had taken at a particular moment of history.

The Poetic Idiom of the Divine

Both Voltaire and the theologians were missing the point about the nature of true religious language. One can tell fairly easily whether a piece of religious language is genuine or not: if it continues to apply with piercing insight to people across a wide variety of cultures and a long succession of historical periods. The parables of Jesus apply everywhere; the Last Supper has as much meaning in Japan or the headwaters of the Amazon as it does in Europe or Palestine. Likewise the Bhagavad Gita, Buddha's Fire Sermon, and the Tao Te Ching.

Let us be clear: this is no polemic against "organized religion." There is no harm if institutional interpreters seek to expound the inner meanings of genuine religious language and practice in their own local ephemeral terms, or even if for the sake of bureaucratic organization rough rules of thumb are generated to guide conduct and keep people on the same page. After all, churches and temples are good things, and they need to be built, paid for, staffed, and maintained; rituals need to be devised, rehearsed, and mounted; and specialists need to be trained, contractually engaged, deployed, organized, and supported. There is no harm either if a voluntary group decides to submit itself to arbitrary and absolute disciplines of law or asceticism, like Orthodox Jews or Indian Saddhus, when that discipline is a glorious gift to the divine whose arbitrariness and explicit non-applicability to others are a warrant of its free voluntariness and a training of the spirit.

As for the general moral law that applies to all, it does not differ much from nation to nation (though it goes through gradual evolution, bringing about, for instance, the abolition of slavery, the emancipation of women, and the emergence of democratic rule) and thus perhaps does not need much official religious definition. Much of it is in our nature and requires only honest self-examination to perceive; the sociobiologists are showing that we do have a biological conscience. That conscience might not tell us not to have slaves, but it does at least tell us to treat our slaves well. The world community is presently engaged in creating a universal bill of human rights, and is having remarkably little trouble in doing so. The difficulty was always in *applying* what we know to be right when we don't want to: that is when we start complicating the law and adverting to cultural relativism in order to muddy the moral waters and thus conceal our intention to cheat. A complex code of moral conduct, when applied by an official religious body to all persons in its communion, is usually a fruitless attempt to anticipate and head off this human tendency to find loopholes. And the really big problems come when the religious authorities decide that it is the presence of *other* codes that is corrupting their faithful, and try to persuade the secular authorities to take them out. An analogy is our own absurdly complex tax code, originally devised to corral the errant human conscience, which is gradually pushing us into imperialistic interventions in other countries so as to eliminate offshore tax havens and thus maintain discipline at home. Totally needless and unbelievably bloody conflicts result from such Big-endian/Small-endian disagreements. The sacrifices of millions of seventeenth-century Germans during the Thirty Years' War between the Catholics and Lutherans were recently—and rightly—shown to be in vain, by a somewhat shame-faced agreement between the two communions that the grace of faith was, as the Lutherans had always maintained, and as the Catholics had never denied, prior to the merit earned by good works. No true poet would have given such rich and beautiful words as grace, faith, merit, etc., the simpleminded, unambiguous, and denotative definitions that got us into the trouble in the first place.

Genuine religious language avoids these morasses. This is not to say that it cannot include elaborate codes of conduct, though these are dangerous temptations to those who think they can buy God's favor, and to those who, with a temperamental talent for extreme self-discipline, want to use that talent to oppress others. As long as we *take* those codes as either a metaphorical description to the many of what voluntary devotion might look like, or as a gift suggestion for the few about what kind of sacrifice to God might be acceptable, the codes are beautiful and appropriate parts of sacred scripture. But we should not blur their difference from the mandatory commands of natural conscience, enshrined in the decalogues of many nations, nor use them to freeze the continuing mind of God. All our great religious leaders have repeatedly warned us against taking the words and actions of religion in a literalistic way, mistaking the husk for the seed—and astonishingly, many of their most zealous adherents persist in doing exactly that. Thus both in the nature of genuine religious language, and in how we should take it, there are crucial understandings that have yet to be arrived at. If we do not arrive at them, we will find ourselves either among the inquisitors or, with Voltaire, the scoffers.

How, then, can we tell genuine religious language when we do not have huge time-scales and vast regions of cultural dissemination to warrant it?—and how should we take it when we find it? The two questions merge into one. It is not enough to say, with St. Paul that the letter killeth, but the spirit giveth life. The rejoinder of Nietzsche and the existentialists, that the spirit killeth but the letter giveth life, is overwhelmingly apt. Not that St. Paul is wrong: both feel right. How can this be? As the physicist Niels Bohr put it, the opposite of a true statement is a false statement, but the opposite of a profound truth is another profound truth. Perhaps a religious truth is of this kind. One type of trope which resembles this description is the metaphor, which asserts in a fictional way an identity between two things that are demonstrably different. Religious language is deeply metaphorical. It is also richly allusive, dense, and often ambiguous, packing centuries or millennia of implication and etymological development into its diction. I am told that the Arabic of the Koran is exemplary in this respect.

Much religious language is in verse. The old Hebrew word for "prophet" also meant poet. Let us seize the bull by the horns and make what may at this stage seem to be a rather obvious point: genuine religious language is poetic. But this is also a deeply controversial point. Is all poetry religious? Is all *good* poetry religious? How do we tell true religious poetry from ordinary poetry? It may be that this is a more important line of investigation than any strictly theological one. We have seen how Voltaire, a highly intelligent and informed man of his times, stumbled over language that was not poetic, and how the theologians to whom he was responding had stumbled themselves by trying to make a logical paraphrase of the poetry they had inherited. The scriptures they disputed remain untouched, as relevant now as they were then. Only the poetry survives. And if we look at it, if any poetry is good enough to survive for long enough, it becomes religious scripture. Over three millennia the *Mahabharata*, an explicitly artificial epic of magic and war, became sacred scripture. So also the erotic poetry of King Solomon. The *Iliad*, the archaic Greek equivalent to a very good violent action movie of the twentieth century, took only about four hundred years to become a religious text, much to the scandal of Plato. An anthropologist from Mars visiting England would probably dismiss the artificiality of our art/religion distinction and describe Shakespeare as a major deity with a strong religious cult. But this point has already been made.

Many religious people would be rightly suspicious of an attempt to "reduce" religion to poetry and metaphors. In a sense, the fundamentalist Baptists, who insist on the literal truth of the Bible, are with Nietzsche and the existentialists on this one: if religious language is a set of pretty stories and metaphors to sugarcoat the pill of a chilly and abstract deism, it is probably not worth having. Indigenous tribal religious leaders are famous for telling well-meaning anthropologists that their myths and rituals are not just symbols but realities. How can we reassure them?

The issue is whether religious metaphors and symbols are "merely" metaphors and symbols. The Catholic Church has a rather neat definition of a sacrament—"the outward and visible sign of an inward and invisible grace." The implication is that there are signs—metaphors, symbols—that are also realities: the "metaphor/reality" distinction simply does not work. Current sociological research on the language of the sciences shows that real effective scientific knowledge is metaphorical and analogical "all the way down"—there is no "pure" scientific knowledge. Even mathematics is one more set of metaphors, though less obvious because of its reductiveness than the vitalistic or intentionalistic metaphors that give such offence. This sociological research usually has an agenda that is, in my view, false: that scientists disguise their own socially constructed prejudices in the mantle of scientific objectivity. This, I think, is for the most part a libel. But the results of the sociological research stand; and they do so, I believe, not because of the metaphorical bent of scientists but because the scientists are right without knowing it: the nature of reality is itself metaphorical and symbolic, and thus any language that accurately describes it must be too. If the universe is made of information, as we have tentatively concluded, then it could scarcely be other than metaphorical and symbolic by nature, since metaphors and symbols are the way in which information is connected, and the universe is by definition connected. So let us correct our statement for Nietzsche, the Baptists, the existentialists, and the tribal spirit doctors, to the effect that by saying religion is metaphorical we do not mean that it is not real. If we accept metaphor as a real constituent of the universe—if we assert that Mrs. Ramsay's shawl is for us at least as real as the skull—then perhaps we can be trusted.

Among the Ndembu people with whom I spent part of my boyhood, the term for a fundamental religious symbol (what Catholics would call a sacrament) was *chinjikijilu*. This word was itself a metaphor: in its literal sense it means a blaze, the mark one would cut on a tree in order to find one's way back from unknown territory. One of the most dangerous aspects of living in a hunting/horticulture society like the Ndembu is getting lost when one is exploring or hunting. So a *chinjikijilu* is a real thing, a physical mark on a tree; it reveals real territory, previously unknown; but it also changes the landscape, adding an area—whatever is within eyeshot of the blaze—to the known territory of the village. One cuts a *chinjikijilu* at the exact boundary between the known and the unknown—in linguistic terms, between the expected terminological formula and the babble of gibberish. It is poetic language; but it is eminently useful, and a real feature of the world once it is made. Shakespeare makes much the same point in *A Midsummer Night's Dream*:

> The poet's eye, in a fine frenzy rolling,
> Doth glance from heaven to earth, from earth to heaven,
> And as imagination bodies forth
> The forms of things unknown, the poet's pen
> Turns them to shapes, and gives to airy nothing
> A local habitation and a name.

Shakespeare and the Ndembu thus solve the pretty paradoxes of Ludwig Wittgenstein, in the *Tractatus Logico-Philosophicus*: "Whereof one cannot speak, thereof one must remain silent"; and "The limits of my language are the limits of my world." (Paradoxes, because in speaking of that whereof one cannot speak, he is not remaining silent; and to speak of limits implies that one has already been in some sense on the other side of them, to make sure they really are the limits.) The deepest religious and poetic language is a blaze that conducts us between the known and the unknown, the not-yet-articulable and the sayable, the past and the future. It is in a sense constitutive of the present moment, to the extent that the present moment is that which mediates between the past and future. Before human beings came along to use words and visual symbols and music and pretence and masks and sacraments to do it, biology was doing it through that unique moment of sexual reproduction when the two different gametes come together (in a "symbolon"—that which is "thrown together") to make a new unique individual. On rare occasions that "symbolon" can be the great grand poem of a new species. And physics was already doing it when it cooked up a new element in the collapsing core of an old star. Poetry is fast evolution: evolution is slow poetry.

Poetic language is not only metaphorical, dense, allusive, and so on, but performative in its essential nature. It makes come into being whatever can do so given the existing stipulations of nature and given a performative community that can assent to its legitimacy. (With poetry I here include all the arts—painting, drama, even music which is the purest of all performatives, directly stipulating an emotional state and making it be through the neurophysiology of audition.) A metaphor itself is a sort of speech act or performative stipulation, since it enacts by its statement, within a community of assent to its provisional authority, a contextual frame for the subject of the metaphor, creating a lexical link in the structure of the language. And all language, with the possible exception of some syntactical fragments, is made of more or less fossilized metaphors. Poetic

religious language is metaphor in its pre-fossilized state, vital, growing, the brilliant live coral that crusts and protects and depends upon
the dead coral of the reef; the molten words that burst out of the
dead structure of stony doctrine. The structure of doctrine may be as
necessary as the dead heartwood is to a tree; but it should always
recognize its subservience to the life of the tree. That life is in the act
of interpretation—both the giving act of the poet speaking out of the
collective mind and the receiving act of the hearer embodying the
text in her own life. A metaphor is a synaptic firing in the brain of
God. It is one of the strange sad ironies of religion that the very
tradition of religious protest, that most boldly proclaimed the need
for individuals to read and interpret the Bible, produced eventually
the Biblical literalists who today make the authority of the Vatican
look squishy by comparison.

But why should interpretation be so necessary? Why should religious language be so dark, so thick, so ambiguous, so thoroughly
odd and scandalous to ordinary reason? In *Huckleberry Finn*, Huck
informs Jim that in France people speak French. Jim is rightly puzzled
by their perversity, the silliness of this elaborate piece of European
etiquette, the unnecessary trouble they must go through whenever
they have a thought to express. "Why do they speak in French?
Why don't they just *say* it?" he wonders. Why doesn't God just say
it? Why must religious language be poetic, and demand a poetic
interpretation, rather than straightforward and definite? There are
several answers to this question, some of which are already implicit
in the need for it to be "all things to all men," as St. Paul has it. The
divine must speak to many nations, periods of history, understandings of science. How might one describe the first ten billion years of
the universe, of the infancy of God, to Mesopotamians of the third
millennium B.C. or Hebrews of the second? Perhaps in terms of a
sequence of creative events, over some kind of divine week and
weekend in *illo tempore*. When Carl Sagan tried to explain the evolution of the universe in his TV series *Cosmos*, he did much the
same thing, imagining the whole history of the universe compressed
into a single year, whose last fraction of a second was given to the
emergence of humankind. It would be unkind to accuse him of a
falsehood in assigning a mere year to the process, and silly to take
him literally. When biologists try to explain natural selection to
laypeople, they usually resort to metaphorical examples that are not
unlike Jesus' parable of the sower. And if physics and biology need

metaphors to explain themselves, a fortiori so does theology. Like the music of Mozart, the divine tongue must transcend local codes and go directly to all people's hearts. It must therefore necessarily have the packed allusiveness and flexibility to adapt itself to different cultural frames of reference. Christianity's own huge success, the stamp of divine approval, is due largely to its repeated and gigantic acts of interpretative genius: to see the history of its rejecting parent as a pattern of prophecy foretelling its own coming; to see the brilliant achievements of the Greeks and Romans as types and expository allegories of the Christian story; to see the pagan philosophers as unconscious transmitters of the Christian message; to see the poetry of Virgil as an augury of the Incarnation. It was only when Christianity ceased to plunge into such dangerous and ambiguous adventures of poetic exegesis that it began to lose its universality. The oddity of religious language comes partly from its need to wire up and connect all realities, cultural as well as natural.

But there are other answers to Jim's question, Why don't they just *say* it? One is that if the divine is as we have speculated it to be, its nature is analogous to the self-organization that emerges out of iterative nonlinear causality and thus breaks free of one-way cause. No merely linear language could therefore capture it. This is not to say that we must abandon reason in speaking of it, but that we must select the instruments of reason carefully, and not try to measure something complex by yardsticks that are simple, or take a sharp-edged photograph of a subtly melded scene. Again like Mozart, our language must do this through some mysterious kind of inner richness, a fractal iterativeness in which every detail is different but recognizably connected and akin. The spirit is best addressed by a connectivity of context that no one element of that context can fix or hold.

Other even more fundamental constraints compel those who speak for the divine to do so in poetry. One is that if the trans-temporal connectivity of all moments in the universe is, as we have speculated, mediated by quantum harmonic coherence, it is subject to the same maddening ambiguity that bedevils programmers when they try to use the formidable powers of the quantum computer to do actual calculations. The problem is that quantum information comes as a superposition of contradictory states, and thus that any communication between different times will tend to be as ambiguous as the Delphic oracle. If one sent anything definite, it would ipso facto be part of the collapsed-information state of the matter world, would no longer have the superluminal properties of quantum information, and would not get through. The trick would have to be to send messages backwards in time that would be appropriately ambiguous, but which when combined with the definite context of an actual historical situation would produce a meaningful intervention—rather as the decoding keys of the Enigma cipher machine in the Second World War could turn apparently random sequences of letters into a meaningful transmission. Thus Jesus' parables were not a mere eccentricity of style, but both an enactment of his incarnation and a hint about the essential metaphoricity of that enactment. But to understand such messages requires a willingness to engage in a terrifying interpretative process: "He that has ears to hear, let him hear." We need rather special ears to hear with. The absurd and charming story of Krishna and his Gopis, the milkmaids whose clothes he stole while they were bathing, when laid with poetic insight over our experience as mortals in the business of life, forms a mysterious moiré pattern that makes us shiver with the divine presence. But with such a message one would always be on the edge of losing one's footing and getting it quite wrong; there would be no assurances except the astonishing promise of faith, that if we go on allowing the story or metaphor to unfold itself in our lives, it will correct itself.

Even more challenging, such a message would have to compete or cooperate with other messages from other futures, themselves empowered to the extent of their probability relative to the time period in which the transmission is received. The message would have to have such a form as to exclude and deny messages from evil futures, but to include and affirm messages from good ones (and to identify each kind as such). And it would have to do all this in the conditions of local misinterpretation and the ancient human tribal tendency toward xenophobia. Tragic conflicts, such as those between Christians and Jews, Jews and Muslims, Muslims and Hindus, Hindus and Christians, and so on would be almost inevitable as different future self-conceptions of the divine wrestled each other in the arenas of the past.

There are many moral reasons for the oddity of religious language. Religion should convince not through past proofs, threats, or promises, but in its immediate practice; it is not that the world contains arcane proofs of God, but that the world to the religious-minded person of impeccable rationality—that is, someone who gives merely adequate recognition to the astonishing wonder of life—is the very body and drama of God. But this needs the poetic sensibility to see it. Religious language is both a training of that sensibility—a kind of indicating, as when someone shows us the significant detail in an Old Master or points out the subtle pattern in the carpet that is obvious once we see it—and at the same time an utterance that is quite comprehensible to that sensibility.

Finally, such messages must be poetic and superficially inscrutable for another reason: if the divine itself is to some infinitesimal degree the result of the actions we take upon hearing its message, that message must be such as to leave open the divine's own free power to continue the active and creative process of intending. God defines herself or himself by those very sendings. If there is an identifiable theme in all such messages, it is that of a more abundant life, that is, an opening of potential rather than a closing of it down. When we cooperate with the message, and allow its exegesis to flow naturally in ourselves, we join as a companion in God's own free intending. Interpretation, metaphorizing, and poetry are not just comments upon the nature of universe-creation; they *are* universe-creation.

An Inordinate Fondness for Beetles: The Divine Language of Nature

What, some readers might ask, are those people to do who do not have the poetic sensibility? I believe that this question implies too narrow a definition of "poetic." We have scarcely scratched the surface of the multitudinous richness of the modes of the divine/natural poetry.

I believe it was the great British biologist J.B.S. Haldane who, on being asked what, after a lifetime studying God's living creations, he could tell us about God, replied that He seemed to have an inordinate fondness for beetles. This delightful response could be taken as irreverent or satirical; but if we do take the notion of God the creator seriously, its truth could scarcely be denied. There are perhaps hundreds of thousands of beetle species, a significant fraction of the world's total biodiversity; Haldane's reply conjures up a God somewhat like a bright little boy who obsessively wants to collect and build every variation of some treasured model or toy. I can remember as a child going again and again to the illustrations in the encyclopedia of the varieties of tropical fish, military medals, tree

leaves, postage stamps, hybrid roses, technical equipment, butterflies, insignia, and indeed beetles, picking out my favorites (I loved
the great stag beetle best of all), and building model aircraft and
plastic ships with their neat nuggety complicated particularity.
Haldane makes us see God putting his head down sideways close to
his latest beetle, to enjoy its fine lines, jointed antennae, elegant
patches of iridescence, and the new mark VI wing-casing design,
and stroking it gently as he adds it to his enormous collection. The
dorky hobbyist is in this perspective quite as much in tune with the
divine (even if quite unaware of it) as the most lachrymose and sigh-
ing aesthete.

Gerard Manley Hopkins has a perception of God's intricate, fas-
cinated, and absorbed craftsmanship that is not unlike Haldane's:

Pied Beauty

Glory be to God for dappled things—
　For skies of couple-colour as a brinded cow;
　　　For rose-moles all in stipple upon trout that swim;
Fresh-firecoal chestnut-falls; finches' wings;
　Landscape plotted and pieced—fold, fallow, and plough;
　　　And áll trádes, their gear and tackle and trim.
All things counter, original, spare, strange;
　Whatever is fickle, freckled (who knows how?)
　　　With swift, slow; sweet, sour; adazzle, dim;
He fathers-forth whose beauty is past change:
　Praise him.

If we look at the second to the last line we can see with splendid
clarity why poetic language is so deeply necessary when it comes to
religion. Nature is God's great ejaculation of seeds into the womb of
nature itself, each one somehow expressing both its own uniqueness and the hereditary stamp of its father; both the unity and the
multiplicity of God's own nature. His beauty is past change: at first
glance, an orthodox statement of the Platonic Catholic theology of
Hopkins' own time and chosen submission. God is changeless, beyond change. But this idea is at once interrogated by the diverse and
protean changeableness of the world that bears its father's likeness.
"Past change" could also mean "all the changes that took place in
the past": God's beauty is precisely the whole history of change and
growth and unfolding. The phrase has one more possible interpretation: to be past something could indeed mean to be no longer within

the realm of that thing, according with orthodox theological definition of eternity; but it could also mean to be even more that thing than that thing was, as when we speak of something going past the speed of sound or light: it is not less fast, but more so. God is *even more* the essence of change than nature is. All three interpretations are in the poem: any one of them would collapse the wave-function of its meaning into something that would falsify the nature of God. In the three meanings of "past change" the trinity is here not a dogma but a live signpost, a blaze pointing us deeper into the forest and still showing us the way back home.

There is, then, a weird surreal poetry in God's conversation with the humans that are the neurons of God—Gopis, weeping statues, African ithyphallic fetishes, and all. The divine language is amateurish, indirect, wayward, "fickle, freckled (who knows how?)." God speaks in the echiura, that sea slug whose male lives as a parasite in the female's kidney; in the grotesque geometry of black holes and subatomic strings; in the animated parachute of a polyp jellyfish, pulsing angelically along; in the rippling animated pelt of the jaguar. Praise Him.

The Queen of Heaven

Or, perhaps, Praise Her.

If the divine is both the attractor, the final cause of the process of natural evolution, and at the same time the process itself—if the inner life of the universe is the biography of God—then we should expect God's character and style to be discernible in the lineaments of nature, as the history of a person comes to be written upon her face. Nature is full of conjunctions or marriages between paired, complementary, and equal opposites—left-handed spin and right-handed spin, positive and negative electromagnetic charge, the two directions of time, yin and yang. In the realm of biology that doubleness is most saliently represented by sex. The word "nature" is cognate with "natal," "generate," "kind" (and indeed "cognate"!): nature is reproduction, or rather "new-production-through-reproduction." The great invention of biological reproduction—sex—is a sort of reprise of the way that natural physics managed to split nothingness into positive and negative somethingness. If nature is both male and female, the divine is both also. Thus it would be as accurate to say "She mothers-forth whose beauty is past change" as "He fathers-forth." It would not be as accurate to say "It neuters-forth;"

there is no neuter personal pronoun in English, nor, I believe, should there be. Neuter animals and plants can only clone themselves, and there is thus less "forth-ness" in their production, less originality. Individuality, sexuality, and original creativity are strongly linked in biological reproduction, and must correspond to some doubleness in the divine nature.

We have many splendid images of the maleness of God; in recent centuries, at least in the West, fewer images of her femaleness. Some of the mainline Christian churches have, with a little jolt of surprise, been awoken to this omission in the last few years. There are plenty of female spirits, angels and saints—not to speak of goddesses—in popular worship, animist, polytheist, and monotheist alike. But the more intellectual religious traditions are not by any means lacking in the seeds of such imagining. Consider Kuanyin, Kannon, the female Bodhisattvas, the Jewish Shekinah, the Virgin Mary, Urania, Hagia Sophia. Any account of the style of God is incomplete without a deep imagining of Her femininity, the more difficult today when we can no longer associate the female with stereotypical social and cultural attributes such as passivity, emotionality, dependency, or an exclusive role in nurturance. The female brings to reproduction at least as much genetic material—the active principle of organic development—as the male, and in those societies in which progress in technology and economics have permitted it, her achievements in traditionally male activities are at least as impressive. Nevertheless, the flavor of female love, of female ingenuity, acceptance, subtlety, depth, generosity, wit, and passion must be combined with the male versions of those characteristics if we would get a fully rounded picture of the divine. Looking at the divine in the female light we see suddenly the astonishing creativity inherent in acceptance; the glory of the moral quality of virginity, of intactness, of immaculateness; the sweetness and delicacy of the divine; her capacity to be wounded by the pain of those she loves; her motherliness; her witchlike, Aphroditic powers of transformation; her familiarity with the dark world of death; her gentle but ruthless sense of humor; her strangely judging nonjudgmentality (if you see what I mean!); even her seductiveness, her own dream of self-enjoyment. Men may have versions of all these qualities, but they are often obscured by other more obvious characteristics. Dezsö Kosztolányi's poem, quoted at the beginning of this book, catches something of this.

Under a lace veil
streamed a mantle, fairy-tale,
from the frail
deeps of twilight, diamond-pale,
blued with such a blue
as the morning dew,
which a lovely lady dons for her surtout,
and a gem, whose hue
dusts with its light the pure peace of the air,
the otherworldly raiment she would wear;
or an angel pins, with virgin grace,
a brilliant diadem into her hair,
and a fine light chaise
rocks to a soft halt and she glides in,
quieter than a dream,
and, its wheels agleam,
on it rolls again,
a flirting smile glimpsed on the face of the queen,
and then the stallions of the Milky Way,
with glittering horseshoes gallop through the spray
of carnival confetti, each flake a star
of bright gold, where hundreds of glass coaches are.

That flirtatious smile on the face of the Queen of Heaven is a masterstroke of truth telling. It is something we must work to understand in our imagination. Let us try to come at it in a logical way. Many of the great religions assert that the closest we can get to the divine is the miracle of another person. If we want to know what God looks like, they say, we must look in the eyes of our neighbor: their innerness is what God is most like. Accordingly, the contact we have with God, or should have if we are not estranged, is imaged in terms of the closest human relationships. God is most often called our father; but the Heavenly Mother is nearly as frequent. Jesus and Krishna are imaged as our brother. In Christianity, and perhaps in Buddhism, the divine is represented as a beloved and holy infant: the gorgeous poetry, the carols, the green and red and gold of the Nativity, clearly convey a large moiety of the joy of religious experience. In our own theological fantasy, the divine is literally our descendant, our Child; Jesus is the Son of Man. The Egyptian Horus, too, is seen as the beloved son, and in the Mesoamerican religions it is often the sacrificed son who is the most perfect image of divinity. A Christian nun becomes the bride of Christ, Psyche is wooed and won by the god of love, Krishna is the divine lover of Radha, and throughout the mysticism and poetry of Islam, Judaism, and Christianity the human soul is described as the girl who becomes a woman through the masterful desire of the divine lover—St. John of the Cross and John Donne spring at once to mind. Donne will never be chaste, "except Thou ravish me." The Shekinah, the spirit of the Jewish people and the spirit also of the Sabbath and the holy Torah, is the bride of Adonai. The relationship of friendship is also called upon as a way of speaking about the comfort and support of our divine companion; and the loyalty of the faithful follower to the generous and heroic leader is implicit in the almost universal term, Lord. God can be our teacher, our tutor, our mentor; even, in the institutions of sacrifice and divine service, a respected trading partner. We have sometimes seen God as a guiding sister, as Odysseus does Athena, and as Milton perhaps saw Urania, the wisdom of God.

But the one relationship we have seemed increasingly to shy away from or repress is the relationship of the human male lover to his divine female beloved. The ancient institutions of the vestal virgin or temple prostitute recognize that relationship: indeed Enkidu dies in *Gilgamesh* because he and Gilgamesh fail to give proper honor to the love-goddess. Adonis is dismembered when he rejects Venus, and Pentheus suffers a similar fate when he profanes the rituals of the Bacchantes. Perhaps we should reconsider the relevance to our own worship of the circum-Mediterranean and middle-eastern cults of the love-goddess: Ishtar, Astarte, Astoreth, Innanna, Isis. In the Middle Ages the cult of the blessed virgin Mary came strangely close, as C.S. Lewis remarked in *The Allegory of Love*, to the idolatry of the Minnesingers and Goliards for their profane mistresses; but the incestuous barrier between holy mother and earthly mistress, and the doctrinal one between divine *latria* and human *dulia*, was never fully breached. Dante's Beatrice is not quite God. Yet if it makes sense for us to call God "master," as we often do, then surely it also makes sense to call God "mistress." In Genesis God creates us in his image, and also male and female: Judaism, Christianity, and Islam, like many other religions, have at their root an admission that the divine is quite as much female as male. Thus any term of respect and love which applies to God in its masculine form must also apply with equal force in its feminine one. If God is a master, then God must also be a mistress. If our lord, then also our lady. If a husband, then also a wife.

What follows from this thought is that if we are to fully round out our imagination of our relationship with the divine, perhaps we must school our fancy to include the passion and submission of a lover before his mistress, of a husband before his wife—when it is the lover, the husband, who is the human partner, and the mistress, the wife, who is the divine one. Mary the Magdalene, the first Apostle to discover the resurrection, may be as valuable an image of God as an image of God's beloved, as Peter the first holy father is both the disciple and the vicar of Christ in traditional Catholic theology. The gentle mastery and tender care and protectiveness and service and honor that a man gives to a wife are not inappropriate for a human being to give God. And, if we are to see sexuality as a metaphor for spiritual relationships, the very hiddenness of female sexual response, the need for tact, patience, humility in the face of the inexplicable moods and desires of a woman that a good lover must learn, the interpretive subtlety and respect he must attain if he would penetrate without violation the intricacy of female emotion, must all be present somewhere in the human love of God. After all, in our fable the very future of God depends upon how we act today; we are helpers in the very shaping of God. Perhaps we could even say that there is a measure of truth in the idea that nature is the virgin god, that we impregnate nature with the idea of the mother god, and that the mother god is born out of nature's womb. Those of us who are men do not need to abandon our own maleness to love and worship God, any more than those of us who are women need to experience God only as the ardent male and not also as the sister female. God is not just the one who must be accepted, but also the one whose own divine acceptance, whose "disponibilité," as the French say, constitutes the unbounded creative principle that we call goodness.

Thus the idea of God as the mother of heaven and the implication from our fable that religion is essentially poetic, metaphorical, interpretative, are deeply and mysteriously linked. God's femaleness is also God's exegetical bottomlessness; the iterative and generative process of interpretation that we must enter when we engage with God's metabolism *is* God's femaleness. The "taking" of how we take a statement, a work of art, a story, is also the "taking" of rapture, the fertile "taking" of virginity.

Glossary

Note: This book necessarily ventures upon the vocabularies and accepted factual material of several disciplines. A glossary is thus provided, with brief definitions of key terms and basic information about major figures, sources, and core concepts mentioned in the text, to help readers who may be unfamiliar with some of the fields referred to. It is not intended for experts, who may well find it oversimplified, overgeneralized, or in places too narrow. Experts may wish to verify in which sense out of many I am using a term, especially if it is a term shared by various disciplines.

Accelerator: Or collider; a device in the science of particle physics whereby subatomic particles are accelerated in speed and energy so as to reveal their structure when they collide.

Acupuncture: The East Asian medical art of stimulating by strategically inserted needles the correct flow of *chi* or energy about the body. Acupuncturists analyze the body into zones or "meridians," that share connections and are the conduits of *chi*; thus they know where needles should be placed to unblock its flow.

Akhenaton: Egyptian pharaoh who briefly established monotheistic belief in the sun, of which all other deities were emanations.

Apoptosis: Death of a living cell.

Aquinas: St. Thomas Aquinas, the great thirteenth-century A.D. theologian who synthesized the philosophy of Aristotle with Christian doctrine.

Arabi: Ibn Arabi, a great Sufi mystic and theologian.

Attractor: The attractor of any dynamical system is the form that its various behaviors trace out in its "phase space"—an imaginary graphical space whose dimensional axes represent the various degrees of freedom of the system, e.g., its temperature, momentum, spatial extent, temporal limits, and speed. For instance, a swinging pendulum, gradually slowing through friction, traces out a simple spiral when its speed and direction are singled out as the axes of its phase space. Complex dynamical feedback systems in which all the elements are interacting demonstrate irregular behaviors that are often called chaotic. The phase space tracings of such chaotic behaviors can be beautiful fractal forms, called "strange" attractors.

Babbage: Charles Babbage, the nineteenth-century scientist who invented the first general computing machine (using brass cams and gears instead of valves or transistors).

Baha'i: Founded by Baha'ullah in the nineteenth century A.D., this religious movement transcends its Islamic roots to seek the religious unity of all humankind.

Big Bang: The theory, largely confirmed by the increase with distance of the red shift of star spectra, that about 10–15 billion years ago the universe was compacted into a single hot dense atom, which exploded outward to form the present cosmos.

Bodhisattva: In Buddhism, an enlightened being; a manifestation of the Buddha in human form. "Bodhi" and "Buddha" are cognates, whose root is the Sanskrit word for wisdom, related to English words such as bid, bode, ombudsman.

Bohm: David Bohm, the quantum physicist who maintained that all events past and future were "enfolded" in an "implicate order" composed of the harmonics of quantum potential fields.

Briss: Jewish circumcision ritual.

Butterfly effect: In chaos theory, the popular phrase denoting the possibility that, because of the sensitive dependence of complex nonlinear systems on their initial conditions, the beating of a butterfly's wing in Brazil could trigger larger turbulences which would in turn escalate into a hurricane.

CAD-CAM: computer-assisted design and computer-assisted manufacture.

Cantor transfinite numbers: The mathematician Georg Cantor proved that there was not one infinite number, but a series of them, each infinitely greater than the last. For instance, the number of possible curves on a plane was larger than the number of points on a line. He named the transfinite numbers aleph zero, aleph one, aleph two, and so on, in order of their "cardinality." A transfinite number of higher cardinality could not be counted off one to one—denumerated—using one of a lower cardinality.

Cargo cult: Melanesian religious practice incorporating elements of Western technology and economics.

Chac-mool: The sacrificial altar of the Mayans, sculpted as a reclining god turning his face to confront the victim.

Chaos theory: Body of understanding devoted to the tracing of hidden order within apparent disorder, and the discerning of disorder within apparent order. Includes such concepts as fractals, catastrophes, bifurcation, iteration, attractors, dynamical systems, nonlinearity, feedback, the butterfly effect, etc. See "Complexity theory," Attractor," "Self-organization," etc.

Chinese Room: A thought experiment proposed by the philosopher John Searle. A worker unable to understand Chinese, yet provided with a set of rules specifying its lexicon, grammar, and rules of usage, is locked in a room and employed to respond to outside utterances in Chinese according to his instructions. The room itself could behave like an intelligent Chinese speaker though nobody in it had any idea of the meaning of the exchange. This thought experiment was intended to demolish automatistic theories of the mind, to reassert the philosophical concept of intentionality, and to act as a critique of computational theories of intelligence.

Clinamen: Or "swerve" in English. Lucretius' Latin term for the initial chance anomaly that disturbed the even fall of matter through the void, and thus initiated the physical universe as it is now.

Commutation, Commutative: Used here in a complex sense, including the legal meaning of a reduced punitive sentence, the economic sense of a substitution of one form of payment for another and the making of small change, and the mathematical meaning of an operation which remains the same in different contexts.

Complexity theory: Body of understanding devoted to complex systems, with many elements and/or nonlinear relations. Such concepts as emergence, dynamical systems, self-organization, etc., link it closely with chaos theory.

Confucianism: Founded by the fifth-century B.C. Chinese sage Confucius, this religion emphasizes personal virtue, piety toward family and the ancestors, and social harmony.

Constantine: The Roman emperor who established Christianity as the official religion of the Roman Empire.

Copenhagen interpretation: Of quantum mechanics, associated with the physicists Niels Bohr and Werner Heisenberg, which emphasized the stranger aspects of quantum theory, such as the observer effect, uncertainty, and complementarity (as opposed to other interpretations, which for instance insisted on the predictability and mathematical certainty of coherent ensembles of elementary particles over time).

Cromwell: Oliver Cromwell, English Protestant dictator who conducted a war of extermination against Irish Catholics.

Deconstructionism: The theory that since words are not their referents or "signifieds," we only know the world as a text, and all words refer only to their paraphrases in other words; thus the world for us can only be a play of differences or deferrals or slippages among "signifiers." To understand is an act of deconstruction into such "traces."

Deism: A belief claiming on the basis of reason that God, having created the universe and set it moving, abandoned it to its own natural processes.

Delphic: Pertaining to the ancient Greek oracle of Delphi, which provided to the Greek world prophecies from the god Apollo, couched in notoriously ambiguous language.

Denumerability: Countability, especially in a context where transfinite numbers are compared. If one number cannot be counted one to one in terms of another, it is said to be nondenumerable.

Derrida: Jacques Derrida, founder of deconstructionism.

Deus absconditus: The doctrine that God, having created the world, abandoned it to its own laws and deterministic or random processes. Characteristic of deistic thinkers.

Dialectical materialism: The philosophical basis of Marxism, in which matter is all that truly exists, human society is an extension of the physical evolution of the universe, and evolution proceeds through the struggle of an existing thesis (or provisional reality) with its own self-generated antithesis to produce a synthesis—which, as a new thesis, repeats the process.

DNA: Deoxyribonucleic acid, the self-replicating double-helix nucleic acid molecule, made up of a sequence of various combinations of four bases or nucleotides (the thymine-adenine pair, and the guanine-cytosine pair) known to encode the genetic instructions for generating all forms of life (except for certain viruses, whose genetic instructions are encoded in RNA, and whose definition as life is under debate).

Dynamical: Pertaining to a system as described by dynamics, the physical science of movement. Dynamics comes in two flavors: classical, dealing with the movements of matter in space, and thermodynamics, dealing with the difference that is made by such factors as heat, entropy, enthalpy, internal energy, phase states, and the statistical properties of pressure and temperature.

Eccles: Sir John Eccles, the neuroscientist whose discovery of an apparently intention-forming area of the brain, that became active before any part of the brain associated with the following action, led him to speculate that the brain was not an autonomous self-motivating entity but rather a complex receiver of commands from, and transmitter of experiences to, a non-physical soul.

Emergence: The core concept of emergentism, the position that argues that new forms of being, such as life and mind, can come into being by natural processes which, crossing certain thresholds of size, complexity, etc., must organize themselves into different kinds of entities displaying new "emergent" properties. As a simple example, the dry gas oxygen, when combined in sufficient quantities with the dry gas hydrogen, produces water, which displays the emergent property of wetness, with its specific characteristics of forming drops and a meniscus, clinging to surfaces, etc. One molecule of water is not wet; yet when enough are added together, wetness emerges. This book generally accepts the emergentist position, but does not draw from it the conclusion that a creator is unnecessary. Rather, however, the creativity is immanent in the process of emergence itself; from a theological point of view, the exquisitely adapted forms of the world are not so much the products of an external designer, as the lineaments of a divine biography.

Entelechy: Used here in its sense of a force directing an entity towards its own completion.

Entropy: Thermodynamic disorder, increasing with time. In thermodynamics, the Second Law dictates that in a closed system work can only be done at the expense of generating waste heat, some of which cannot itself be used to do work. Thus a thermodynamic world with a finite endowment of free energy to do work is one which is running down or decaying toward an eventual heat-death. The increase of entropy takes place over time, and thus time and entropy provide definitions for each other, time's direction being set by the increase of entropy, and entropy being that which increases over time. Information theory also contains a version of the concept of entropy, in which the generation of information must pay the cost of increasing informational disorder elsewhere; the two uses of the idea nicely coincide in the heating of a computer when it is doing calculations. However, contemporary information theorists are now pursuing concepts of computation in which vanishingly small amounts of entropy are produced; and various researchers have pointed out that all such theory applies only to closed systems. Ilya Prigogine, for instance, has argued that in open systems chance variations can reset the high availability of work energy.

Enzyme: A biochemical catalyst made of proteins, used by living organisms to conduct their various metabolic operations.

Event horizon: On approaching a black hole, the zone where the velocity created by gravitational attraction exceeds the speed of light, so that no matter, energy, or information can escape.

Existentialist: One who believes that all value and reality inhere in the immediate experience of existence, and that essences are mere counters of mental discourse.

Exponentially: See "Polynomially."

Fractal: An irregular geometrical shape that continues to reveal significant detail at any scale of magnification and cannot be represented by classical geometry. Fractals are said to be "self-similar"—that is, like coastlines, branching trees, river tributaries, or clouds, they show similar shapes at different scales, whether close up or far away. This property is also called "scaling symmetry" or "internal symmetry," since this is a symmetry denoting invariance under changes of scale, rather than invariance under changes of angle or rotation. Since such forms can have the odd property of filling up the space available to them with more and more detail, a line densely kinking to fill up a plane, or a surface densely folding to fill up a volume, they seem to defy the conventionally absolute distinctions between one-dimensionality and two-dimensionality, two-dimensionality and three-dimensionality, and so on: mathematicians have thus been able to classify fractals in terms of how densely they fill the next dimension up, thus generating the concept of a fractal dimension. As well as one-dimensional lines, two-dimensional sheets, and three-dimensional volumes, for instance, there might be forms like electrical discharges, corals, or bronchi that would have a fractal dimension of 1.85 or 2.37.

Ganesh: Or Ganesha, the Hindu god of counting, categories, wealth, and prosperity. Originally created out of her own body dirt by the goddess Parvati, he was beheaded because of a misunderstanding by Shiva, Parvati's divine husband; his head was replaced by that of an elephant.

Gautama: Personal name of the Buddha.

Genii: In ancient Roman religion, a "genius" was the resident spirit of a locality or an entity, c.f. a "kami" in Shintoism.

Geodesic: Albert Einstein and Hermann Minkowski proposed that any physical entity could be described as a four-dimensional solid, existing in three spatial dimensions and one temporal one, visualizing it as a sort of long sausage whose two ends were its creation and its destruction. The trajectory it traced out in space-time was its world-line or "geodesic."

Gluon: An elementary particle that mediates the force that sticks other subatomic particles together in the atomic nucleus.

Gödel: Kurt Gödel's Incompleteness Theorem, sometimes referred to as Gödel's paradox, has been very fruitful in the field of mathematical logic. It shows that any system of logic rich enough to be used to draw conclusions, one whose axioms are explicit enough to be used to prove or disprove statements, must generate propositions of the general form of "This statement is unprovable." Such a statement is both true and unprovable, indicating that truth is not identical with proof and that no system of logic can prove its own axioms, thus suggesting that there are truths that are prior to any text. The logical form of the problem sentence emerges when we ask the question: "*Which* statement is unprovable?"—which results in an interesting infinite regress of nested quotation marks, reminiscent of the nonlinearity of the equations that generate fractal attractors: "This statement: 'This statement: "This statement: . . . is unprovable" is unprovable' is unprovable." If religion is defined as belief without proof, and if Gödel's theorem shows that no belief can be proved, and if all humans have beliefs, then all humans are religious.

Grand Inquisitor: The benevolent dictator in Dostoyevsky's fable (recounted in *The Brothers Karamazov*) who, when Christ returns, decides to crucify him once again, in order to protect the people against the unbearable freedom that he would bring.

Graviton: The hypothetical particle thought to conduct gravitational energy.

Gunas: In Hindu natural philosophy, the three Gunas—light, matter, and fire—constituted the elements out of which the perceived universe is made.

Habermas: Jürgen Habermas, German philosopher who believes that all truth claims are subject to the social legitimation of the claimant.

Hagia Sophia: The holy wisdom of God in Byzantine Christianity, imaged in female terms and constituting in some theological traditions a feminine aspect of the divine.

Hebbian circuits: Donald Hebb, the Canadian scientist known as the father of cognitive psychobiology, suggested that thoughts, memories, etc., were constituted by highly complex and unique—but stable—circuits of neurons, whose synaptic connections to each other had by previous experience been calibrated in the weighting of their ability to transmit nerve impulses. Such circuitry is obviously iterative and nonlinear. Later work on the mind-brain connection—including the study of artificial and natural neural networks, genetic algorithms, and neural Darwinism—has extended and deepened this body of theory, while remaining true to its basic nonlinear, self-organizing principles.

Hegelian state: G.W.F. Hegel's idea that the state—in his view, the Prussian state—was an important milestone in the emergence of a perfectly rational universe, the triumph of reason, and spirit over chaos and materiality.

Higgs field: The hypothetical field that bears an analogous relationship to mass as electromagnetic fields bear to electricity.

Hilbert Space: A mathematical concept proposed by the nineteenth-century mathematician David Hilbert. A topological space is made up of as many dimensions as are required to describe some real or imaginary object (see "phase space") and/or the environment in which it is embedded. Hilbert space is the space of all spaces, that is, the space sufficient to describe all and any spatial entities and environments of whatever number of dimensions and of whatever topological form.

Hobbes: Thomas Hobbes, English seventeenth-century philosopher who based his politics on the need for absolute sovereign power to protect human beings from each other in their natural struggle for advantage.

HOX: (Homeobox) genes guide the fetal development of cellular organisms, including animals and plants. Each HOX gene is responsible for a particular zone of the body.

Huichol: A Mexican ethnic group known for the richness of their religious ideas and practice.

Hunapúh and Ixbalanqué: The heroic brothers in the Mayan epic the *Popol Vuh*, who played the ball game against the lords of Xibalba, the house of Death.

Hydrosphere: By analogy with "atmosphere," a term used by planetary ecologists and others to describe the layer of water in the oceans, lakes, and artesian reservoirs that covers the Earth.

Iconoclasm: In its original meaning, advocacy of the destruction of any images of the divine.

Illo tempore: Literally, "that special time": as used by Mircea Eliade and others, the sacred time described by many traditional religions that existed before the present universe and still exists "around the corner" of the quotidian world we live in.

Inflation theory: The theory that the universe went through a brief period of extremely fast expansion at an early moment of the Big Bang; one implication is that many parallel "universes" (if that term can be used in the plural) might have emerged at the same time.

Iteration: The repeating of an operation or process, essential in many branches of chaos and complexity theory. Iteration need not produce a dull uniformity of product, but can generate unexpected new forms of order.

James: William James' *The Varieties of Religious Experience* is a classic in the study of the psychology of religion, one which does not demean its subject.

Julia set: A subset of the Mandelbrot set, or a blowup of some part of the visual representation of the set. Like its parent set, it reveals infinite varieties of new detail at different scales.

Kalevala: The Finnish epic, collected together from oral tales by the nineteenth century scholar Elias Lönnrot, which tell the stories of Väinämöinen, the "eternal sage," Ilmarinen, the primeval smith, and Lemminkäinen, who seek wives from the dark land of Pohjola.

Kami: A spirit or ghost in the Shinto religion, often a nature spirit.

Kantian: Follower of Kant; one who believes that we cannot experience things in themselves but only in terms of the categories of our perception, especially the categories of space and time; one who believes in the necessary disinterestedness of moral action.

Knox: John Knox, Scottish anti-Catholic puritan who led the movement to destroy the images and decorations of the Scottish Church.

Koan: In Zen, a paradox or riddle designed to deflect the mind from narrow habits of thought into meditative insight.

Krishna: The beautiful hero of many Hindu sacred stories, including the *Mahabharata* and the Bhagavad Gita; an avatar of the god Vishnu; the lover of the milkmaid Radha.

Kuanyin: Or Kannon, the East Asian Buddhist goddess or Bodhisattva of divine compassion.

Kuhn: Thomas Kuhn, philosopher/historian of science who proposed that the acceptance of scientific theories depended upon successive "paradigms" of "normal science" that were sociologically determined.

Lao Tse: Or Lao Tzu, the sixth-century B.C. founder of Taoism.

Laplace calculator: Or Laplace computer, an imaginary device invented by the eighteenth-century French natural philosopher Pierre Simon de Laplace. He proposed that all events in the universe could be explained by the collisions among its fundamental particles, whose properties uniquely determined their motions and the effect of their collisions. The Laplace calculator contained a complete list of all the particles in the universe, together with a record of their motions at any one time. Given this information, the calculator could predict all future events in the universe, including, presumably, all human thoughts, intentions, and actions.

Loa: A divine or demonic spirit in the religion of Vodun, especially one who can take possession of an adept.

Machiavelli: Renaissance Italian political philosopher who advocated an amoral policy of expediency on the part of rulers so as to maintain peace and order.

Maimonides: Moses Maimonides, the great twelfth-century A.D. Jewish scholar who reconciled the philosophy of Aristotle with the religion of the Talmud.

Mandelbrot set: The most familiar of all fractals. Benoit Mandelbrot discovered this set, usually represented by a color-coded diagram of surprising beauty (the "radiant snowman"). It is obtained by taking a field of complex numbers (i.e., ones with both real and imaginary components), squaring each one, adding the result to itself, and then feeding the end product back into the equation as the initiating variable. The numbers are color-coded to indicate how quickly they either increase to infinity or approach some limit, and displayed on a plane.

Masada: The stronghold where the remnants of the Jewish Zealot rebellion held out heroically against a Roman army until A.D. 73, when they committed mass suicide rather than surrender.

Meridians: See "Acupuncture."

Metempsychosis: The doctrine, held by various religious, philosophical, and mystical traditions, including the Hindus, the Buddhists, and some members of Socrates' school, that maintains that the soul can transmigrate from one body to another, and even be incarnated in the form of an animal.

Misologic: A Socratic concept, referring to the kind of mistrust of logic displayed by his grieving followers when, on his deathbed, he attempts to prove the immortality of the soul.

Moroni: The angel and resurrected prophet in the theology of the Church of the Latter-Day Saints who revealed the sacred scriptures of the Book of Mormon to Joseph Smith.

Nanotechnology: Technology on a molecular (nanometer) scale. Abbreviated to "nanotech" or "nano."

Neurocybernetic interface: System for connecting living nerve and brain cells with cybernetic computing devices. Still in early developmental phase, though advances have been made in restoring hearing loss and in military control of weapons by these methods.

Neurotransmitter: A chemical used by the brain to affect the transmission of neural impulses across the synapse (the gap between neurons), so as to pass messages or to reset whole areas of the brain into different brain states.

Neutrino: A particle with no charge and vanishingly small mass, that can pass through the earth without being affected.

Nominalism: The philosophical position that general abstract terms have no referents and exist only as names.

Nonlinear: Used here in the senses it is used in dynamics and mathematics. In a nonlinear physical process—often called a feedback process—the various elements all affect each other and there is no clearly determinable origin or priority of cause and effect; or an object affects itself and thus governs its own behavior. In a nonlinear mathematical equation, the solution to the equation is fed back again into the equation as one of its original variables, and the result is sometimes a set of values which when plotted in a phase space denoting how quickly the solutions increase to infinity or converge to a single value, produces a fractal form of great beauty. The Mandelbrot set, the most familiar of such fractals, is the product of the Mandelbrot equation, a classic nonlinear equation in the sense in which I am using the word.

Nucleotide: The basic building block and code unit of DNA, composed of a phosphate group, a sugar, and a purine or pyramidine base.

Observer problem: In quantum mechanics, the uncertainty that results when the only available means of measuring an event is comparable in magnitude to the event itself, and thus alters it so that its unobserved state cannot be known. Further research has suggested that the mere state of an observer's knowledge can be a factor in the reality being observed, a reality such as the polarization or charge of one member of an entangled particle pair when that of the other member is known, or the difference in behavior of a subatomic entity depending on whether it is being measured by wave-detecting or particle-detecting instruments, or the position of a particle whose momentum is exactly known. The observer problem in other fields of knowledge, for instance the study of animal behavior where the naturalist may be changing the animal's conditions, or anthropology, where the anthropologist's own knowledge may be a factor, in the social situation, may or may not be analogous to the problem as it arises in quantum physics.

Parmenides: The Greek philosopher from Elis in Italy who proposed that time and change were illusions and that the universe was a single, motionless block.

Penrose tilings: "Tiling the plane" is a mathematical concept describing the ability of certain shapes—such as equilateral triangles, squares, and hexagons—to cover an infinite plane space without gaps. Traditional tiling theory dealt with repeating patterns made up of shapes or combinations of shapes, with their attendant axes of symmetry or rotation. A new branch of this theory, popularized by the math-physicist Roger Penrose, deals with groups of shapes which, though never repeating, can be proven to tile the plane. One of these, a rather elegant combination of fat parallelograms and thin ones, produces such a tiling with a general but not exact five-axis rotational symmetry (although obviously the regular pentagon, unlike the triangle, square, and hexagon, cannot tile the plane). Intriguingly the ratio of thin to fat parallelograms in this tiling approaches the golden section ratio with greater and greater exactness as the tiled area increases. The golden section ratio—1 : 1.618...—is a universal in all living systems; its derivation from the ratios of the dimensions of a regular five-pointed star, and from the square root of five, leads to an interesting speculation about the role of what one might call "fiveness" in the emergence of life in the cosmos. Whereas other tilings merely repeat mechanically, a Penrose tiling grows in an unpredictable way, as do evolving living organisms.

Phase changes: Changes in phase state, such as freezing, boiling, melting, subliming, condensation, the formation of a plasma, or alterations in the general molecular, crystalline, or electrochemical orientation of a body of matter.

Phase space: An imaginary space whose axes are the various variables required to describe an object—e.g., the three dimensions of its location, its speed, momentum, direction, temperature, pressure, density, phase state, etc. Obviously this often requires more dimensions than the familiar three of space, making the whole hard to visualize; and thus phase spaces are usually carefully edited to show only the variables of interest to the observer, or those which make a significant difference to the object's behavior.

Phase state: In physical chemistry, the physical state of a piece of matter—solid, liquid, gas, plasma, its crystalline orientation or molecular structure.

Picaro: The hero of a picaresque fiction or story, that is, one constructed as a series of relatively disconnected episodes in which a clever central figure, often an unprincipled one, undergoes various adventures and experiences.

Planck's constant: Max Planck discovered this constant, one of the fundamental quantities in quantum physics. It describes the relationship of the energy of a photon to its frequency.

Polarity: Of an elementary particle, the handedness of its spin. Illustrated by holding out one's two hands with the thumbs up: the two hands have opposite polarity.

Polynomially: Refers here to the rate of change: a polynomial increase is one in which one or more of the quantities increases; an exponential increase is much greater, in which the exponent—that is, the number of times a quantity is multiplied by itself—increases.

Popol Vuh: The Mayan epic, which recounts the creation of the world and the adventures of Hunapúh and Ixbalanqué.

Positivist: One who believes that the only truth we can know is provable empirical fact based on sensory evidence and exact logic.

Poststructuralist: Describes a set of intellectual movements, including deconstructionism and various forms of discourse analysis including Foucauldian, feminist, postcolonial, and "queer studies" versions: usually committed to exposing the inconsistencies of traditional value systems by revealing them as based on political power interests. It followed structuralism, which maintained that the meaning of something was constituted by its structural and contextual elements, but departed from it in locating that meaning in its contradictions, and in discrediting meaning as meaningful term.

Privation: A term in classical philosophy denoting the absence or relative absence of some property, an absence which could itself have specific properties; for instance, evil might be a relative privation of good, time might be a privation of being (if being is conceived of as necessarily eternal).

Probability: A mathematical and logical field of study, in which a probability of one means certainty, and a probability of zero means impossibility. All normal probilities are thus expressed by some decimal, e.g., .35.

Proustian: Referring, here, to the experience (described in Marcel Proust's *À la recherche du temps perdu*) of complex and vivid memories triggered by some evocative association, such as the taste of Sunday madeleine cake.

Pyrrhonian: A skeptic who believes in the indefinite postponement and suspension of final judgment.

Quantum foam: In some versions of quantum theory, the state of a vacuum at very small scales: since reality, according to quantum theory, is always approximate, even nothingness itself is in its finest resolution a foam of tiny deviations in the direction of matter or antimatter, continually annihilating each other at a rate that constitutes one measure of the energy of the "quantum vacuum." One such deviation from absolute nothingness is thought by some cosmologists to have provided the seed of the Big Bang.

Quantum mechanics: The established theory governing the smallest components of matter and energy. It includes such concepts as uncertainty, or the unknowability of certain minute quantities; the granular quality of reality at very small scales; complementarity, or the mutual dependence of different measures at such scales; the wave-particle duality of matter; entanglement, by which two remote particles might be mutually dependent upon each other for their state of being, even if separated by too great a distance to communicate in time to inform each other of that state; the description of unobserved matter as a probabilistic wave function, collapsed into actuality only by observation; superposition, the ability of very small entities to be in more than one informational state at once;

and the highly ordered and predictable behavior of elementary particles—uncertain and unpredictable in themselves—when in ensembles connected in space or time.

Quantum vacuum: See "Quantum foam."

Quark: An elementary particle, a component of the hadrons of which matter is made.

Quasicrystals: Crystal-like arrangements of matter that, unlike ordinary crystals whose basic structures repeat regularly and symmetrically, achieve stability in a nonrepeating and asymmetrical array of generally similar though not identical connections. Penrose tilings display the principle at work in two-dimensional geometry.

Quechua: The linguistic and ethnic group containing the ancient Incas and their modern descendants.

Rational expectations: The complicating factor in such fields as economics, sociology, law theory, and road traffic control, whereby the expectations and predictive efforts of intelligent participants in a process such as the market, a society, a legal system, or a highway can confuse or frustrate any attempt to regulate or control it, or can generate new structures of general practice not given in the initial conditions.

Reflexive: A term beginning to come into use in anthropology and other disciplines, referring to the underlying characteristic of self-reference, self-consciousness, self-inclusion, iteration, and the quotation marks implicit in rehearsed social behavior.

Renormalization: The ingenious mathematical device by which awkward infinitudes in such fields as astrophysics, cosmology, and particle physics can be cancelled out, giving testable predictions.

Ribosome: The protein-factory of the living cell, made up of RNA and protein.

RNA: Ribonucleic acid, which transmits genetic information to living cells and when organized into ribosomes synthesizes the proteins that make up living organisms.

Rorty: Richard Rorty, American philosopher who believes in the priority of conversation and its continuance over any other activity, including the pursuit of truth.

Savonarola: Florentine preacher whose attack on idolatry led to the destruction of much Renaissance art.

Schleiermacher: Friedrich Schleiermacher's *On Religion: Speeches to Its Cultured Despisers* defended the merits of pious practice and local particular religion against the abstract philosophical deism and absolute reliance on reason advocated by the Enlightenment.

Schrödinger's cat: The quantum physicist Erwin Schrödinger proposed an odd thought experiment to illustrate a possible paradox in quantum theory. A cat is hidden in a box, accompanied by a vial of poison gas which is released by a mechanism if and when a radioactive source, also hidden from any observer, emits a particle. Quantum theory maintains that such a particle has only a virtual existence until it is observed, that is, it exists as the superposition of two states—not having been emitted, and having been emitted, according to relative degrees of probability. Since the only way an observer can know whether the particle has been emitted is by whether the cat is alive or dead, the cat itself must share the virtual superposed state of the particle—that is, it is both alive and dead, with some level of probability for each. Only when the box is opened does the cat's superposed state, like the particle's, collapse into one of two values, alive and dead.

Scientology: A religion which believes in the subjection of matter to spirit, and thus in a nonphysical basis for sickness and disease.

Searle: See "Chinese Room."

Self-organization: A process in which, through the interaction of all its elements with each other and with themselves, a relatively stable system emerges. The rolling boil of a pot of heated water is a good example of the result; another is the Great Red Spot of Jupiter, a storm that has raged in the same form and at the same latitude for hundreds of years at least; a third is a living organism, whose gestating cells have through their mutual interaction specialized themselves to produce a functioning plant or animal. There is evidence that the brain establishes coherent and retrievable memories in the same general way.

Self-similar: See "Fractal."

Sephiroth: The Cabbalistic mystical diagram depicting the tree of heaven, that indicates how the divine essence is mediated to its creation.

Shahnameh: The Epic of Shahnameh Ferdowsi, by Hakim Abol-Ghasem Ferdowsi Toosi (940–1020), recounts among other things the tragic story of Sohrab and Rustem.

Shekinah: In Judaism, the spirit of the Sabbath and of the holy people as the bride in her divine wedding with Adonai; even the feminine manifestation of God.

Shinai: Bamboo sword used in Japanese martial arts practice.

Shinto: Japanese traditional religion, emphasizing the divine spirits of nature and piety towards ancestors.

Sidney: Sir Philip Sidney, English renaissance poet, critic, statesman, and war hero, author of *The Defense of Poetry*.

Sikh: One who believes in Sikhism, a religion combining elements of Islam and Hinduism.

Singularities: In mathematical physics and cosmology, these are objects that break the normal continuity of space or time, in such a way that at certain points or surfaces there are no gradations between one part of the object and another, or between it and its local environment. A black hole is a familiar kind of singularity—or rather, different kinds of black holes contain different kinds of singularities. The origin of the universe is often referred to as a singularity.

Society of mind: Phrase popularized by Marvin Minsky, the MIT computer scientist, who described the human mind not as a single integrated entity but as a collection of competencies, loosely organized under ad hoc executive control.

Sociobiology: The study of the behavior of humans and other social animals in the light of their biological inheritance and the psychological requirements imposed by the need to reproduce their genes into the next generation.

Solipsism: The theory that the self is the only reality, as it is the only thing we can know.

Species, genus, family, order, class, phylum, kingdom: The taxonomical classification system of animals, in ascending order of generality and temporal remoteness of first evolutionary appearance. There is a slightly different terminology for plants, bacteria, etc., and interspecies gene transfer somewhat muddies the clear picture.

St. Bartholomew's Day Massacre: Massacre of about 100,000 Protestants by French Catholics during the Reformation.

Structuralist-functionalist: Describes a position adopted by some anthropologists and other social scientists in the twentieth century, according to which political, kinship, and ideological structures in society are the result of a functional adjustment of the available technology to the local ecology, and the chief currency of society is economic power.

Sufism: A form of Islamic mysticism dating from the eighth century A.D., containing a lofty poetic and philosophical account of the relationship of the natural, the human, and the divine.

Suttee: Traditional Indian practice involving the voluntary self-immolation of wives at the funeral of their husbands.

Synaptic circuit: the circuitry formed when a number of neurons, or brain cells, fire in sequence, setting each other off by electrochemical impulses across the synapse (the gap between neurons).

Tai chi: The traditional Chinese exercise, deriving from the martial arts, designed to encourage the flow of *chi* or spiritual energy about the body.

Tao, Taoism: An originally Chinese religion dating from the sixth century B.C., which perceives the inner generative forces of nature as alive and divine.

Telomeres: The sections at the ends of the chromosomes (the lengths of DNA that carry the genes which build the bodies of living organisms); telomeres become frayed away with age, a fraying thought to have an important role in aging.

Theism: Abstract philosophical position claiming to prove the existence of God or gods.

Thermodynamic decay: See "Entropy."

Theromorphism: In the form of a beast; often in reference to representations of gods and spirits, e.g., Set, Quetzal, Ganesha, the Lamb of God, etc.

Thick description: An anthropological term associated with the anthropologist Clifford Geertz, denoting a kind of ethnography that richly depicts the details of another society without drawing conclusions or imposing "western" categories. It is an attempt to avoid generalizations and judgments that might carry a neocolonial bias.

Three Unities: The doctrine—attributed by its European literary adherents to Aristotle—that well-made tragic dramas ought to exhibit unity of time, place, and action.

Tiamat: The creation goddess in ancient Mesopotamian religion; the universe is her dismembered body.

Tlaloc: The Mayan storm-god.

Totalize: To commit what contemporary poststructuralist thinking regards as one of the worst sins—to arrange all experience and information with respect to a single organizing principle.

Transfinite number: See Cantor.

Tridentine: Pertaining to the Catholic Church and doctrine as it has been constituted since the codifications of the Council of Trent (1545–63).

Turing machine: Alan Turing, British inventor of the first modern programmable computer (and also of the system that broke the Nazi Enigma Code), was able to do so partly because he had proved mathematically that all computational systems or devices worked according to the same basic principles. Any other computational device could thus be simulated in its operation by an imaginary "Turing machine," which consisted of an infinite reversible tape marked with instructions in the form of zeros and ones, passing through a tape head which, according to the tape instructions, would move the tape forward or back or print a zero or one.

Turing test: Hypothetical test for artificial intelligence devised by Alan Turing. If a human interlocutor could not tell, after a typed conversation of a given length with a computer, whether he was conversing with a human being or a computer, the computer could be said to be artificially intelligent.

Umbanda: A Brazilian religion, combining African, Amerindian, and Christian elements.

Umwelt: Used here in the sense given by Jacob von Üxkull and J.T. Fraser: literally, "about-world": the universe affected by an entity's effectors and registered by its receptors; whatever is required for an entity to exist.

Unification Church: Founded by Sun Myung Moon in the twentieth century, this religious movement seeks to unify all world religions.

Urania: The ancient Greek muse of astronomy, but also conceived of by some thinkers, including John Milton, as the heavenly goddess of wisdom.

Vedic tradition: The most ancient roots of Hinduism, based on the Vedas, its sacred poetic and liturgical texts.

Vodun: Popularly known as Voodoo and much misunderstood under that name, this religion emphasizes ritual, spirit possession, and direct manifestation of divine spirits.

Whig: The "Whig view of history" as it was known to its opponents, saw the world as evolving toward a state of enlightened democracy, law and order, usually with advanced western technological nations leading the way.

Will to power: The fundamental motivation of life, according to Nietzsche and other philosophers.

Wittgenstein: Ludwig Wittgenstein, major twentieth-century linguistic philosopher, whose basic questions concerned the extent to which our language constrains our reality.

Yogi: Practitioner of traditional Indian ascetic discipline.

Zen: A sophisticated form of Buddhism, whose highest value for the practitioner is enlightenment; properly seen by a meditating adept, the world as it is is already full of the perfection of being.

Further Reading

Alexander Argyros, *A Blessed Rage for Order* (University of Michigan Press, 1991).
The best book to date on how the new ideas in evolution and chaos theory might revolutionize contemporary philosophy.

John Armstrong, *The Paradise Myth* (Oxford University Press, 1969).
A brilliant and profound work on the caduceus and on our conception of the Arcadian paradise.

A. Dwight Baldwin, Jr., Judith de Luce, Carl Pletsch, eds., *Beyond Preservation: Restoring and Inventing Landscapes* (University of Minnesota Press, 1993).
Two long essays, by William Jordan and Frederick Turner, define the new paradigm in environmental philosophy; an interdisciplinary panel of experts discusses these essays from various points of view.

Greg Bear, *Queen of Angels* (Warner Books, 1990).
Perhaps the most fully realized of Bear's imagined world cyber-technology futures.

The Bible (any standard edition).
The scripture which, in whole or part, is central to the religion of about half of the human species.

Derek Bickerton, "Creole Languages," *Scientific American*, July 1983.
Language is not an arbitrary cultural invention, but an inborn natural capacity.

William Blake, *The Complete Poetry and Prose of William Blake* (David Erdman, ed.; Anchor, 1982).
Blake is a true prophet, and his work, especially *The Marriage of Heaven and Hell,* is foundational to this book.

Maurice Bloch, Jonathan Parry, eds., *Money and the Morality of Exchange* (Cambridge University Press, 1989).
A path-breaking collection of essays in economic anthropology, implying that every human society probably has some version of a marketplace that anchors one end of its moral system.

Daniel Botkin, *Discordant Harmonies* (Oxford University Press, 1990).
This book by a distinguished ecological scientist dispells many contemporary environmentalist myths with its clear exposition of the nonlinear feedback systems in nature, and its refusal to separate human and natural activities.

William Buck, trans. and ed., *Mahabharata* (University of California Press, 1981).
An accessible abridgement of the great Indian epic poem that evolved into a profound religious scripture.

Walter Burkert, *Homo Necans: the Anthropology of Ancient Greek Sacrifical Ritual and Myth*, trans. Peter Bing (Berkeley: University of California Press, 1983).
—. *Greek Religion* (Harvard University Press, 1987).
The foremost authority on Greek religion.

David Channell, *The Vital Machine* (Oxford University Press, 1991).
How our mechanistic and vitalistic explanations of nature converged in the late twentieth century.

Pierre Teilhard de Chardin, *The Phenomenon of Man* (HarperCollins, 1980).
A pathbreaking evolutionary interpretation of religion.

Confucius, *Analects,* trans. Arthur Waley (Vintage, 1989).
The core text of Confucianism.

Robert P. Crease and Charles C. Mann, *The Second Creation: Makers of the Revolution in Twentieth-Century Physics* (Macmillan, 1986).
A good introduction to the new physics up to the advent of chaos theory.

E.G. D'Aquili, C.D. Laughlin, Jr., and J. McManus, eds., *The Spectrum of Ritual: A Biogenetic Structural Analysis* (Columbia University Press, 1979).
A pathbreaking book about the neurobiology of religion.

Charles Darwin, *The Origin of Species* (Collier; Macmillan, 1962)
Every serious student of religion ought to reread this profound and splendid book.

Paul Davies, *God and the New Physics* (Touchstone, 1983).
—. *The Cosmic Blueprint* (Simon & Schuster, 1988).
—. *The Mind of God: The Scientific Basis for a Rational World* (Touchstone Books, 1993)
Accessible introductions to the new cosmology.

Richard Dawkins, *The Selfish Gene* (Oxford University Press, 1990).
The classic work of biological reductionism.

Koen DePryck, *Knowledge, Evolution, and Paradox* (State University of New York Press, 1993).
A brilliant and profound book about the philosophy, esthetics, and neuropsychology of interdisciplinary studies.

David Deutsch and Michael Lockwood, "The Quantum Physics of Time Travel," *Scientific American*, March 1994.
An accessible contemporary account of the parallel universes theory proposed by Hugh Everett III.

Bryce S. DeWitt, R. Neill Graham, eds., *The Many-Worlds Interpretation of Quantum Mechanics* (Princeton Series in Physics, Princeton University Press, 1973).
The explication of Hugh Everett III's many-worlds theory.

Fyodor Dostoyevsky, *The Brothers Karamazov*, trans. Constance Garnett (Modern Library, 1996).
This great novel explores the conflict between rationalism and religion and the problem of evil.

Émile Durkheim, *Suicide: A Study in Sociology* (Free Press, 1997)
Society as God: one of the founding works of sociology.

Sir John Eccles, Roger Sperry, Ilya Prigogine, Brian Josephson, *Nobel Prize Conversations* (Saybrook, 1985).
A fascinating book about the new brain science: mental causality is neither purely bottom-up nor purely top-down, but constitutes a nonlinear feedback system with unpredictable yet ordered emergent features.

Irenäus Eibl-Eibesfeldt, *Human Ethology* (Aldine de Gruyter, 1989).
The classic, yet at the time very controversial, work that showed how universal is much of human behavior, and that rooted human behavior in natural evolution.

T.S. Eliot, *Four Quartets* (Harcourt Brace, 1974).
A great twentieth-century religious poem which draws together themes and images from several world religions.

Stephen Erickson, *The (Coming) Age of Thresholding* (Springer, 1999).
A prophetic survey of the new era we are presently entering.

R.O. Faulkner, trans., *The Ancient Egyptian Book of the Dead* (University of Texas Press, 1990).

Abulqasem Ferdowsi, *The Shahnameh* (Mazda, 1993).
The great Persian tragic-epic poem.

Paul Feyerabend, *Against Method* (Verso Books, 1993).
A radical pluralist critique of science.

Robin Fox, ed., *Biosocial Anthropology* (Malaby Press, 1975).
—. *Encounter with Anthropology* (Transaction Publishers, 1991).
—. *The Challenge of Anthropology* (Transaction Publishers, 1994).
Robin Fox has been the clearest advocate for the fact that we are an animal species reflecting the history of our evolution.

J.T. Fraser, "Out of Plato's Cave: The Natural History of Time," *Kenyon Review*, Winter 1980.
—. *Time as Conflict* (Birkhäuser, 1978).
—. *Time, Conflict, and Human Values* (University of Illinois Press, 1999).
Fraser's theory of the composite nature of time, as a concentrically nested hierarchy of temporalities, is in my opinion the most important contribution to fundamental philosophy of this half-century.

William Gibson, *Neuromancer* (Ace, 1986).
—. *Count Zero* (Ace, 1987).
—. *Mona Lisa Overdrive* (Ace, 1998).
Splendidly crafted glitzy-grungy cyberpunk novels about the neural-cybernetic interface, its dangers, corruptions, and mystical possibilities.

James Gleick, *Chaos: Making a New Science* (Viking, 1987).
The classic overview of the new nonlinear science, which, however, puzzlingly leaves out Prigogine.

Vladimir Gontar, "Theoretical Foundation for the Discrete Dynamics of Physicochemical Systems: Chaos, Self-Organization, Time and Space in Complex Systems." *Discrete Dynamics in Nature and Society*, vol. 1, no. 1, p. 31.
A technical but brilliant explanation of how if time and space are quantized and the constituents of the universe can thus behave like a game with counters and turns, new forms of self-organization can emerge.

Jane Goodall, *The Chimpanzees of Gombe: Patterns of Behavior* (Belknap Press of Harvard University Press, 1986.
—. *Visions of Caliban: on Chimpanzees and People,* with Dale Peterson (Boston: Houghton Mifflin, 1993).
There is not so great a gap between us and our primate relatives as the social constructionists would like to believe.

Stephen Jay Gould, *The Flamingo's Smile* (W. W. Norton, 1985).
—. *Eight Little Piggies* (W. W. Norton, 1994).
Gould's insistence on the nonlinear and sometimes sudden processes of evolution has been a useful corrective to more determinist views, but his ideological distaste for teleology makes him miss some of the more exciting implications of his approach.

David Ray Griffin, ed., *The Reenchantment of Science* (SUNY Press, 1988).
—. *God and Religion in the Postmodern World* (SUNY Press, 1989).
Griffin's attempt to recruit a reconstructive postmodernism based on a sophisticated Whiteheadian religious worldview is an important part of the emerging religious world picture.

Jürgen Habermas, *Between Facts and Norms: Contributions to a Discourse Theory of Law and Democracy* (MIT Press, 1996).
An intelligent and conscientious attempt to derive values from the requirements for a democratic society.

Charles Hartshorne, *Born to Sing: an Interpretation and World Survey of Bird Song* (Indiana University Press 1973).
Natural esthetics.

Václav Havel, *The Power of the Powerless: Citizens Against the State in Central-Eastern Europe* (M.E. Sharpe, 1985).
—. *Open Letters: Selected Writings, 1965–1990* (Knopf, 1991).
Havel points the way toward a future society of evolutionary hope.

Stephen W. Hawking, *A Brief History of Time* (Bantam, 1988).
One look at the new physics of time.

N. Katherine Hayles, *Chaos and Order: Complex Dynamics in Literature and Science* (University of Chicago Press, 1991.
Hayles' work is full of interesting insights about the humanistic implications of the new science.

G. W. F. Hegel, *Reason in History* (Bobbs-Merrill, 1953).
A concise exposition of Hegel's concepts of dialectic and the evolution of spirit and reason through history.

Martin Heidegger, *Being and Time*, trans. Joan Stambaugh (SUNY Press, 1997).
The founding work of postmodern philosophy, by a Nazi thinker.

Hesiod, *Theogony, Works and Days*, ed. M.L. West (Oxford University Press 1999).

James Hillman, *The Soul's Code: In Search of Character and Calling* (Warner Books, 1997).
Hillman is one of the leaders of the current "soul movement" in America.

Thomas Hobbes, *Leviathan* (Prentice Hall, 1958).
The classic of political philosophy in which the state of nature is described as a war of each against all.

Douglas Hofstadter, *Gödel, Escher, Bach* (Vintage, 1979).
This book has not lost any of the wonderful surprise, playfulness, and originality of its investigation of self-referential processes and structures.

Gerard Manley Hopkins, *Poetry and Prose* (Everyman, 1999).
No poet has more richly demonstrated the immanence of the divine in nature.

Ivan Illich, *H2O and the Waters of Forgetfulness: Reflections on the Historic-
ity of Stuff* (Dallas Institute of Humanities and Culture, 1985).
Illich's critique of modernity cannot be ignored.

William James, *The Varieties of Religious Experience* (Macmillan, 1997).
The classic work on the psychology of religion.

Immanuel Kant, *Fundamental Principles of the Metaphysic of Morals*
(Prometheus Books, 1987).
—. *Critique of Pure Reason* (Everyman, 1990).
Works in which Kant respectively sets forth (among many other things) his
theory of the necessary disinterestedness of true ethical behavior, and his skep-
ticism regarding our access to the world through the senses.

L.W. King, ed., *Enuma Elish, vol. 1 & 2: The Seven Tablets of Creation; The
Babylonian and Assyrian Legends Concerning the Creation of the World
and of Mankind* (Book Tree, 1999).

Thomas Kuhn, *The Structure of Scientific Revolutions* (University of Chicago
Press, 1996).
An important book that led many of its followers to regard scientific knowl-
edge as subject to sociological pressures.

Lao Tse, *Tao Te Ching,* trans. Stephen Mitchell (HarperPerennial, 1992).
A good translation of the Taoist classic.

Leon M. Lederman and David N. Schramm, *From Quarks to the Cosmos* (Scientific American Library, 1989).
A useful introduction to the converging visions of cosmological and particle
physics.

Vladimir Lefebvre, "The Fundamental Structures of Human Reflexion," in *Journal of Social and Biological Structures* 10 (1987).
Lefebvre's interesting speculations trace the nonlinear mathematics of human
ethical and veridical judgments.

C.S. Lewis, *Out of the Silent Planet* (Scribner's, 1996).
—. *Perelandra* (Scribner's, 1996).
Even more eloquently than in his essays, these novels outline a deep critique of
technology as it concerns salvation.

David Lindsay, *A Voyage to Arcturus* (Ballantine Books, 1963).
A visionary and deeply poetic science fiction novel, which suggests a view of the universe as the actual battleground of spiritual forces.

Elias Lönnrot, *The Kalevala* (Oxford University Press, 1999).
The Finnish national epic poem.

James Lovelock, *Gaia: A New Look at Life on Earth* (Oxford University Press, 1979).
The Gaia Hypothesis, that all life on this planet constitutes a superorganism that regulates its own life support.

James Lovelock and Michael Allaby, *The Greening of Mars* (Warner Books, 1984).
A remarkable book about the practical work of transforming a dead planet into a living one.

Niccolo Machiavelli, *The Prince* (Oxford University Press, 1998).
The classic work on political power and the god-state.

Benoit Mandelbrot, *The Fractal Geometry of Nature* (Freeman, 1977).
One of the most original books ever written, this beautifully illustrated and eccentric treatment of nonlinear and discontinuous mathematics is still at the leading edge of contemporary natural philosophy.

Lynn Margulis and Dorion Sagan, *Microcosmos: Four Billion Years of Evolution from Our Microbial Ancestors* (Summit, 1986).
An original reconception of the dynamics of evolution on this planet, which by implication refutes the "fragile balance of nature" theory and emphasizes the creativity of nature.

David Marr, *Vision* (Freeman, 1982).
A pathbreaking book on the nature of visual perception, with striking implications for esthetics; now slightly outdated, but still very useful.

Juan Mascaro, trans., *The Upanishads* (Viking, 1965).
A good though small selection of the classic works of Hindu meditation.
—. *Bhagavad Gita* (New York: Viking, 1983).
The mystical conversation between Krishna and Arjuna on the battlefield of life.

Herman Melville, *Moby Dick* (Buccaneer Books, 1960).
In a sense, Melville's great novel asks all the questions about religion that this book attempts to answer.

John Milton, *Paradise Lost* (Buccaneer Books, 1983).
The greatest religious epic poem in the English language.

Gregory Nagy, *The Best of the Achaeans; Concepts of the Hero in Archaic Greek Poetry* (Johns Hopkins University Press, 1979).
This book marvelously catches the unflinchingness, pragmatism, and dignity with which the Greeks confronted divine reality.

Rudolf Otto, *Idea of the Holy* (Oxford University Press, 1958).
Religion as the experience of terrifying and fascinating mystery.

Blaise Pascal, *Pensées*, trans. A.J. Krailsheimer (Penguin Classics, 1995).
A passionate defense of religion in a time of rationalism.

Arthur Peacocke: *Theology for a Scientific Age: Being and Becoming-Natural, Divine and Human* (Augsburg Fortress Publishers, 1993).
A pioneering study of the relationship between science and religion

Arthur Peacocke ed., *In Whom We Live and Move and Have Our Being: Panentheistic Reflections on God's Presence in a Scientific World* (Eerdmans, 2004).
An excellent collection of recent work on the divine in nature.

Roger Penrose: *The Emperor's New Mind: Concerning Computers, Minds, and the Laws of Physics* (Oxford University Press, 1989).
This book purports to show the impossibility of artificial intelligence, but it is actually a brilliant exploration of the new implications of nonlinearity.

Stephen Pinker, *The Language Instinct* (HarperPerennial, 1995).
A brilliantly written book showing how language is an evolved capacity of the human animal, and therefore part of nature.

Sir John Polkinghorne, *The Faith of a Physicist: Reflections of a Bottom-Up Thinker* (Princeton University Press, 1994).
In the Gifford Lectures, Polkinghorne gives a major summary of his work on the implications for the creator of the creation and for the creation of the creator.

Ilya Prigogine and Isabelle Stengers, *Order Out of Chaos: Man's New Dialogue with Nature* (Bantam, 1984).
The most important book on the emergent properties of nature.

Willard V. Quine, *From Stimulus to Science* (Harvard University Press, 1998).
Some interesting and awkward questions about how we get scientific knowledge from the world we sense—if indeed we do.

Miklós Radnóti: *Foamy Sky: The Major Poems of Miklós Radnóti*, trans. Zsuzsanna Ozsváth and Frederick Turner (Princeton University Press, 1992).

Walpola Sri Rahula, *What the Buddha Taught* (Grove Press, 1986).
A standard introduction to Buddhism.

Angelo S. Rappoport, *Ancient Israel: Myths and Legends* (Bonanza Books,1987)

Ingo Rentschler, Barbara Herzberger, David Epstein, eds., *Beauty and the Brain: Biological Aspects of Aesthetics* (Birkhauser, 1988).
The first major book on the evolution, neurobiology, and psychophysics of beauty.

Paul Reps, Nyogen Senzaki, eds., *Zen Flesh, Zen Bones: A Collection of Zen and Pre-Zen Writings* (Shambhala, 1994).
A fine collection of Zen classics.

Rainer Maria Rilke, *Letters to a Young Poet* (W.W. Norton, 1994).
—. *The Duino Elegies and the Sonnets to Orpheus*, trans. A. Poulin (Houghton Mifflin, 1977).
Rilke has not been recognized sufficiently for his greatness as a religious poet of science and evolution. The best translation of the *Duino Elegies* is that of Spender and Leishman.

John M. Robson, ed., *Origin and Evolution of the Universe: Evidence for Design?* (McGill-Queen's University Press, 1987).
A serious and interesting discussion of the possible role of intention and consciousness in the evolution of the universe.

Richard Rorty, *Philosophy and Social Hope* (Penguin, 2000).
Replaces the search for truth with a search for a democratic conversation.

William Ryan and Walter Pitman, *Noah's Flood: The New Scientific Discoveries About the Event That Changed History* (Simon and Schuster, 1998).
See chapter 4.

Padma Sambhava, Robert A. Thurman trans., *The Tibetan Book of the Dead* (Bantam, 1994).

Jeffrey Satinover, *The Quantum Brain: The Search for Freedom and the Next Generation of Man* (Wiley, 2001).
A daring and learned argument that free will can be derived from a combination of classical determinism and quantum indeterminacy amplified into the macrocosm in the brain.

Friedrich D. Schleiermacher, *On Religion: Speeches to Its Cultured Despisers* (Cambridge Texts in the History of Philosophy, 1996).
Among other things, this powerful and original work defends local and ritualized forms of religion against abstract theism.

Gershom Scholem, ed., *Zohar: The Book of Splendor: Basic Readings from the Kabbalah* (Schocken, 1995).
An ancient, labyrinthine, and poetic work of Jewish textual exegesis, full of strange wisdom.

J. William Schopf, ed., *Earth's Earliest Biosphere: Its Origin and Evolution* (Princeton University Press, 1983).
A magisterial collection of essays that shows how catastrophic the great experiment of organic life can be.

Erwin Schrödinger, *Science and Humanism: Physics in Our Time* (Cambridge University Press, 1951).
Schrödinger's attempt to find a place for human freedom in the universe through quantum uncertainty anticipates Penrose's similar work. Until the science of nonlinear and complex systems came along, this was the best hope for a theory of freedom.

John Searle, *Minds, Brains, and Science* (Harvard University Press, 1986).
A good exposition of the inadequacies of traditional philosophical language—though not always aware that it is—in dealing with the mind/brain, mind/matter problem, itself a problem created by philosophical definitions.

George A. Seielstad, *At The Heart of the Web: The Inevitable Genesis of Intelligent Life* (Harcourt Brace, 1989).
The ontoepistemological necessity of observers in the universe.

Lynda Sexson, *Ordinarily Sacred* (Crossroad, 1982).
The religious and ritual dimensions of ordinary life: written with great charm and insight.

William Shakespeare, *The Complete Works,* David Bevington, ed (Addison-Wesley, 1997).
A spiritual achievement fully as great as any religious scripture in the world.

Philip Sidney, *The Defence of Poesie, Astrophil and Stella, and Other Writings,* ed. Elizabeth Porges Watson (Tuttle, 1997).
The most eloquent advocate for the prophetic virtues of poetry.

Brian Skyrms, *Evolution of the Social Contract* (Cambridge University Press, 1996).
Using elegant game-theory computer models, this book shows how evolution in a reproducing population can bring about apparently moral behavior.

Joseph Smith, trans., *The Book of Mormon* (Church of Jesus Christ of the LDS, 1981).

Elliott Sober and David Sloan Wilson, *Unto Others: The Evolution and Psychology of Unselfish Behavior* (Harvard University Press, 1998).
With Skyrms' book (see reference), this work shows convincingly how values can emerge from facts in an evolving population of reproducing organisms.

Sorin Sonea and Maurice Panisset, *A New Bacteriology* (Jones & Bartlett, 1983).
Like Margulis and Sagan's book, this work demonstrates the close kinship of all life on earth.

Dennis Tedlock, trans., *Popol Vuh: The Mayan Book of the Dawn of Life* (Touchstone, 1996).
The strange but poetic story of the Mayan creation and of two heroic brothers' descent into the underworld.

H.S. Thayer, "The Right to Believe: William James's Reinterpretation of the Function of Religious Belief," *Kenyon Review*, Winter, 1983.
An interesting discussion of an early precursor of the anthropic principle.

Henry David Thoreau, *Walden* (Charles E. Merrill, 1969).
The human as part of nature.

Lionel Tiger, *Optimism: The Biology of Hope* (Simon and Schuster, 1979).
Hope is an essential activity of the human brain.

Paul Tillich, *Biblical Religion and the Search for Ultimate Reality* (University of Chicago Press, 1964).
A powerful attempt to make religion reasonable without reductiveness.

Frederick Turner, *Genesis, an Epic Poem* (Saybrook Publishers, 1988).
—. *Natural Classicism* (University Press of Virginia, 1991; first published 1985).
—. *Rebirth of Value: Meditations on Beauty, Ecology, Religion, and Education* (SUNY Press, 1991).
—. *Tempest, Flute, and Oz: Essays on the Future* (Persea Books, 1991).
—. *Beauty: The Value of Values* (University Press of Virginia, 1991).
—. *The Culture of Hope: A New Birth of the Classical Spirit* (Free Press, 1995)

Victor W. Turner, *Schism and Continuity in an African Society* (Manchester University Press, 1957).
—. *The Forest of Symbols* (Cornell University Press, 1967).
—. *The Drums of Affliction* (Oxford University Press, 1968).
—. *The Ritual Process* (University of Chicago Press, 1969).
—. *Dramas, Fields, and Metaphors* (Cornell University Press, 1974).
—. *From Ritual to Theatre* (PAJ Publications, 1982).

Victor Turner's deeply humanistic anthropology is an excellent corrective against all power-based theories of social construction.

Mark Twain, *The Adventures of Huckleberry Finn* (Penguin, 1986).
Among other things, this great novel shows the creative mechanism by which morality and conscience can evolve as living species do.

The Vatican, *Catechism of the Catholic Church* (Libreria Editrice Vaticana, 1994).
The blueprint of contemporary Catholicism.

Voltaire, *Philosophical Dictionary* (Penguin Classics, 1984).
The classic work of religious debunking.

Judith Wechsler, ed., *On Aesthetics in Science* (M.I.T. Press,1978).
An excellent collection of essays on the intricate beauty that science uncovers in nature. The essay by Cyril Stanley Smith on crystallography and visual beauty is especially recommended.

Richard Westfall, *Never at Rest: A Biography of Isaac Newton* (Cambridge University Press, 1983).

John Archibald Wheeler, "World as System Self-Synthesized by Quantum Networking," *IBM Journal of Research and Development,* 32, no. 1 (1988).
A summary of Wheeler's somewhat misnamed "Anthropic Principle" of cosmology, in which the initial conditions of the universe are constrained by the necessity to bring about observers of it that will collapse its wave function.

Alfred North Whitehead, *Science and the Modern World* (Cambridge University Press, 1967).
An amazingly prescient look at the intellectual currents that are bringing about new era of the divine.

Andrew Wilson, ed., *World Scripture: A Comparative Anthology of Sacred Texts* (Continuum Publishing Group, 1995).
Compiled under the patronage of the Unification Church, this excellent collection of texts is a fine introduction to what the various recognized world religions have in common.

Edward O. Wilson and Charles J. Lumsden, *Promethean Fire* (Harvard University Press, 1983).
A lively and controversial introduction to human sociobiology.
Edward O. Wilson, *Biophilia* (Harvard University Press, 1984).
—. *Consilience: The Unity of Knowledge* (Random House, 1999).
Wilson's courageous and original work sets human values within the context of biological evolution.

Ludwig Wittgenstein, *Tractatus Logico-Philosophicus* (Routledge, 1995).
—. *Philosophical Investigations* (Prentice Hall, 1999).
—. *On Certainty* (HarperCollins, 1986).
Wittgenstein's work constitutes the bar and standard that any account of religious meaning must surmount; but it also provides hints about how to do so.

Virginia Woolf, *To the Lighthouse* (Harcourt Brace, 1955).
Woolf's novel is eloquent proof, if any were needed, that a deeply spiritual and moral point of view is possible without the theological structures of traditional religion.

Robert Wright, *Nonzero: The Logic of Human Destiny* (Pantheon, 2000).
Excellent discussion of games-theoretical and emergentist implications of evolution.

Wu Cheng-En, *Monkey: Folk Novel of China*, trans. Arthur Waley (Grove Press, 1994).
More usually titled *The Journey to the West*, this abridged translation is accessible and catches the mixture of comedy and religious depth in this remarkable work.

E.C. Zeeman, "Catastrophe Theory," *Scientific American*, April 1976.
A lucid presentation of the ideas of René Thom. One of the first appearances in the United States of the new science of nonlinear geometry.

Index

Abraham, 28, 62, 161, 189, 190
Accelerator, 245
Achilles, 201
Acupuncture, 245, 252
Adam and Eve, 27, 187
Adonai, 109, 243, 257
Aesculapius, 51, 52, 54, 60
Africa, 1, 9, 10, 20, 21, 35, 50, 113, 164, 190, 208, 224, 240, 259, 271
afterlife, 46, 114, 116, 179, 194, 197, 198, 201, 202, 203
aging, 64, 66, 172, 258
Aikido, 168
Akhenaten, 21
Akhenaton, 10, 152, 245
Alcestis, 168, 194
alchemy, 32
Allah, 10, 19, 175, 181, 204, 211
Alpha, 175, 211
Amazon, 15, 36, 229
American Revolution, 88
Ammon, 20
angakoq, 55
Angel, 168, 175
Anglo-Saxon, 20
animism, 20, 138, 182, 241
Anthropic Principle, 120, 123, 273
anthropology, 258
antichaos, 77
Aphrodite, 241
Apollo, 20, 53, 54, 55, 57, 151, 247
apoptosis, 245
Aquinas, 28, 160, 245
Arabic, 211, 232
Ararat, 49
Argyros, Alexander, 261
Aristotle, 40, 245, 252, 258
Arjuna, 6, 219, 224, 267
Armstrong, 51
Armstrong, John, 261

art, 15, 35, 42, 45, 57, 58, 62, 63, 73, 75, 81, 83, 90, 110, 111, 112, 115, 141, 151, 155, 172, 178, 196, 207, 211, 232, 244, 245, 256
Artemis, 52, 167, 169
asceticism, 212
Asia, 9, 48, 50, 51, 184, 194, 208
atheism, 181
atheist, 177, 180
Athena, 29, 52, 53, 243
Athens, 21, 29, 40
atom, 37, 111, 121, 127, 129, 170, 227, 246
attractor, 26, 78, 83, 84, 85, 86, 87, 95, 119, 133, 179, 189, 213, 240, 245, 246
Auschwitz, 208
Austin, 228
axiom, 29, 69, 108, 109, 110, 111, 229
Aztec, 44

Babbage, Charles, 131, 245
Babits, 170
Bacchantes, 53, 243
Baha'i, 10
Baha'i, 204, 246
Baha'ullah, 174, 246
Baldur, 151, 167
Baldwin, A. Dwight, 261
Bali, 198, 220
baptism, 33
Baptist, 34, 44, 212, 218, 232, 233
Bear, Greg, 160, 261
Beatrice, 243
Bellini, 188
Bendis, 20
Bhagavadgita, 6, 27, 99, 114, 116, 193, 212, 219, 229, 252
Bible, 8, 49, 60, 61, 63, 99, 114, 193, 208, 232, 235, 261

Bickerton, Derek, 36, 261
Big Bang, 97, 100, 103, 106, 121, 128, 144, 175, 221, 228, 246, 251, 256
Bio-engineering, 166
biology, 17, 22, 31, 34, 37, 38, 39, 40, 53, 57, 59, 61, 63, 66, 67, 68, 75, 76, 86, 87, 90, 91, 95, 105, 106, 111, 112, 119, 136, 139, 141, 147, 148, 158, 160, 166, 167, 183, 184, 185, 187, 192, 193, 198, 199, 200, 214, 220, 221, 230, 240, 241, 248, 250, 256, 257, 262, 266, 269, 273
biotechnology, 32, 163, 192
Black Sea, 49, 207
Blake, 117, 168, 203, 261
blessing, 63, 187
Bloch, Maurice, 154, 261
bodhisattva, 246, 252
Bohm, David, 132, 134, 135, 136, 141, 173, 175, 203, 217, 219, 246
Bohr, Neils, 120, 231, 247
bond, 66, 156
Botkin, Daniel, 262
bowerbird, 111, 127
Brahman, 10, 138, 175, 184
brain, 12, 30, 31, 34, 55, 75, 76, 77, 80, 83, 85, 86, 87, 96, 98, 106, 108, 110, 118, 119, 122, 138, 139, 141, 144, 147, 150, 151, 162, 169, 174, 180, 185, 186, 199, 209, 213, 221, 235, 248, 250, 253, 257, 258, 263, 270, 271
brain chemistry, 12, 56
branching, 57, 68, 69, 79, 117, 121, 134, 177, 249
Braudel, Fernand, 89
Buck, William, 262
Buddha, 19, 32, 35, 41, 116, 145, 174, 181, 191, 208, 212, 224, 229, 246, 249, 269
Buddhism, 20, 43, 169, 175, 212, 242, 246, 259, 269
Buddhist, 9, 10, 99, 168, 198, 212, 252
Buddhists, 13, 35, 179, 190, 201, 252
bulla, 67
Burkert, Walter, 262
business, 15, 25, 41, 64, 136, 153, 154, 155, 156, 157, 159, 160, 166, 167, 237
butterfly effect, 78, 135, 222, 246
Byzantine, 10, 250

CAD-CAM, 129, 246
caduceus, 51, 52, 53, 54, 55, 57, 59, 60, 61, 65, 66, 67, 69, 139, 144, 152, 261
Caesar, 42
candle, 45
Cantor, Georg, 26, 246, 247, 259
cargo cult, 246
Cartesian, 12, 17, 178, 182
Catechism, 205, 272
Catholic, 9, 20, 33, 147, 169, 184, 190, 200, 204, 205, 206, 210, 211, 218, 223, 224, 227, 229, 230, 231, 232, 233, 239, 244, 259, 272
Catholicism, 14, 44, 272
causality, 70, 118, 119, 122, 236, 263
celebration, 38, 65, 106, 157
Chac-mool, 246
chakra, 51
Channell, David, 262
chaos, 47, 71, 76, 77, 78, 79, 80, 81, 87, 95, 132, 173, 182, 205, 246, 247, 250, 251, 261, 262, 264, 265, 268
chaos theory, 246
Chardin, Teilhard de, 224, 262
Chaucer, 35
chemistry, 3, 48, 70, 91, 104, 110, 120, 122, 128, 146, 166, 227, 228, 254
Ch'i, 213
Chicxulub, 19
China, 20, 21, 34, 84, 89, 113, 147, 183, 198, 208, 212, 246, 247, 257, 258, 273
Chinese room, 246
chinjikijilu, 233
Chomsky, 36
Christendom, 207, 209
Christian, 8, 13, 19, 20, 33, 42, 115, 116, 169, 179, 190, 191, 201, 202, 204, 205, 206, 207, 209, 211, 212, 213, 223, 224, 236, 241, 242, 245, 259
Christianity, 21, 22, 43, 141, 168, 169, 183, 197, 202, 207, 208, 209, 210, 212, 214, 223, 224, 225, 236, 242, 243, 247, 250
Christmas, 8, 183
chromosome, 31
circumcision, 33, 62, 65, 66, 246
Clarke, Arthur C., 161
Clarke, Arthur C., 31
clinamen, 247
clitoridectomy, 16, 33

cognitive, 23, 53, 71, 93, 150, 159, 169, 182, 250
communion of saints, 160, 162
communist, 15
commutation, 190, 191, 247
complexity, 1, 246, 247
computation, 129, 130, 131, 133, 136, 137, 141, 249
Confucian, 99, 201
Confucianism, 20, 43, 44, 147, 247, 262
Confucius, 114, 169, 247, 262
Constantine, 19, 247
Constitution, 88
contemplation, 44, 45, 48, 115, 116, 117, 163, 214, 215
Copenhagen interpretation, 136, 247
corporation, 159, 160, 167
Coyote, 146
Crease, R. P., 262
Creed, 223
cremation, 33
Crichton, 166
Cromwell, 9, 247
cross, 60, 168, 175, 197, 214, 221
crusade, 163
Cupid and Psyche, 195
cypher, 237

dance, 4, 5, 17, 45, 170, 201
Dante, 195, 243
D'Aquili, E. G., 262
Darwin, 13, 37, 56, 67, 105, 106, 262
Darwinism, 250
Davies, Paul, 262
Dawkins, Richard, 37, 262
de la Rochefoucauld, 46
de Luce, Judith, 261
de Man, Paul, 13
death, 2, 8, 16, 34, 50, 52, 59, 64, 65, 111, 114, 115, 147, 151, 171, 178, 179, 186, 190, 197, 200, 204, 208, 241, 245, 248
deconstruction, 85, 247
deconstructionist, 12, 13
deism, 247
deist, 247
deity, 10, 20, 31, 46, 108, 141, 152, 174, 182, 232
Delphic, 54, 173, 236, 247
denumerability, 247
dePryck, Koen, 128, 263
Derrida, Jacques, 247

determinism, 1, 42, 74, 75, 90, 91
determinist, 37, 76, 91, 136, 264
deus absconditus, 247
Deutsch, David, 263
devil, 46
DeWitt, Bryce, 263
Diana, 52
Dickinson, Emily, 168
Dionysus, 8, 53, 54, 190
Dioscuri, 194
Dis, 188
disponibilité, 244
Divine Comedy, 27
DNA, 18, 38, 48, 52, 53, 57, 61, 76, 109, 129, 131, 140, 146, 179, 184, 192, 199, 248, 253, 258
domestication, 62
Donne, 203, 243
Dostoyevsky, 27, 113, 205, 250, 263
doubt, 1, 7, 12, 13, 14, 15, 60, 113, 223, 224
drug, 45
Durkheim, 149, 159, 263
dynamical, 78, 248

Easter, 8, 20, 183, 197
Eccles, John, 84, 248, 263
economics, 64, 153, 156, 157, 241, 246, 256
ecumenism, 10, 19, 43
Eden, 27, 53, 60, 154, 164, 208
education, 35, 40, 48, 91, 164
Edwards, Jonathan, 70
Egypt, 60, 61, 63, 147, 183
Eibl-Eibesfeldt, Irenaeus, 69, 263
Einstein, 26, 100, 127, 129, 140, 249
Eliade, Mircea, 194, 251
Eliot, T. S., 172
Eliot, T. S., 14, 35, 195, 263
Elohim, 20, 109, 112, 211
Elysian Fields, 58
emergence, 248
emergent, 18, 76, 80, 81, 83, 85, 105, 108, 126, 132, 136, 137, 138, 141, 144, 145, 146, 147, 148, 149, 150, 151, 152, 160, 162, 179, 180, 218, 248, 263, 268
Enki, 51
Enlightenment, 1, 10, 39, 42, 48, 125, 152, 178, 219, 229, 256
Enlil, 20
entelechy, 248

entropy, 64, 75, 80, 81, 104, 135, 151, 248, 258
enzyme, 249
Epicureanism, 42
epistemology, 14, 18, 128, 270
Epstein, David, 269
Erickson, Stephen, 263
eschatology, 208
eternity, 26, 114, 115, 116, 117, 143, 214, 215, 217, 240
ethology, 53
Eucharist, 33, 227, 228
Europe, 9, 10, 20, 40, 48, 50, 89, 169, 178, 193, 207, 208, 229, 265
Eurydice, 54
Eve, 27, 175, 187
event horizon, 249
Everett, Hugh III, 98, 117, 263
evil, 25, 27, 46, 113, 118, 160, 180, 200, 201, 202, 209, 237, 255, 263
evolution, 5, 13, 22, 23, 34, 37, 39, 48, 49, 56, 57, 63, 64, 66, 67, 75, 88, 90, 95, 101, 105, 106, 109, 110, 111, 143, 148, 149, 164, 169, 170, 174, 175, 182, 185, 187, 193, 196, 205, 208, 209, 224, 228, 230, 234, 235, 240, 247, 261, 263, 264, 265, 267, 269, 270, 272, 273
exegesis, 244
Existentialism, 13, 43
existentialist, 12, 95, 99, 172, 179, 249
Exodus, 6, 27, 60

facticity, 47
faith, 13, 29, 30, 37, 39, 50, 69, 170, 181, 205, 209, 213, 222, 229, 231, 237
Fall, 3, 27, 154, 161, 205, 212
Father, 114, 169, 206
Faulkner, R. O., 263
Faust, 118
feedback, 55, 58, 59, 67, 68, 77, 78, 82, 84, 85, 87, 88, 89, 91, 102, 109, 116, 119, 128, 132, 179, 185, 213, 217, 222, 245, 246, 253, 262, 263
Ferdowsi, 263
fetish, 35
Feyerabend, Paul, 15, 17, 263
finance, 64, 156
flood, 47, 48, 269
food, 33, 34, 90, 189
footbinding, 33

Foucault, Michel, 14, 215
Fox, Robin, 264
fractal, 26, 68, 77, 78, 79, 82, 86, 102, 117, 133, 213, 217, 236, 245, 249, 250, 253, 257, 267
Fraser, J. T., 101, 102, 103, 104, 105, 116, 133, 259, 264
freedom, 1, 6, 27, 29, 30, 34, 37, 38, 40, 41, 42, 48, 55, 56, 57, 60, 68, 73, 74, 75, 76, 88, 89, 91, 94, 95, 96, 104, 107, 109, 112, 113, 115, 117, 120, 122, 123, 132, 134, 136, 137, 138, 141, 149, 150, 154, 155, 156, 160, 165, 171, 172, 191, 193, 205, 222, 230, 236, 238, 245, 248, 250, 270
Freemason, 34
Freud, 9

Gaia, 107, 108, 110, 111, 112, 144, 183, 267
game, 17, 30, 37, 41, 93, 99, 133, 136, 145, 162, 164, 229, 251, 264, 270
Ganesha, 175, 249, 258
Gautama, 28, 249
Geertz, Clifford, 258
gene, 37, 38, 39, 40, 66, 106, 136, 139, 140, 167, 192, 213, 251, 258
Genesis, 64, 68, 187, 243, 270, 271
genius, 142, 162, 181, 214, 236, 249
Germany, 35, 40
Gibbon, Edward, 207
Gibson, William, 145, 160, 264
gift, 32, 44, 53, 58, 87, 153, 154, 156, 172, 183, 195, 196, 230, 231
Gilgamesh, 50, 51, 194, 195, 243
Gleick, James, 264
glossolalia, 45
gluon, 249
god, 10, 11, 20, 21, 26, 27, 28, 29, 31, 35, 38, 43, 50, 51, 54, 55, 57, 58, 60, 61, 62, 63, 70, 84, 94, 98, 99, 100, 101, 107, 109, 110, 112, 114, 117, 120, 123, 125, 138, 139, 141, 142, 143, 147, 149, 150, 151, 152, 161, 166, 174, 175, 178, 179, 181, 183, 188, 204, 205, 206, 207, 208, 209, 210, 211, 214, 215, 216, 218, 219, 220, 222, 223, 225, 227, 231, 235, 237, 238, 239, 240, 241, 242, 243, 244, 246, 247, 249, 250, 252, 257, 258, 262, 263, 265, 267
Gödel, 29, 69, 77, 102, 250

golden bough, 55, 86
Gontar, 133
Gontar, Vladimir, 264
Goodall, Jane, 264
Gopis, 237, 240
Gospel of John, 60
Gospels, 27, 206
Gould, Stephen Jay, 264
Graham, Neill, 263
gravitation, 13, 15
graviton, 250
Greek, 42, 51, 54, 65, 66, 85, 147, 168,
    190, 201, 206, 212, 232, 247, 253,
    259, 262, 268
Grendel, 189
Griffin, David ray, 265
Gudea, 51
Gulag, 9, 14, 16, 93, 210
Gunas, 138, 250
gusler, 54

Habermas, Jurgen, 265
Habermas, Jürgen, 16, 17, 250
Hades, 58, 195, 201
Hagia Sophia, 241, 250
Haldane, J. B. S., 238, 239
Handel, 188
Hartshorne, Charles, 265
Hasid, 34, 175
Havel, Vaclav, 265
Hawking, Stephen, 131, 265
Hayles, Katherine, 265
heaven, 5, 27, 41, 59, 63, 114, 116, 140,
    157, 168, 170, 172, 184, 195, 202,
    209, 234, 240, 242, 244, 257, 261
Hebb, Donald, 84, 86, 250
Hebrew, 51, 54, 59, 60, 62, 65, 66, 141,
    191, 204, 208, 211, 232, 235
Hecate, 167, 169
Hegel, 92, 149, 159, 250, 265
Heidegger, Martin, 10, 265
Heisenberg, Werner, 247
helix, 52, 61, 67, 129, 199, 248
hell, 41, 172, 196, 202, 210
Hera, 52, 53
Hercules, 52, 61, 147, 151, 152
hermeneutic, 14, 66
Hermes, 51, 52, 54, 66
Herzberger, Barbara, 269
Hesiod, 68, 265
Hesperides, 52
Higgs, 130, 250

Hilbert, 100, 250
Hillman, James, 164, 265
Hindu, 9, 10, 19, 20, 33, 34, 51, 99, 116,
    138, 151, 168, 169, 191, 193, 201,
    237, 249, 250, 252, 267
Hinduism, 20, 21, 42, 152, 161, 212,
    224, 257, 259
Hiroshima, 50, 210
Hitler, 8, 40, 42, 159, 167
Hobbes, 16, 149, 164, 251, 265
Hofstadter, Douglas, 265
Holocaust, 9, 14, 16, 27, 48, 192, 208,
    209, 210
holy, 25, 169, 197, 206, 207, 268
Holy Spirit, 169, 197, 206, 207
Homer, 232
Hopkins, Gerard Manley, 142, 168, 239,
    266
HOX, 213, 251
Huckleberry Finn, 113, 235, 272
Huichol, 20, 169, 251
humanism, 25, 180, 181, 182, 225
Hunahpú, 175, 251, 255
Hunapúh, 194

I Ching, 28
Ibn Arabi, 28, 207, 245
Icon, 251
Iconoclasm, 183
Illich, Ivan, 164, 266
illo tempore, 251
immortality, 46, 51, 163, 172, 252
Inanna, 167
indeterminacy, 95
Indo-European, 50, 53, 85
infinite, 10, 26, 68, 79, 84, 94, 100, 132,
    133, 141, 197, 214, 215, 216, 217,
    219, 222, 246, 250, 251, 254, 259
infinite regress, 84
inflation theory, 251
Inquisition, 8
Ireland, 8, 35
Ishtar, 243
Islam, 21, 42, 43, 141, 169, 203, 204,
    207, 208, 209, 211, 212, 214, 224,
    243, 257
iteration, 80, 251
iterative, 236
Ixbalanqué, 175, 194, 251, 255

Jacob, 61, 62, 63, 64, 65
Jaguar, 146, 188

Jahweh, 59, 60, 62, 65, 109
James, William, 9, 128, 251, 266, 271
Japan, 147, 198, 212, 229
Jerusalem, 208, 211
Jesus, 19, 20, 32, 35, 41, 47, 48, 60, 61,
    63, 64, 116, 145, 157, 161, 168, 170,
    174, 175, 181, 190, 194, 197, 202,
    204, 205, 206, 208, 210, 211, 221,
    223, 227, 228, 229, 235, 237, 242,
    244, 250, 270
Jew, 33, 66, 209, 211
Jewish, 6, 13, 20, 59, 60, 61, 109, 116,
    169, 193, 208, 218, 224, 241, 243,
    246, 252, 270
Jews, 21, 34, 62, 192, 201, 204, 207,
    208, 209, 210, 211, 230, 237
jihad, 18, 22, 163
Job, 10, 27, 29, 168
Jordan, William R. III, 261
Josephson, Brian, 263
joy, 5, 45, 110, 118, 143, 172, 222, 225,
    242
Joyce, James, 195
József, Attila, 150, 196
Judaism, 43, 141, 201, 207, 209, 210,
    211, 212, 214, 224, 243, 257

Kaaba, 8, 33, 175
Kabbala, 61
Kalevala, 194, 251, 267
kami, 251
Kant, 2, 27, 29, 41, 89, 202, 251, 266
Kantian, 12, 251
karma, 42, 200
Kashmir, 9
Kazantzakis, Nikos, 161
Kepler, 134
King, L. W., 266
Kingdom, 157, 202
Knox, John, 10, 251
koan, 19, 35
Koran, 27, 99, 114, 232
Kosztolányi, Deszö, 3, 241
Krishna, 19, 43, 47, 141, 191, 219, 224,
    237, 242, 252, 267
Kuanyin, 151, 161, 167, 241, 252
Kuhn, Thomas, 17, 252, 266
Kundera, Milan, 113

Laban, 61, 62, 63, 64
Lagash, 51
lama, 225

Lao Tse, 32, 252, 266
Laplace, 135, 141, 252
Last Supper, 228, 229
Laughlin, C. D., 262
law, 28, 36, 39, 40, 58, 61, 77, 81, 100,
    102, 150, 154, 161, 167, 185, 228,
    230, 256, 259
Lederman, Leon, 266
Lefebvre, Vladimir, 266
Lewis, C. S., 164, 243, 266
liberty, 40, 113
limbic, 56, 186
Lindsay, David, 113, 266
Lockwood, Michael, 263
Lonnrot, Elias, 267
Lorenz attractor, 78, 95
Lorenz, Konrad, 53
love, 12, 14, 22, 34, 36, 39, 41, 52, 110,
    113, 116, 127, 143, 151, 152, 153,
    155, 156, 160, 164, 168, 169, 172,
    177, 187, 189, 193, 200, 203, 212,
    215, 218, 223, 224, 241, 242, 243,
    244
Lovelock, 107
Lovelock, James, 267
Lumsden, Charles J., 272
Lutheran, 230, 231
Lyons, Harriet, 62
lyre, 54, 55, 56, 57, 65, 66, 86, 194

Machiavelli, 16, 252, 267
madonna and child, 188
Magdalen, 244
magic, 30, 31, 32, 33, 55, 59, 86, 232
Mahabharata, 193, 194, 196, 232, 252,
    262
Maimonides, 28, 252
mandala, 117, 213
Mandelbrot, 68, 77, 79, 84, 251, 252,
    253
Mandelbrot, Benoit, 267
Mao, 8, 42, 150, 159
Margulis, Lynn, 267, 271
market, 6, 57, 58, 64, 66, 67, 144, 152,
    153, 154, 156, 157, 158, 160, 166,
    173, 195, 222, 256
Marr, David, 267
Marx, 88
Marx, Karl, 153, 158
Marxist, 21, 57
Mary, 20, 161, 168, 174, 175, 195, 206,
    218, 221, 241, 243, 244

Masada, 22, 252
Mascaro, Juan, 267
materialism, 21, 42, 178, 247
materialist, 39, 74, 182
mathematics, 26, 28, 47, 69, 79, 91, 96, 99, 102, 105, 106, 109, 135, 175, 190, 207, 214, 215, 217, 247, 250, 253, 254, 255, 256, 257
Maya, 20, 147
McManus, J., 262
meaning, 12, 15, 18, 20, 22, 31, 32, 35, 37, 38, 48, 50, 52, 53, 54, 57, 62, 65, 70, 74, 82, 84, 85, 86, 91, 93, 98, 99, 116, 133, 143, 156, 162, 170, 176, 178, 179, 180, 184, 190, 191, 192, 193, 221, 222, 228, 229, 232, 240, 246, 247, 251, 255, 273
Mecca, 33
meditate, 213
meditator, 117
Mediterranean, 49, 53, 66, 69, 89, 184, 208, 243
Melville, Herman, 121, 196, 267
menopause, 64, 185
merchant, 58, 59, 158
Mercury, 51, 54, 57, 58, 59, 130, 152, 159
metaphor, 22, 31, 38, 85, 86, 102, 190, 231, 233, 234, 237, 238, 244
metatron, 60, 61, 62
metempsychosis, 252
Mexico, 34, 35
Michael, 161
middle class, 1, 35
Middle East, 49
Midori, 198
Milton, John, 61, 161, 195, 243, 259, 267
Minerva, 20
Minkowsky, 249
Minsky, Marvin, 257
miracle, 2, 3, 11, 30, 31, 32, 76, 146, 170, 174, 228, 242
miracles, 4, 30, 31, 33, 151, 216, 221
Mithras, 20, 191
modernism, 10, 178
Mohammed, 19, 32, 145, 174, 204
money, 58, 63, 64, 65, 153, 154, 155, 156, 157, 158, 190
Monkey, 6, 20, 146, 147, 273
monotheism, 10, 20, 21, 46, 145, 152, 208, 212, 224

monotheist, 212
moral, 6, 8, 13, 16, 22, 27, 29, 31, 32, 33, 34, 36, 37, 39, 40, 41, 42, 45, 48, 53, 73, 111, 112, 113, 114, 115, 122, 148, 153, 154, 156, 158, 168, 171, 189, 193, 194, 200, 204, 213, 217, 222, 223, 224, 230, 237, 241, 251, 261, 270, 273
morality, 36, 37, 39, 40, 41, 42, 46, 48, 112, 113, 118, 153, 157, 159, 191, 207, 215, 272
Mormon, 253, 270
Moroni, 175, 253
Moses, 6, 21, 32, 51, 59, 60, 61, 62, 66, 145, 174, 196, 208, 252
Mozart, 32, 56, 198, 236
multicultural, 14, 16
Muslim, 8, 9, 10, 13, 20, 33, 34, 141, 204, 211, 217, 228, 237

Nagy, Gregory, 268
nakedness, 184, 185, 187
nanotechnology, 253
naturalistic, 23, 39, 109
nature, 43, 67, 108, 110, 111, 133, 145, 192, 203, 238, 239, 240, 264, 267, 268
Nazi, 13, 16, 192, 259, 265
Ndembu, 34, 147, 151, 183, 233, 234
negative obligation, 155
neoteny, 62
neuroanatomy, 55, 90
neuron, 98, 120, 150, 180
neurotransmitter, 31, 56, 253
neutrino, 37, 253
New Testament, 6, 193
Newton, 10, 13, 100, 101, 125, 127, 135, 272
Nietzsche, 74, 113, 231, 232, 233, 259
Ningizzida, 51, 60
Noah, 47, 48, 50, 269
nominalism, 253
nominalist, 12
nonlinear, 26, 47, 68, 77, 78, 79, 83, 85, 95, 100, 116, 120, 136, 167, 168, 222, 236, 246, 247, 250, 253, 262, 263, 264, 266, 267, 270, 273
nonlinearity, 78, 222, 246, 250, 268
nucleotide, 253
Nzambi, 10

obligation, 41, 153, 156, 158

observer problem, 253
Odysseus, 188, 195, 243
Oedipus, 57, 68, 118, 189, 197
O'Keeffe, Georgia, 177
Omega, 175, 200, 211
omnipotence, 26, 27
omniscience, 26, 27, 214
oracle, 54, 68, 247
Oresteia, 29
Orpheus, 53, 54, 87, 195, 196, 269
Orphic journey, 194
Orthodox, 5, 8, 34, 204, 211, 218, 230
Otto, 43
Otto, Rudolph, 268
Ozsváth, Zsuzsanna, 3, 86, 268

Padma Sambhava, 268
Panisset, Maurice, 271
Paraclete, 206, 207
paradise, 27, 51, 161, 261, 267
Paradise Lost, 27, 161, 267
paradox, 6, 77, 101, 105, 107, 114, 136,
    222, 234, 250, 252, 256, 263
parallel universes, 98, 117, 263
Parmenides, 253
Parry, Jonathan, 154, 261
Parvati, 249
Pascal, 209, 215, 268
passover, 32, 35
Paul, 17, 43
Peacocke, Arthur, 268
Penrose, Roger, 77, 122, 254, 256, 268,
    270
Pentecost, 6
Pentecostal, 206
performative, 90, 228, 234
Persephone, 167, 195
person, 3, 5, 21, 31, 35, 44, 74, 81, 99,
    107, 116, 118, 147, 148, 149, 158,
    160, 174, 179, 200, 206, 213, 217,
    218, 220, 222, 223, 225, 238, 240,
    242
Peter, 244, 262
pharmakon, 54
phase, 254
phenomenological, 12
philosophy, 1, 10, 12, 28, 42, 141, 165,
    178, 191, 207, 245, 250, 252, 255,
    261, 263, 264, 265, 267
physics, 2, 15, 47, 48, 64, 68, 70, 74,
    100, 102, 109, 120, 121, 128, 129,
    130, 132, 136, 138, 146, 178, 227,
    228, 234, 235, 240, 245, 253, 254,
    256, 257, 262, 265, 266
Pilate, 168
Pinker, Stephen, 36, 268
Pitman, Walter, 48, 49, 269
Planck, 69, 121, 126, 140, 254
Plato, 10, 20, 41, 101, 157, 232, 264
Pletsch, Carl, 261
pluralism, 2, 14, 15, 16, 17, 18, 22
poetry, 31, 54, 55, 56, 57, 65, 66, 67, 73,
    84, 86, 87, 90, 145, 151, 167, 175,
    178, 192, 193, 194, 198, 199, 200,
    205, 207, 211, 212, 216, 232, 233,
    234, 235, 236, 237, 238, 239, 240,
    242, 244, 258, 259, 267, 270, 271
Pol Pot, 8, 42
Polkinghorne, John, 268
polytheism, 19, 20, 21, 42, 46, 147, 152,
    208, 211, 212, 224
polytheistic, 21, 109, 152, 161, 167, 175,
    212, 224
Popol Vuh, 6, 99, 193, 251, 255, 271
positivist, 12, 179, 255
poststructuralist, 255
Pound, Ezra, 35
prayer, 44, 48, 99, 163, 194, 218, 219,
    220, 222
predestination, 42
Prigogine, 80, 100, 249, 263, 264
Prigogine, Ilya, 268
probability, 255
prophecy, 46, 52, 53, 123, 150, 153, 194,
    196, 236
prophet, 46, 174, 204, 210, 232, 253,
    261
Proserpina, 188
Protestant, 9, 10, 42, 202, 206, 224
Proust, 84, 255
psychopomp, 51, 58, 60
punishment, 28, 46, 53, 187, 190
Purgatory, 200
pyramid, 44
Pyrrhonian, 12, 255
Python, 54
Quakers, 44
quantum, 15, 47, 74, 77, 95, 97, 98, 100,
    101, 103, 117, 120, 121, 122, 128,
    131, 132, 134, 136, 137, 141, 145,
    147, 151, 168, 173, 174, 175, 179,
    203, 211, 217, 219, 220, 221, 236,
    246, 247, 253, 254, 255, 256, 270
quasicrystals, 256

Quechua, 20, 256
Queen of Heaven, 242
Quetzal, 69, 167, 258
Quine, 17
Quine, W. v. O., 268

Radnóti, Miklós, 210, 268
Rahula, Walpola Sri, 269
Rand, 179
Rappoport, Angelo S., 269
Rastafarian, 34
rational expectations, 256
Real Presence, 227, 229
realism, 23
reason, 1, 8, 28, 29, 30, 35, 42, 50, 54,
    70, 86, 96, 111, 117, 125, 133, 146,
    149, 151, 180, 184, 189, 215, 219,
    229, 235, 236, 238, 247, 250, 256,
    265
rebirth, 65
reductive, 70, 126, 158, 179
reflexive, 256
reformation, 48, 229
Renaissance, 33, 141, 159
renormalization, 256
Rentschler, Ingo, 269
replication, 17, 37, 67
representational, 15, 186
revelation, 6, 205
Rifkin, Jeremy, 166
Rilke, 54, 55, 56, 57, 86, 143, 269
ritual, 18, 20, 33, 34, 35, 36, 38, 44, 45,
    46, 53, 56, 65, 66, 99, 106, 125, 185,
    186, 187, 188, 191, 192, 193, 194,
    212, 218, 220, 224, 246, 259, 270
RNA, 129, 130, 248, 256
Robson, J. M., 269
Rolle, Richard, 45
Roman, 19, 21, 22, 32, 51, 52, 54, 59,
    147, 152, 168, 169, 174, 191, 197,
    207, 212, 227, 247, 249, 252
Roman Empire, 19, 21, 32, 207
Rorty, Richard, 16, 256, 269
Rube Goldberg, 11, 19, 47, 134
Ryan, 48, 49
Ryan, William, 269

sacrament, 32, 214, 224, 227, 232, 233
sacrifice, 2, 8, 14, 28, 38, 44, 99, 151, 156,
    163, 171, 173, 189, 190, 191, 192, 193,
    208, 218, 220, 221, 231, 243
Sagan, Carl, 235

Sagan, Dorion, 267, 271
saint, 31, 147, 172
saints, 31
salvation, 5, 6, 21, 33, 36, 83, 112, 148,
    164, 181, 214, 223, 266
Samedi, 161, 175
Samoa, 36
Santa Claus, 170
Santiago de Compostela, 35
Satan, 161, 195
Satinover, Jeffrey, 122, 269
save, 63, 114, 116, 156
savior, 44, 46, 60
Savonarola, 10, 256
scaling, 79, 249
Schleiermacher, Friedrich, 8, 256, 269
Schliemann, Heinrich, 69
Scholem, Gershom, 270
Schopf, J. William, 270
Schramm, David N., 266
Schrödinger, Erwin, 122, 136, 256, 270
Scientology, 16, 257
Searle, 84, 246, 257
Searle, John, 270
Second World War, 237
secular, 1, 2, 3, 14, 25, 32, 40, 46, 49,
    99, 114, 180, 209, 230
Seielstadt, G. S., 270
Selene, 169
Self-organization, 257
self-similar, 257
sensory, 11, 23, 45, 84, 86, 128, 139,
    183, 255
Sephiroth, 137, 257
serpent, 51, 52, 54, 60, 63, 196
Seville, 207, 211
sex, 11, 52, 53, 66, 67, 185, 186, 240
Sexson, Lynda, 270
Shahnameh, 193, 257, 263
Shakespeare, 2, 80, 81, 89, 119, 148, 153,
    155, 156, 158, 170, 193, 199, 200,
    201, 223, 228, 232, 233, 234, 270
shaman, 53, 55, 194, 196
shamanic, 46, 55, 115, 194
shame, 45, 53, 107, 154, 186, 187, 188,
    191, 193
Shaolin, 198
Shekinah, 62, 65, 241, 243, 257
Sheldrake, Rupert, 220
Shinto, 8, 14, 45, 249, 251, 257
Sidney, Philip, 21, 257, 270
Sikh, 257

singularity, 97, 121, 257
skepticism, 13, 14, 15, 18, 22, 266
Skyrms, Brian, 17, 37, 270, 271
Smith, Cyril Stanley, 272
Smith, Joseph, 270
snake, 51, 52, 53, 59, 60, 61, 65, 66, 67, 68, 69, 175
Sober, Elliott, 17, 270
sociobiogy, 230
sociobiology, 53, 257
Socrates, 21, 30, 40, 41, 252
Solidarnösc, 165
solipsism, 258
Solomon, 196, 232
Son, 169, 206, 242
Sonea, Sorin, 271
soul, 5, 13, 32, 34, 38, 42, 46, 51, 59, 83, 84, 99, 108, 112, 116, 119, 125, 140, 150, 171, 181, 200, 201, 203, 208, 213, 220, 243, 248, 252, 265
sower, 64, 235
Spain, 35, 60, 61, 137, 169, 207, 221
Sperry, Roger, 263
Spielberg, Steven, 161, 166
St Francis, 41
St. Bartholomew's Day massacre, 8, 258
St. Francis of Assissi, 197
St. Paul, 170, 231, 235
staff, 51, 52, 53, 59, 60, 61, 67
Stalin, 8, 42, 159
Stevens, Wallace, 14, 201
Stoicism, 42
structuralist, 258
Sufi, 19, 168, 169, 175, 224, 245, 258
Sumerian, 50, 51
supersymmetry, 22
survival, 18, 34, 37, 38, 65, 92, 95, 104, 139, 140, 185, 187, 188, 228
suttee, 258
Swift, Jonathan, 9
symbol, 67, 234
symmetry-breaking, 65, 100, 135
synapse, 31, 32, 86, 119, 139, 153, 235, 250, 258
syncretism, 19, 20, 21, 22, 23, 25, 26, 36, 224
syncretist, 19, 21

Tai Chi, 31, 213, 258
talents, 32, 63, 93
Talmud, 65, 252
tantric, 11

Tao, 98, 169, 175, 179, 224, 229, 258, 266
Taoism, 20, 138, 252, 258
Taoist, 10, 197, 224, 266
tattooing, 33
taxonomy, 258
technology, 1, 2, 21, 30, 31, 32, 33, 56, 66, 70, 86, 90, 92, 96, 111, 112, 128, 141, 151, 153, 154, 157, 160, 164, 165, 167, 168, 170, 173, 182, 191, 192, 193, 194, 206, 207, 214, 241, 246, 253, 258, 259, 261, 266
Tedlock, Dennis, 271
teleology, 38, 264
telomere, 31, 258
temporality, 106, 214
Thayer, H. S., 271
The Journey to the West, 6, 20, 273
The Merchant of Venice, 59
theism, 258
theodicy, 27, 193
theology, 1, 10, 11, 27, 28, 31, 42, 44, 48, 108, 109, 113, 120, 141, 144, 169, 178, 190, 208, 212, 217, 219, 236, 239, 244, 253
thermodynamic, 81, 258
Theseus, 56
Thirty Years' War, 230
Thirty Years' War, 8
Thom, René, 273
Thoreau, 271
three second line, 55
Thurman, Robert A., 268
Tiamat, 69, 258
Tibetan Book of the Dead, 268
Tiger, Lionel, 271
Tillich, Paul, 43, 271
time, 5, 6, 10, 12, 17, 18, 19, 22, 26, 27, 28, 31, 32, 35, 37, 41, 46, 47, 49, 52, 58, 62, 64, 65, 67, 68, 69, 75, 77, 81, 82, 92, 97, 100, 101, 102, 103, 104, 105, 106, 107, 108, 112, 114, 116, 117, 118, 119, 120, 123, 128, 130, 131, 132, 133, 134, 138, 140, 141, 143, 144, 153, 159, 162, 163, 165, 167, 168, 169, 170, 171, 173, 175, 181, 182, 189, 190, 191, 196, 199, 200, 202, 207, 208, 209, 210, 214, 215, 216, 217, 219, 221, 222, 227, 229, 231, 237, 238, 239, 240, 247, 248, 249, 251, 252, 253, 255, 257, 258, 263, 264, 265, 268

timeless, 26, 27, 106, 109, 135, 137, 141, 155, 203, 208, 215, 217
Tiresias, 52, 53
Tlaloc, 8, 147, 258
Tolstoy, 5
top-down, 70, 119, 144, 150, 263
Torah, 66, 204, 243
tourist, 35, 36
trade, 44, 54, 57, 63, 64, 65, 154, 208
trance, 5, 31, 45, 54, 61
transcendence, 44, 63, 65, 147, 197, 215, 216, 217
transcendent, 14, 15, 94, 99, 100, 196, 197, 214
transfinite, 26, 246, 247, 259
transsubstantiation, 227
transubstantiation, 32, 227, 229
tree of knowledge, 51
Trent, Council of, 227, 229, 259
trinity, 169, 174, 211, 224, 240
Tripitaka, 20, 169
Trismegistus, 66
Trojan War, 69
True Thomas, 195
Turing, 39, 77, 135, 136, 141, 147, 175, 220, 259
Turner, Frederick, 261, 268, 271
Turner, V. W., 271
Twain, Mark, 272

Umbanda, 20, 44, 212, 259
umwelt, 101, 103, 105, 106, 107
Unification, 10, 33, 175, 259, 272
Unification Church, 10, 175, 259, 272
Unitarian, 99
universalism, 11, 18, 22
Upanishad, 99, 172, 213
Upanishads, 19, 175, 212, 267
Urania, 241, 243, 259
Üxkull, 101, 259

value, 2, 35, 36, 37, 38, 39, 41, 42, 48, 51, 73, 74, 79, 83, 87, 89, 92, 93, 94, 96, 103, 121, 141, 144, 149, 154, 155, 156, 157, 159, 178, 201, 215, 249, 253, 255, 259
Vanini, Lucilio, 219
Vatican, 223, 235, 272

Vedic, 259
Venus, 20, 56, 152, 243
Virgil, 195, 236
virgin, 241, 244
Virgin Mary, 184
virtue, 36, 39, 61, 83, 94, 112, 211, 215, 247
Vishnu, 167, 169, 252
Vodun, 8, 14, 20, 34, 152, 161, 167, 169, 252, 259
Voltaire, 10, 219, 227, 229, 231, 232, 272
Vyasa, 196

Wahhabist, 26
Wakan Tanka, 10
Wechsler, Judith, 272
Wheeler, John Archibald, 120, 121, 122, 135, 273
Whig, 92, 259
Whitehead, Alfred North, 273
Wilde, Oscar, 46, 182
Wilson, Andrew, 272
Wilson, David, 17
Wilson, David Sloan, 270
Wilson, Edward, 183
Wilson, Edward O., 272, 273
Wittgenstein, 12, 15, 17, 178, 234, 259
Wittgenstein, Ludwig, 273
Woolf, Virginia, 148, 177, 178, 179, 217, 233, 273
worship, 9, 10, 18, 31, 44, 141, 152, 181, 182, 183, 214, 218, 224, 241, 243, 244
Wright, Robert, 273
Wu Cheng-En, 20, 273

Yeats, 114, 115, 150, 210
Yggdrasil, 51, 183
Yoga, 117
yogi, 31

Zeeman, E. C., 273
Zen, 13, 19, 99, 117, 172, 175, 179, 213, 252, 259, 269
Zeus, 52, 53, 152
Zipporah, 63, 196
Zohar, 60, 62, 270